Colonial Violence and Monuments in Global History

This book tackles the historical relationship between colonial violence and monuments in Africa, Europe, the Indian subcontinent, North America, and Australia.

In this volume, the authors ask similar questions about monuments in each location and answer them following a parallel structure that encourages comparison, highlighting common themes. The chapters track the contested histories of monuments, scrutinizing their narrative power and examining the violent events behind them. It is both about the history of monuments and the histories the monuments are meant to commemorate. It is interested in this nuanced relationship between violence, monuments, memory, and colonial legacies; the ways different facets of colonial violence—conquest, resistance, massacres, genocides, internments, and injustices—have been commemorated (or haven't been), how they live in the present, and how pertinent they are in the present to different peoples. Legacies of colonial violence, and continued reinterpretations of the past and its meanings remain very much ongoing. They are still very much unsettled questions in large parts of the world.

Colonial Violence and Monuments in Global History will be essential reading for students, scholars, and researchers of political science, history, sociology and colonial studies. The book was originally published as a special issue of the *Journal of Genocide Research*.

Cynthia C. Prescott is Professor of History at the University of North Dakota, USA. She is the author of *Pioneer Mother Monuments: Constructing Cultural Memory* (2019), and *Gender and Generation on the Far Western Frontier* (2007).

Janne Lahti is a historian working at the University of Helsinki as Academy of Finland Research Fellow. He has published seven books, including *Cinematic Settlers: The Settler Colonial World in Film*, with Rebecca Weaver-Hightower (2020), and *The American West and the World: Transnational and Comparative Perspectives* (2019).

Colonial Violence and Monuments in Global History

Edited by
Cynthia C. Prescott and Janne Lahti

Routledge
Taylor & Francis Group

LONDON AND NEW YORK

First published 2024
by Routledge
4 Park Square, Milton Park, Abingdon, Oxon OX14 4RN

and by Routledge
605 Third Avenue, New York, NY 10158

Routledge is an imprint of the Taylor & Francis Group, an informa business

British Library Cataloguing in Publication Data
A catalogue record for this book is available from the British Library

ISBN13: 978-1-032-50219-9 (hbk)
ISBN13: 978-1-032-50222-9 (pbk)
ISBN13: 978-1-003-39745-8 (ebk)

DOI: 10.4324/9781003397458

Typeset in Myriad Pro
by Newgen Publishing UK

Publisher's Note
The publisher accepts responsibility for any inconsistencies that may have arisen during the conversion of this book from journal articles to book chapters, namely the inclusion of journal terminology.

Disclaimer
Every effort has been made to contact copyright holders for their permission to reprint material in this book. The publishers would be grateful to hear from any copyright holder who is not here acknowledged and will undertake to rectify any errors or omissions in future editions of this book.

Contents

Citation Information

The chapters in this book were originally published in the *Journal of Genocide Research*, volume 24, issue 4 (2022). When citing this material, please use the original page numbering for each article, as follows:

Chapter 6

The Ajnala Massacre of 1857 and the Politics of Colonial Violence and Commemoration in Contemporary India
Mark Condos
Journal of Genocide Research, volume 24, issue 4 (2022), pp. 568–585

Chapter 7

Belgian Monuments of Colonial Violence: the Commemoration of Martyred Missionaries
Idesbald Goddeeris
Journal of Genocide Research, volume 24, issue 4 (2022), pp. 586–603

For any permission-related enquiries please visit:
www.tandfonline.com/page/help/permissions

Notes on Contributors

Mark Condos is an historian interested in the intersections between violence, race, and law within the British and French empires. His previous research has examined the relationship between militarism, violence, and state-building in colonial Punjab and along the North-West Frontier of British India. He is currently working on a new project that looks at how concepts of prestige, dignity, and honor informed imperial practices of retributive violence, and the ways that imperial powers attempted to justify these within legal, moral, and other normative frameworks.

Ann Curthoys is Professor Emerita at the Australian National University and an honorary professor at the University of Western Australia. She writes about many aspects of Australian history including Indigenous history, and about genocide theory and historical writing. Her most recent book, co-authored with Jessie Mitchell, is *Taking Liberty: Indigenous Rights and Settler Self-Government in the Australian Colonies, 1830–1890* (2018).

Alison Fields is the Associate Director of the OU School of Visual Arts and the Mary Lou Milner Carver Professor of Art of the American West, Associate Professor of Art History at the University of Oklahoma. Fields is the author of *Discordant Memories: Atomic Age Narratives and Visual Culture* (2020).

Idesbald Goddeeris is Professor of Imperial History at the University of Leuven (KU Leuven), Belgium. He mainly works on mission history and postcolonial debates.

Shino Konishi is Associate Professor in the Institute for Humanities and Social Sciences at the Australian Catholic University. Her research examines Indigenous and early colonial history, and her publications include *The Aboriginal Male in the Enlightenment World* (2012), and the edited collections *Indigenous Intermediaries: New Perspectives on Exploration Archives* (2015) and *Brokers and Boundaries: Colonial Exploration in Indigenous Territory* (2016).

Janne Lahti is a historian working at the University of Helsinki as Academy of Finland Research Fellow. He has published seven books, including *Cinematic Settlers: The Settler Colonial World in Film*, with Rebecca Weaver-Hightower (2020), and *The American West and the World: Transnational and Comparative Perspectives* (2019).

Cynthia C. Prescott is Professor of History at the University of North Dakota, USA. She is author of *Pioneer Mother Monuments: Constructing Cultural Memory* (2019), and *Gender and Generation on the Far Western Frontier* (2007).

Bruce Scates is Fellow of the Academy of the Social Sciences at the Australian National University. He is the author of several major studies on conflict and commemoration and provided extensive public commentary on Australia's Statue Wars. His work on dialogical memorialization and investigation of frontier violence in Western Australia received special commendation in the First Report of the Council for National Reconciliation.

Marcus B. Weaver-Hightower is Professor of Foundations of Education at Virginia Tech. His research focuses on qualitative methods, food politics, boys and masculinity, sociology of education and policy, and comics and graphic novels. He the author of *Unpacking School Lunch; How to Write Qualitative Research; The Politics of Policy in Boys' Education*; and other articles and collections.

Rebecca Weaver-Hightower is Professor of English specializing in postcolonial studies and Chair of English at Virginia Tech. Her recent books, *Frontier Fictions: Settler Sagas and Postcolonial Guilt* (2018) and *Cinematic Settlers: The Settler Colonial World on Film* (co-edited with Janne Lahti, 2020) analyze and compare global settler colonial literatures, especially of South Africa, Canada, the US, and Australia. A theme of her research has been examining the psychological and social work literature does during times of colonial conflict.

Peter Yu is the Vice-President, First Nations, at the Australian National University. He has over 35 years' experience in Indigenous development and advocacy in the Kimberley and at the state, national, and international level. He was the Executive Director of the Kimberley Land Council, part of the national leadership group negotiating the Federal Government's response to the 1992 Mabo High Court judgment on native title, and a delegate to the First Nations Constitution Convention in 2017.

Introduction: Looking Globally at Monuments, Violence, and Colonial Legacies

Cynthia C. Prescott and Janne Lahti

On 9 March 2015, the University of Cape Town campus was abuzz with unexpected excitement. One of the black African students of this formerly white-only university had just hurled a bucket of excrement on the statue of Cecil Rhodes. The statue of this famous colonizer, once revered for his boundless ambition and energetic expansion of the British realm, had figured prominently on campus since the statue's inauguration in 1934, located just downhill from the convocation hall. Calls for its removal dated back at least to the 1950s, when Afrikaner students objected to Rhodes as an advocate of British supremacy. In the post-apartheid years, economic and social inequality has continued to mar South Africa. In 2015, growing anger at the silence over historical injustices and a refusal to rectify years of systematic racism, violence against black Africans, and land theft boiled over into protests. It sparked a wildfire, a global Rhodes Must Fall movement. A few days after being tarnished by feces, more than 1,000 people gathered for a rally at the monument, demanding the university to remove the statue (which it did a month later). Meanwhile the protests spread to other campuses in South Africa, and then to Oxford University in Great Britain. What sparked the protests, according to decolonization scholar Sabelo J. Ndlovu-Gatsheni, was "the continued existence of Rhodes' memorials and statues in South Africa as a sign of colonial/apartheid arrogance and refusal by those who benefitted from his colonial plunder to express repentance and tolerance of the feelings of those who Rhodes abused."[1] In post-apartheid society Rhodes has become perhaps the most potent symbol of the inequalities stemming from past colonial violence that resonate in modern South Africa and across the world. In short, Rhodes stands for all the greedy, violent colonizers who took away the natives' lands, killing, enslaving, and exploiting them.[2]

The Rhodes Must Fall movement is a pertinent example of how in recent years questions and debates surrounding colonial durabilities and legacies have become both increasingly visible and increasingly global. Gaining new steam in the summer of 2020 with the Black Lives Matter protests, there now exists widespread and multilayered

---

[1] Sabelo J. Ndlovu-Gatsheni, *Epistemic Freedom in Africa: Deprovincialization and Decolonization* (London: Routledge, 2018), 221-222.

[2] On "Rhodes Must Fall," see Roseanne Chantiluke, Brian Kwoba, and Athinangamso Nkopo, eds., *Rhodes Must Fall: The Struggle to Decolonise the Racist Heart of Empire* (Exeter: Zeb Books, 2018); Eve Fairbanks, "The Birth of Rhodes Must Fall," *The Guardian* 15 November 2015, https://www.theguardian.com/news/2015/nov/18/why-south-african-students-have-turned-on-their-parents-generation (accessed 9 August 2021).

calls for racial justice and for decolonization of European knowledge, higher education, museums, public spaces, and historical narratives in different parts of the world.[3] This phenomenon frequently relies on grassroots civic activism in exposing and addressing the consequences of the colonial past in the present, and it continues to be symbolized by the highly visible eruptions against public monuments, the toppling of statues.[4]

Protests against statues of Rhodes and other colonizers quickly spread to the United Kingdom and continental Europe. Simultaneous calls to remove Confederate war monuments in the United States raised similar questions.[5] In 2020, the Black Lives Matter protests again pushed monuments to the center of heated debates not only in the United States, but also in nations around the world where less privileged ethnic groups identified with the label "Black," including France, Nigeria, Brazil, India, and Australia.[6] Singaporeans questioned veneration of British colonial officer Stamford Raffles, calling instead for greater respect for their Asian heritage. And Greenlanders targeted a statue of missionary Hans Egede, vanguard of Danish-Norwegian colonization three hundred years ago. Protesters have toppled statues, rallied for justice, and clashed with authorities.

While most of these protests have portrayed the subjects and erectors of such statues as racist colonizers, the fevered pitch of these debates has often missed more complex aspects of identity politics that helped motivate their erection. Protesters argue that explorer Christopher Columbus enslaved Indigenous peoples in the Caribbean and initiated colonization – or even genocide – of Native Americans. But many of the statues honoring Columbus were erected a century ago by Italian Americans seeking to counteract discrimination by claiming their place within Euro-American society. Similarly, as Alison Fields points out in this special issue, at the turn of the twentieth century, New Mexicans claiming Spanish-American heritage commemorated conquistador Juan de Oñate to align themselves with European conquest — a notion that became hotly contested a century later, producing violence between protesters and counter-protesters in 2020.

Meanwhile, public institutions have begun to reevaluate monuments, removing some at a fast pace. For example, in June 2021 the American Museum of Natural History (AMNH) received permission from the City of New York to remove a controversial statue of US

---

[3] The literature here is broad and nuanced. See, for instance, Lars Jensen, *Postcolonial Europe* (London: Routledge, 2020); Dan Hicks, *The Brutish Museums: The Benin Bronzes, Colonial Violence, and Cultural Restitution* (London: Pluto Press, 2020); Alice Procter, *The Whole Picture: The colonial story of the art in our museums & why we need to talk about it* (London: C. Cassell, 2020); Alan Lester, *Deny and Disavow: Distancing the Imperial Past in the Culture Wars* (London: SunRise, 2022); Britta Schilling, *Postcolonial Germany: Memories of Empire in a Decolonized Nation* (Oxford: Oxford University Press, 2014); Sandra Ponzanesi and Gianmaria Colpani, eds., *Postcolonial Transitions in Europe: Contexts, Practices and Politics* (London: Rowman & Littlefield International, 2016); Amy Lonetree, *Decolonizing Museums: Representing Native America in National and Tribal Museums* (Chapel Hill: University of North Carolina Press, 2012).

[4] On decolonial/postcolonial civic movements and initiatives, see https://www.kolonialismus.uni-hamburg.de/2015/09/10/postkoloniale-initiativen-in-deutschland-2/ for Germany and https://www.splcenter.org/data-projects/2020-confederate-symbol-removals for US Confederate monuments. See also https://contestedhistories.org/, and https://umap.openstreetmap.fr/it/map/viva-zerai_519378#6/41.508/11.096. On frontier violence in Australia, see https://c21ch.newcastle.edu.au/colonialmassacres/.

[5] Southern Poverty Law Center, "Whose Heritage? Public Symbols of the Confederacy," 1 February 2019, https://www.splcenter.org/20190201/whose-heritage-public-symbols-confederacy.

[6] Black Lives Matter is a decentralized political and social movement that dates back at least to 2013. It began in the US but is transnational today. Christopher J. Lebron, *The Making of Black Lives Matter: A Brief History of an Idea* (Oxford: Oxford University Press, 2017); Barbara Ransby, *Making All Black Lives Matter: Reimagining Freedom in the Twenty-First Century* (Berkeley: University of California Press, 2018); Jelani Cobb, "The Matter of Black Lives," *The New Yorker*, 6 March 2016, https://www.newyorker.com/magazine/2016/03/14/where-is-black-lives-matter-headed (accessed 19 June 2021).

President Theodore Roosevelt. Though Roosevelt is lauded for his work on environmental conservation, limiting the power of big business, and protecting workers, his racial views and promotion of American imperialism were less praiseworthy, and his conservation policies were devastating for Indigenous peoples. Moreover, many found the AMNH statue's hierarchical depiction of Roosevelt on horseback, flanked by scantily-clad African and a Native American men, to be racist.[7] Similarly, in Gisbourne, New Zealand, a controversial statue of explorer James Cook, who claimed Australia and New Zealand for Great Britain, was moved from Tītīrangi Hil – where Māori and Europeans first encountered one another, and where Cook's crew killed nine Māori after a misunderstanding – to a nearby museum. Yet other colonial statues remain in place throughout the nation, including another Cook statue in Gisbourne.

Arguably, monuments hold a key role in present endeavors to confront colonial injustices and when seeking to counter past wrongs. An interesting question is why? More specifically, why and how does past colonial violence resonate through monuments? Why and how do monuments matter when making claims for colonial authority or when challenging and rebutting those claims?

Academics have sought to answer these questions, bringing them to bear on specific historic and cultural contexts. Dozens of scholars have commented on individual statues and writing on statues of a certain country or empire.[8] Yet, they rarely have adopted a global outlook.[9] Nor have they focused on the relationship between specific historical acts of colonial violence and specific monuments. This special issue seeks to do just that. It tackles the historical relationship between colonial violence and monuments in Africa, Europe, the Indian subcontinent, North America, and Australia. We ask similar questions about monuments in each location, and answer them following a parallel structure that encourages comparison, highlighting common themes. It tracks the contested histories of monuments, scrutinizing their narrative power and examining the violent events behind them. It is both about the history of monuments and the histories the monuments are meant to commemorate. It is interested in this nuanced relationship between violence, monuments, memory, and colonial legacies; the ways different facets of colonial violence – conquest, resistance, massacres, genocides, internments, and injustices – have been commemorated (or haven't been), how they live in the present, and how pertinent they are in the present to different peoples. Legacies of colonial violence, and continued reinterpretations of the past and its meanings remain very much ongoing. They are still very much unsettled questions in large parts of the world

---

[7] American Museum of Natural History, https://www.amnh.org/exhibitions/addressing-the-theodore-roosevelt-statue (accessed 12 May 2021).

[8] Much of what academics have written has been in newspapers, blogs, social media, and other public forums. Monographs on the topic include Matthew Stanard, *The Leopard, the Lion, and the Cock: Colonial Memories and Monuments in Belgium* (Leuven: Leuven University Press, 2019); Robert Aldrich, *Vestiges of the Colonial Empire in France: Monuments, Museums, and Colonial Memories* (New York: Palgrave Macmillan, 2005); Lisa Blee and Jean M. O'Brien, *Monumental Mobility: The Memory Work of Massasoit* (Chapel Hill: University of North Carolina Press, 2019); Karen L. Cox, *No Common Ground: Confederate Monuments and the Ongoing Fight for Racial Justice* (Chapel Hill: University of North Carolina Press, 2021); Cynthia Culver Prescott, *Pioneer Mother Monuments: Constructing Cultural Memory* (Norman: University of Oklahoma Press, 2019). See also https://pioneermonuments.net/.

[9] On studies that situate colonial memory in transnational contexts and touch on monuments as part of the memory landscapes, see Dominik Geppert and Frank Muller, eds., *Sites of Imperial Memory: Commemorating Colonial Rule in the Nineteenth and Twentieth Centuries* (Manchester: Manchester University Press, 2015).

as attested, for example, by the recent debates between Germany and Namibia over recognition and compensation over the Herero and Nama genocide in 1904-1907.

In many instances, monuments enable unjust violent colonial pasts to live in the present. Monuments matter; debates and reconciliations gain meaning through monuments, on what we choose to commemorate and how. What is at stake is nothing less than mastery over the past – who owns it and what do we make of it – and the paths we chart toward unknown futures.

Furthermore, bringing different memorials to colonial violence into discussion with each other and to the same analytical frame reveals that memorialization is a global phenomenon. While there are many different kinds of monuments erected by distinct groups around the world, they nonetheless raise parallel questions about who gets remembered and how, and how commemoration has been reinterpreted and contested over time. They speak of a shared history, a joint narrative of conquest, othering, and celebration of white pioneers and colonizers.

Violence of Monuments

Bringing together writings about the relationships of monuments and violence in different empires and in different settings reveals several common themes that emphasize the violence of colonial monuments. For one, focusing on monuments to colonial violence highlights the overlapping forms and fluid boundaries of extreme violence being commemorated. Cycles of asymmetrical violence, such as explorer Maitland Brown's punitive expedition against the Karajarri of Western Australia were commemorated, while other events were completely ignored, as in the case of the Ajnala Massacre during the Indian Uprising in the mid-nineteenth century. Instances of genocide have also been celebrated as victories and heroic expansions around the world, such as the Spanish slaughter of the Acoma Pueblo in the sixteenth century, or the German extermination of the Herero and Nama in southwest Africa in the early twentieth century.

It is easy to see that most monuments were erected by colonial powers seeking to celebrate settler advancement, the civilizing mission, and/or colonial exploitation, and to reinforce their power over Indigenous groups. There typically was little room for self-critique because colonial monuments in India, Belgium, South Africa, Namibia, the United States, and Western Australia commemorate individual named colonizers, specific groups, and particular events. They often embody narratives of settler righteousness as well as victimhood and sacrifice, as did the Explorers' Memorial in Fremantle, Western Australia or the *Reiterdenkmal* in Windhoek, South West Africa (Namibia), as examined here by Bruce Scates and Peter Yu and by Janne Lahti. They carefully documented "massacres" of colonial soldiers and settlers, and their "responding" with violence intended both as retribution and education: to punish Native groups – seen as unruly children and/or as untamed savages – and to discourage future violence against their colonizers. Colonizers often sought to teach the colonized a lesson through violence and thus to justify disproportionate violence. This notion of exemplary violence – even violence as pedagogy – rises as one key thread connecting the individual articles in the issue.

So does the tendency to depict Indigenous peoples as uncounted dangerous hordes to be feared, or as anonymous numbers killed. Although individual settler victims are identified and commemorated, Indigenous figures are typically nameless, faceless masses to be overcome, as in the Voortrekker Monument in Pretoria, South Africa. Often they and their side of the story remain erased from the monuments and their narrations altogether, as was the case initially with the Explorers' Memorial and the *Reiterdenkmal*. And as Rebecca and Marcus Weaver-Hightower's essay in this volume demonstrates, even colonial monuments such as the 1820 Settlers National Monument in Makandha (formerly Grahamstown), South Africa, that do not directly depict such disproportionate violence nonetheless enact cultural violence upon Indigenous persons and groups.

On the other hand, many violent genocides and massacres by the colonizers have been left without a monument, sometimes regardless of the petitions of locals. Idesbald Goddeeris shows that there still exist no monuments to colonial atrocities that happened in Congo during the colonization of King Leopold II and Belgium. Instead, there are numerous monuments to Belgian missionaries killed during the decolonization struggles. Mark Condos reveals that a brutal massacre in Ajnala, British India, was largely forgotten from the memory of the former colonial rulers but also ignored by the decolonized Indian nation as it did not fit the national (Hindu) ethos it celebrated. Refusal to erect monuments to horrific violence can also be seen to exhibit Indigenous agency, their preferences. This is the case at Wounded Knee, South Dakota where no monument stands to the massacre of the Lakotas in the hands of the US cavalry in 1890, except a marker that Lakotas erected in 1903 at the nearby site of the mass grave where the cavalry's victims were interred.[10]

Monument form also tells of the complex relationship between colonial violence and memory. Many colonial monuments rely on representational sculpture to emphasize white dominance. Equestrian statues of conquistador Juan de Oñate or Namibia's *Reiterdenkmal* declare colonizers' power over the colonized. Bas-reliefs placed around a statue's base – such as those depicting colonial punitive justice beneath the *Explorers' Monument* – or those lining the walls of the *Voortrekker Monument* portray white colonists as rightful settlers vanquishing savage indigenes. Less representational forms are open to more diverse interpretations. Boulders mounted with interpretive plaques can celebrate colonial settlement, such as those placed throughout the United States by the Daughters of the American Revolution to mark Euro-American westward expansion, or mourn local incidents of colonial violence, as at the *Pinjarra Massacre Memorial* at Pinjarra, Western Australia. Local Belgian monuments to colonial missionaries serve as surrogate gravesites. And a Sikh temple was built to mark the Ajnala Massacre mass grave.

Monument location likewise demonstrates the complex relationship between colonial violence and memory. Statues to colonizers placed in front of capitols or in other prominent locations in urban centers, like Namibia's *Reiterdenkmal*, link government and commercial might to those colonizers. Placing the Voortrekker Monument near the seat of British colonial government at Pretoria, rather than the site of the military victory that it celebrates, emphasized Afrikaner political and economic power. So did the choice to erect the statue of James Stirling, the "founding father" of Western Australia involved in the Pinjarra Massacre, at the heart of the business district of Perth. Rejecting commemoration of Indigenous figures near such seats of power reinforce colonial dominance. The statue of Indigenous leader Yagan was not allowed to be put alongside white colonial

---

[10] David Grua, "'In Memory of the Chief Big Foot Massacre': The Wounded Knee Survivors and the Politics of Memory," *Western Historical Quarterly* 46, no. 1 (2015): 31-51.

figures at Perth's Kings Park, but it found space on an important Indigenous meeting place instead, as Shino Konishi and Ann Curthoys notice. Such monuments placed far from urban centers serve more intimate local commemorative practices. Belgian missionary monuments exist not in the Congo, where they served and died in bloodshed following Congolese independence, but, Goddeeris reveals, in rural, peripheral areas of Belgium, where they function as empty tombs and sites of family gathering and mourning. They appear in regional clusters, suggesting that such monuments inspired neighboring municipalities to erect their own commemorations.

In some ways, monuments around the world concretize a single version of history. They mark – or commemorate at a distance – a site worthy of remembering. The monument thus creates a faux historical space, where visitors or residents can be taught a particular interpretation of the past. While a bronze statue appears permanent and unchanging, the physical, cultural, and political landscape in which it stands are ever-changing. Monuments are reinterpreted, removed, and destroyed. New kinds of monuments spring up.

Yet in creating a physical symbol of a particular narrative, monuments also provide an opportunity for people to interact with that narrative in divergent ways. Its meaning depends on the perspective of the viewer. Moreover, the narratives the monuments tell seldom remain fixed, but are open to reinterpretation. While memorial statues and structures imply permanence, these *lieux de memoire* (sites of memory)[11] are not settled and are always changing. While a representative commemorative sculpture declares who counts as a hero or martyr, monuments offer opportunities for dialogical memorialization. As surrounding physical and cultural landscapes change, monuments are carefully maintained or are forgotten.[12] Oppressed groups deface or damage statues, or erect counter-memorials that change the original monument's meaning. Indigenous peoples can write against the colonial narratives the monuments advance. As Alison Fields' essay shows, Native American artist Nora Noranjo Morse's contribution to a project commemorating the four hundredth anniversary of Spanish colonization of New Mexico challenges that celebration. Her *Numbe Whageh*, a spiral-shaped landscape installation that emphasizes Indigenous understandings of time and place, juxtaposes against the bronze statues of Don Juan de Oñate and other Spanish settlers designed by white and Hispanic artists.

Contested Powers of Monuments

Monuments to colonial violence remain at the center of hotly contested and debated identity politics. They both divide and bring together communities, and they have done so throughout their histories. This becomes evident in the articles in this special issue too. First, Alison Fields situates the statues of the Spanish explorer and settler expansionist Juan de Oñate in the murky legacies of multiple colonial pasts in North America. By emphasizing Spanish colonial violence, instead of US killing of Native Americans, Fields reveals layers of colonial violence that easily escape our attention when we think of

---

[11] Pierre Nora, "Between Memory and History: Les Lieux de Mémoire," *Representations*, no. 26 (1989), 7–24.
[12] Paul Connerton, *How Modernity Forgets* (New York: Cambridge University Press, 2009); Adrian Forty and Susanne Küchler, eds., *The Art of Forgetting* (Oxford; New York: Berg, 1999).

monuments, racializations, and colonial reckonings in the modern-day United States. Her discussion of three different *lieux de mémoire* highlights highly contested memories of Oñate.

Such contestation over commemorating colonizers appears throughout the essays in this special issue. Pairing two essays on settler monuments in Western Australia similarly emphasizes continued reinterpretations and debates over the Australian pioneer myth and the power of dialogical commemoration. Through their history of the origins and afterlife of the *Explorers Monument*, Bruce Scates and Peter Yu highlight the potential for counter-memorialization to transform a site commemorating white retaliatory violence into one of reconciliation. Ann Curthoys and Shino Konishi likewise explore monuments to white perpetrators of the 1834 Pinjarra Massacre and efforts by the Bindjareb Noongar to commemorate the Aboriginal victims of that massacre.

Some of the most explicit monuments to European colonial violence were erected in Sub-Saharan Africa, including the *Reiterdenkmal* in Windhoek, Namibia, and the Voortrekker Monument in Pretoria, South Africa. Like statues of Juan de Oñate and British military leaders in Western Australia, these monuments justified white dominance in their respective regions by celebrating punitive violence against Indigenous populations. Janne Lahti's piece on the *Reiterdenkmal* in Windhoek, a monument celebrating German settler rule over African land and camouflaging genocidal violence committed by the *Kaiserreich* against Herero and Nama peoples, reveals both the ways that a statue can justify colonial violence by celebrating colonizers as triumphant innocents, and also points to the limits of such narrative constructions. Rebecca and Marcus Weaver-Hightower's comparison of the Voortrekker Monument with the 1820 Settlers National Monument reveals Anglophone South Africans' attempts to frame themselves as "good colonizers," in the face of supposedly more violent indigenes and Afrikaner nationalism portrayed in the Voortrekker.

Our final two essays focus on more local memorials to victims: colonized peoples in India and colonizing missionaries in their Belgian homelands. Mark Condos highlights grassroots efforts to commemorate Sikh "martyrs" of the Indian Uprising at Ajnala. He reveals a forgotten massacre that during this age of polarized debates surrounding the legacies of the British Empire and divisive debates over national identity in multiethnic India, holds little political traction beyond the local minority community. Then we end our world tour in Europe, examining relations of power between the colonizer and the colonized as they manifest in the public spaces and memory of contemporary Europe. Idesbald Goddeeris reveals a culture of amnesia, erasure, and selective memorialization, where individual white Europeans killed by black Africans or Chinese persons are commemorated as heroes and martyrs through a plethora of local monuments, but where the mass genocide in Congo remains hidden from public spaces and thus from collective memory.

Taken together, these seven essays reveal both the power of monuments to celebrate or camouflage histories of colonial violence as well as their power to enact cultural violence, and the ways in which that power can be challenged. They demonstrate that monuments come with narrative power, where both the narrative and the power the monument embodies and resonates change over time and remain open to multiple interpretations (regardless of the monument's original intentions). Monuments carry colonial legacies or racism and violence into the present, but their existence also enables the people in the present (scholars, activists, and others) to question the prevalent narratives of the past. This is what happened with Rhodes Must Fall and other such movements. They focus our attention on the injustices of the past resonating in the present, and make us challenge the status quo. Monuments allow us to critically look at the past, to contest any given truths and to create dialogue for potentially less divisive and less violent futures. They can demonstrate the importance of amplifying Indigenous and minority voices as we remember and teach about our societies' difficult pasts, up to and including genocide.

Disclosure Statement

No potential conflict of interest was reported by the author(s).

Visualizing Juan de Oñate's Colonial Legacies in New Mexico

Alison Fields

ABSTRACT

In 2005, the *Cuarto Centenario* memorial in Albuquerque, New Mexico was installed, comprised of *La Jornada*, a sculptural grouping honouring Spanish conquistador Juan de Oñate's 1598 settlement in New Mexico, and *Numbe Whageh*, an earthwork reflecting a Native response to Oñate's colonial legacies. This essay considers the June 2020 removal of Oñate from the memorial's sculptural grouping, after a protestor was shot in a standoff with a New Mexico citizen "militia." I will also examine other visual representations of Oñate in the state, including an equestrian statue in Alcade that was also removed in June 2020, as well as the inclusion of "Oñate's foot" in the 2018 SITE Santa Fe exhibition *Casa Tomada*. These representations, and their active histories, demonstrate how Oñate's colonial violence continues to resonate in the present day.

When I drive through Alcade, I always look there, where the Oñate sculpture was once placed. And he's still there. He may not be there physically, but he's there.

– Nora Naranjo-Morse, artist, Santa Clara Pueblo

Introduction

At midday on 15 June 2020, Rio Arriba County road and building maintenance staff applied a torch to the hooves of the twelve-foot bronze equestrian statue of Spanish conquistador Juan de Oñate, the focal point of the Northern Rio Grande National Heritage Center in Alcade, New Mexico. Pried away from its concrete pedestal, a bulldozer quickly transferred the statue to a flatbed truck, carrying it down the highway to a "top-secret" location.[1] Then-county manager Tomas Campos described the action as a pre-emptive move, to protect county property from a planned afternoon protest calling for the statue's removal, and a counter-protest by members of a right-wing militia.[2] It came days after an online petition calling for the statue's removal, drafted by local artist Luis Peña in honour of "missing and murdered indigenous women (MMIW)

---

[1] Molly Montgomery, "County Takes Down Oñate Monument," *Rio Grande Sun*, 15 June 2020, http://www.riograndesun.com/news/county-takes-down-o-ate-monument/article_2530ed9c-af2f-11ea-b2e9-4f1a4633c37b.html?utm_medium=social&utm_source=facebook&utm_campaign=user-share&fbclid=IwAR1Xp51DKuj_IlpDUWwTdcZ6hdY-A4Df28ZQb3AqQXWs3mJbZyuEON6CqGA (accessed 17 April 2021).

[2] Montgomery, "County Takes Down Oñate Monument."

and LGBTQ2+ relatives lost to continued colonial violence, and in solidarity with Black Lives Matter," garnered over 650 signatures from Rio Arriba residents.[3] Among the small group that watched as the Oñate statue was pulled from its perch and shuttled away, were several older Hispanic men carrying a conquistador hat and standing solemnly, fists over their chests.[4]

Later that evening, a crowd of over 100 gathered to celebrate the statue's removal.[5] Those in support of the statue's removal recognized an ongoing legacy of violence against Native bodies and lands, traceable to Spanish and Euro-American colonization of New Mexico. The statue, then, had served as a symbolic extension of Oñate's historical violence, embodying the colonizer in the present day. While celebrating the statue's removal as a moment of liberation from colonialism, indigenous activists also memorialized losses across time, stamping red handprints and the letters "MMIW" on the now-empty pedestal. Tewa Women United Environmental Justice Coordinator Beata Tsosie-Peña, of nearby Santa Clara Pueblo and El Rito, reflected, "This is a very solemn day, because we're also remembering missing and murdered indigenous relatives, at the hands of this legacy, we're also remembering a lot of lives lost and that continue to be lost," she said.[6] Through the conflicting and deeply felt responses to the removal of the statue, events occurring over the course of 400 years – Oñate's 1598 settlement in New Mexico and contemporary protests calling for racial justice – can be understood as part of a historical continuum.

The day after that the statue in Alcade was removed, a second statue of Oñate was dismantled in Albuquerque, New Mexico. Part of the larger Cuarto Centenario memorial, this removal occurred after a protestor was shot by counter protestor Steven Ray Baca in the midst of a standoff with a citizen militia. The series of events that led to the two statue removals, along with their uncertain aftermaths, speak to the complex task of publicly remembering Oñate and Spanish colonization of the present US-Mexico borderlands. In this article, I examine three visual representations of Oñate in New Mexico, in both their presence and absence: the 1993 equestrian statue in Alcade sculpted by Reynolda "Sonny" Rivera and the surrounding visitor centre, the inclusion of "Oñate's foot" in the 2018 SITE Santa Fe exhibition *Casa Tomada*, and the 2005 *Cuarto Centenario* memorial in Albuquerque, comprised of *La Jornada*, a sculptural grouping honouring Oñate's 1598 settlement in New Mexico, and *Numbe Whageh*, an earthwork reflecting a Native response to Oñate's colonial legacies.[7] I consider each site's original purpose and intent, the narratives they convey and obscure, their history of interpretation, and their current situations. These representations, and their active histories, demonstrate how Oñate's colonial violence continues to carry emotional weight in the present day.

---

[3] Molly Montgomery, "Hundreds Petition Country to Remove Oñate Monument," *Rio Grande Sun*, 11 June 2020, http://www.riograndesun.com/news/hundreds-petition-county-to-remove-o-ate-monument/article_2863c708-ab80-11ea-9 33f-f7569a3463df.html (accessed 17 April 2021).

[4] As described by Nora Naranjo-Morse, who attended the removal. Nora Naranjo-Morse, interview with author, 23 March 2021.

[5] Montgomery, "County Takes Down Oñate Monument."

[6] Ibid.

[7] This essay updates my previous examination the *Cuarto Centenario* memorial to consider related representations of Oñate in New Mexico, as well as the events that have occurred since the memorial's installation. See Alison Fields, "New Mexico's Cuarto Centenario: History in Visual Dialogue," *The Public Historian* 33, no. 1 (February 2011): 44–72.

Oñate in New Mexico History and Memory

In 1598, Juan de Oñate led an expedition of nearly 600 colonists, including soldiers and their families, to what is now northern New Mexico, establishing the first permanent European settlement in today's continental United States. The group, which was made up of "Spaniards, other Europeans, mestizos, and indigenous peoples from what was then New Spain" occupied the pueblo Ohkay Owingeh (San Juan Pueblo) before establishing the capital of San Gabriel.[8] As the first territorial governor of New Mexico, Oñate has been credited for introducing horses, cattle, sheep, new crops and technologies to the area inhabited by numerous Pueblo peoples. He also opened a major trade route between New Mexico, Chihuahua, and Mexico City, and enabled the spread of Christianity to the area. However, in his engagement with the region's Native people, Oñate left a violent legacy. In December 1598, a group of Oñate's men ascended Acoma Pueblo in search of supplies against the wishes of the community. After they engaged in theft and the violation of a Pueblo woman, warriors from Acoma Pueblo attacked, killing twelve Spanish soldiers, including Juan de Zaldívar, Oñate's nephew and field marshal.[9] In retaliation, Oñate made a formal declaration of war against the people of Acoma. The resulting three-day invasion led to an estimated 800 deaths at Acoma, the destruction of ceremonial sites, and the enslavement of women and girls. Infamously, in an effort to deter further rebellion, it also saw Oñate order his men to remove the right foot of twenty-four surviving Acoma men. Because of his brutal treatment of the people of Acoma, Oñate was tried as a war criminal by the Spanish government and permanently banished from New Mexico.

Centuries later, Oñate's presence New Mexico has continued in cultural memory – "a field of cultural negotiation through which different stories vie for a place in history."[10] Oñate remains entrenched in New Mexico remembrance as the state's first colonial governor – in street and building names, school mascots, ballads, and festivals. In 1933, the Española Valley Fiesta (known as the Fiesta de Oñate until 1986) was established in honour of Oñate's arrival in northern New Mexico.[11] For the 1998 *Cuarto Centenario*, the four hundredth anniversary of Oñate's settlement in New Mexico, celebrations across the state included parades, performances, and a commemorative stamp. A re-enactor dressed as Oñate even retraced the steps of the colonizer, walking from Zacatecas, Mexico to Española.[12] Oñate's legacies were granted more lasting form in the equestrian statue in Alcade, and as part of the Albuquerque *Cuarto Centenario* Memorial's figurative grouping, *La Jornada*. These efforts were in keeping with other celebrations of Spanish presence in the state. While Oñate faced narrow resistance from the Acoma in 1598, the 1680 Pueblo Revolt was a collective rebellion against Spanish systems of governance and religion. Led by the holy man and war captain Po'Pay of Ohkay Owingeh, the armed revolt temporarily drove the Spanish from New Mexico. Today, the Santa Fe Fiesta holds

---

[8] Michael L. Trujillo, "Oñate's Foot: Remembering and Disremembering in Northern New Mexico," *Aztlán: A Journal of Chicano Studies* 33, no. 2 (Fall 2008): 92.

[9] Trujillo, "Oñate's Foot," 95.

[10] Marita Sturken, *Tangled Memories: The Vietnam War, the Aids Epidemic, and the Politics of Remembering* (Berkeley: University of California Press, 1997), 1.

[11] For more on heritage in the Española Valley, see Thomas H. Guthrie, *Recognizing Heritage: The Politics of Multiculturalism in New Mexico* (Lincoln: University of Nebraska Press, 2013), Chapter 3.

[12] Trujillo, "Oñate's Foot," 93.

an annual reenactment, put on by the group "Los Caballeros de Vargas," celebrating the 1692 return of Spanish forces to New Mexico following the Pueblo Revolt.[13]

Through such commemorative activities, conflicting cultural memories of Oñate were amplified. Scholars, including Philip B. Gonzales, John M. Neito-Phillips, and Charles Montgomery, have detailed the rise of a "Spanish-American" identity in New Mexico in the late nineteenth and early twentieth century.[14] As Neito-Phillips writes, this identity had origins in struggles against political and social marginalization by Anglo Americans, and emerged in response to persistent denigration of New Mexico's Spanish-speaking population as racially mixed, inferior, and not fit for statehood.[15] Out of these conditions, some Spanish-speaking New Mexicans began to "define their racial identify as Spanish, in part by resurrecting archaic notions about 'purity of blood' that dated to the conquest."[16] This definition emphasized European heritage, while creating distance from negative stereotypes of Mexicans. Montgomery writes that both Hispanos and Anglos "used the visual and rhetorical symbolism of the state's colonial past" to define New Mexico's modern Spanish heritage.[17] This reinforced what, in 1948, Carey McWilliams called a Southwest "fantasy heritage," which denied ethnic intermingling and lauded Spanish colonizers as heroes.[18]

Spanish-American identity is distinct from other identities such as "Mexican-American," "Chicano," "Latino," and "Hispanic," which each signal distinctive connections to heritage in Latin America and Spain and carry political and social implications.[19] For instance, Frank G. Pérez and Carlos F. Ortega explain that "Mexican American" identity indicates Americans of Mexican descent, while those that identify as "Chicana/o" see themselves as members of "historically and structurally oppressed group and advocate for social justice."[20] Both "Hispanic" and "Spanish-American" identities, while carrying different class connotations, downplay indigenous ancestry and generally "share a cultural orientation that supports the fantasy heritage of the Southwest."[21]

In New Mexico, fantasy heritage glorified Oñate's contributions as a noble founding father.[22] Among the state's Native communities, however, which include nineteen Pueblos, three Apache tribes, and the Navajo Nation, Oñate was remembered more frequently as the perpetrator of horrific colonial violence and as a convicted war criminal. These memories, resurfaced during planning for the *Cuarto Centenario*, are particularly charged at Acoma Pueblo. As Gonzales concludes, "It was the emotional identification

---

[13] Simon Romero, "Statue's Stolen Foot Reflects Divisions Over Symbols of Conquest," *New York Times*, 30 September 2017, https://www.nytimes.com/2017/09/30/us/statue-foot-new-mexico.html (accessed 1 April 2021).

[14] See Phillip B. Gonzales "History Hits the Heart: Albuquerque's Great *Cuartocentenario* Controversy, 1997–2005" in *Expressing New Mexico: Nuevomexicano Creativity, Ritual, and Memory*, ed. Phillip B. Gonzales (Tucson: University of Arizona Press, 2007); John M. Nieto-Phillips, *The Language of Blood: The Making of Spanish-American Identity in New Mexico, 1880s–1930s* (Albuquerque: University of New Mexico Press, 2004); and Charles Montgomery, *The Spanish Redemption: Heritage, Power, and Loss on New Mexico's Upper Rio Grande* (Berkeley: University of California Press, 2002).

[15] Nieto-Phillips, *The Language of Blood*, 2.

[16] Ibid.

[17] Montgomery, *The Spanish Redemption*, 4.

[18] See Carey McWilliams, *North to Mexico: The Spanish-Speaking People of the United States* (Westport, CT: Praeger; 3rd edition, 2016), Chapter 2.

[19] Trujillo, "Oñate's Foot," 92.

[20] Frank G. Pérez and Carlos F. Ortega, *Deconstructing Eurocentric Tourism and Heritage Narratives in Mexican American Communities: Juan de Oñate as a West Texas Icon* (New York: Routledge, 2020), 33.

[21] Ibid.

[22] Erika Doss, *Memorial Mania: Public Feeling in America* (Chicago: University of Chicago Press, 2010), 313.

with actual and cultural ancestors that rendered the symbolic violence in the Oñate controversy a virtual extension of the real violence of the past."[23]

Originating in tourist efforts emphasizing a romantic Spanish past, the state's public rhetoric often employs a trope of tri-cultural harmony between New Mexico's Native American, Hispanic, and Anglo populations. Central to what Chris Wilson identifies as "the myth of Santa Fe," such unifying rhetoric "obscures long-standing cultural and class frictions."[24] Further, Pérez and Ortega argue that this tri-cultural emphasis "downplays the state's Mexican/American peoples," while exiling Indigenous people to the past.[25] This approach "allows vendors to sell and tourists to consume without having to engage the messiness of colonial exploitation, violence, injustice, and related issues."[26] Robert Trapp, publisher of the *Rio Grande Sun* in Española affirms that lived experience in New Mexico is very different from its marketing: "The racism here is real, multidirectional and simmers just below the surface."[27]

Of course, the realities of long simmering racial tensions and debates over public remembrance are not confined to New Mexico. Over the past several years, protesters across the U.S. have targeted visible symbols of white supremacy, calling specifically for the removal of public statues of Confederate soldiers, slave owners, and conquistadors.[28] Violent counter protests formed, such as the 2017 "Unite the Right" white supremacist rally in Charlottesville, Virginia, which had a stated goal of opposing the removal of a statue of General Robert E. Lee from a local park. During the summer of 2020, when much of the nation endured a locked down due to the COVID-19 pandemic, the May 25 death of George Floyd at the hands of a Minneapolis police officer sparked protests for racial justice across the nation, and revived debates over public statues. In the weeks that followed, dozens of statues and memorials to Confederate soldiers and generals, and other figures of historical oppression, were vandalized or removed. In Boston, for instance, the head of a statue of Christopher Columbus was pulled off during a June protest.[29] Then-President Trump responded to these events in a divisive speech delivered at Mount Rushmore on July 3, criticizing the removal and defacement of these statues as an attack on national heritage.[30] Activist and professor Moises Gonzoles commented that this national movement "has triggered a lot of reflection on some of these monuments and how these monuments portray, at least in New Mexico, this idea of Spanish American white supremacy."[31]

---

[23] Gonzales "History Hits the Heart," 208.

[24] Chris Wilson, *The Myth of Santa Fe: Creating a Modern Regional Tradition* (Albuquerque: University of New Mexico Press, 1997), 8.

[25] Pérez and Ortega, *Deconstructing Eurocentric Tourism and Heritage Narratives in Mexican American Communities*, 1.

[26] Ibid., 34.

[27] Quoted in Romero, "Statue's Stolen Foot Reflects Divisions Over Symbols of Conquest."

[28] "Monumental Lies," *Reveal News*, 15 August 2020, https://revealnews.org/podcast/monumental-lies-update-2/ (accessed 20 March 2021).

[29] Alan Taylor, "The Statues Brought Down Since the George Floyd Protests Began," *The Atlantic*, 2 July 2020, https://www.theatlantic.com/photo/2020/07/photos-statues-removed-george-floyd-protests-began/613774/ (accessed 20 April 2021).

[30] Annie Karni, "Trump Uses Mount Rushmore Speech to Deliver Divisive Culture War Message," *New York Times*, 3 July 2020, https://www.nytimes.com/2020/07/03/us/politics/trump-coronavirus-mount-rushmore.html (accessed 20 April 2021).

[31] John Burnett, "Statues Of Conquistador Juan De Oñate Come Down As New Mexico Wrestles With History," *NPR*, 13 July 2020, https://www.npr.org/2020/07/13/890122729/statues-of-conquistador-juan-de-o-ate-come-down-as-new-mexico-wrestles-with-hist (accessed 5 January 2022).

The conditions that gave rise to the statue removals, both in New Mexico and across the nation, reinforce what memory scholars have long argued: that understandings about the past are shaped by the conditions of the present. Art historian Kirk Savage claims that by tracing the history of commemoration, the fixed notion of the memorial is destabilized, and a history of transformation and change is revealed. Through this process, he writes,

> Grand plans are transformed into actual places, and those places are in turn transformed by the people who occupy and use them. The ground perpetually shifts as changes in the land-scape and in the world around it open up new possibilities of engagement.[32]

Through this continued engagement, memorials marking the past remain open to new meanings. In his study of the Alamo, Richard Flores writes that through the process of memorialization, cultural memories and historical discourse are entangled, embodied in specific sites, and expressed through shifting social practices. In order to understand these relationships, he suggests that we must "cast a glance in two directions at once: toward the past and the narrative entwinement of memory and history and toward the present, so as to examine the construction of place in terms of discursive formation and physical representation."[33] In this article, I trace the commemorative histories of the Oñate statues in New Mexico through this dual lens, calling upon agents of the past and present, as they set the stage for an undetermined future.

Alcade

Before the equestrian statue of Oñate in Alcade was placed on a flatbed truck and hauled to an unnamed garage for safekeeping in June 2020, it attracted relatively few visitors. Just north of Española, a city of about 10,000 people, Alcade has a population of less than 300. Located on rural Highway 68, along the modern scenic route to Taos, the statue was created as part of the Oñate Monument Resource and Visitor Center. The centre was built at the directive of then-Democratic Party boss and longtime State Senator, Emilio Naranjo, influenced in part by the impending *Cuarto Centenario*. In the early 1990s, Naranjo envisioned developing a publicly funded complex to honour Hispanic history and culture in the state that would include a museum, visitor centre, and a towering statue of Oñate.[34] A personal crusade, Naranjo secured over $1,300,000 tax dollars from state legislators to fund the centre in his district, along with major contributions from Rio Arriba County and the U.S. Business Administration.[35] The intent of the visitor centre was to promote the "Hispanic heritage of the Española Valley and Rio Arriba County" near the site of Oñate's initial settlement.[36] In 1993, a dedication ceremony was held to unveil the statue, drawing hundreds to hear speeches from key New

---

[32] Kirk Savage, *Monument Wars: Washington, D.C., the National Mall, and the Transformation of the Memorial Landscape* (Berkeley: University of California Press, 2005), 11.

[33] Richard R. Flores, *Remembering the Alamo: Memory, Modernity, and the Master Symbol*, 18. Also see Laura Hernández-Ehrisman, *Inventing the Fiesta City: Heritage and Carnival and San Antonio* (Albuquerque: University of New Mexico Press, 2008).

[34] Larry Barker, "State's $2M visitor center Oñate's final folly," *KRQE*, 8 February 2016, https://www.krqe.com/news/states-2m-visitor-center-onates-final-folly/ (accessed 17 April 2021).

[35] Barker, "State's $2M visitor center Oñate's final folly."

[36] Rio Arriba County, Oñate Center, http://www.rio-arriba.org/departments_and_divisions/onate_center.html (accessed 25 April 2021).

Mexico politicians. As Naranjo gave thanks to the legacy of Oñate in Northern New Mexcio, some members of the crowd chanted "Viva Don Juan de Oñate. Viva Emilio Naranjo."[37]

After winning a design competition, Reynaldo "Sonny" Rivera, an Albuquerque-based figurative sculptor, was commissioned to create the 12-foot bronze statue, at the cost of approximately $120,000. Rivera modeled the statue after an equestrian statue of ancient Roman emperor Marcus Aurelius, featuring Oñate on horseback wearing battle armour.[38] The horse's muscular legs are frozen in mid-step, its head held high. Oñate is perched forward, staring out to the side, as his hands pull back the reigns and his spurred boots hover at the horse's side. In choosing to depict Oñate, Rivera recognized his complex legacy, acknowledging that he was not a "saint." However, he argues that Oñate's contributions should still be honoured: "I celebrate the courage and spirit of people who confront challenges and overcome obstacles in life."[39] From Rivera's chosen model of Aurelius, to his imposing larger-than-life bronze form, elevated on horseback and ready for battle, Rivera marks Oñate as a masculine and heroic figure dominating the landscape. The statue's heroic narrative is in line with many other monuments marking colonial and westward expansion.[40] Though the equestrian statue and the visitor centre were uniformly celebratory, hiding Onate's legacy of violence, enslavement, and forced labour, the active history of the site is more complex (Figure 1).

While the crowd of the dedication day was an isolated occasion at the rural site, the statue became well known across the state for an incident that occurred several years after its unveiling. On 29 December 1997, in protest of the coming *Cuarto Centenario* celebrations, two anonymous activists slipped into the visitor centre's grounds at night and sawed off the right foot of the Oñate statue. Twenty years later, the self-described foot thief, who wished to remain anonymous, detailed to a *New York Times* reporter how he and his accomplice hiked miles to Alcade to complete their act.[41] He had imagined that the removal would bring Oñate's war crimes into focus, but initially, even the statue's caretakers overlooked the missing foot. So, identifying themselves as "Friends of Acoma," they began to contact local newspapers.[42] Columnist Larry Calloway at *The Albuquerque Journal* was one journalist who received this "combination of a press release and a ransom note," along with a Polaroid photograph of a bronze boot and spur.[43] The note said, "We took the liberty of removing Oñate's right foot on behalf of our brothers and sisters at Acoma Pueblo. We will be melting this foot down and casting small medallions to be sold to those who are historically ignorant."[44] The story of the vandalism soon reached newspapers across the country, as well as in Spain and

---

[37] Barker, "State's $2M visitor center Oñate's final folly."

[38] Doss, *Memorial Mania*, 314. No likeness of Onate has survived, impacting Rivera's approach. See Pérez and Ortega, *Deconstructing Eurocentric Tourism and Heritage Narratives in Mexican American Communities*, 28.

[39] Reynaldo "Sonny" Rivera, "Oñate sculptures need context, not banishment," *MSN*, 28 June 2020, https://www.msn.com/en-us/news/us/oñate-sculptures-need-context-not-banishment/ar-BB163Ruh (accessed 1 April 2021).

[40] Cynthia Prescott, *Pioneer Mother Monuments: Constructing Cultural Memory* (Norman: University of Oklahoma Press, 2019), 10.

[41] Simon Romero, "It Takes a Foot Thief," *New York Times*, 2 October 2017, https://www.nytimes.com/2017/10/02/insider/new-mexico-statue-conquistador-foot-thief.html?action=click&module=RelatedCoverage&pgtype=Article&region=Footer (accessed 1 April 2021).

[42] Romero, "It Takes a Foot Thief."

[43] "Monumental Lies," *Reveal News*.

[44] Stan Alcorn, "Onate's Foot," *99% Invisible*, 4 December 2018, https://99percentinvisible.org/episode/onates-foot/ (accessed 1 April 2021).

Figure 1. Equestrian Statue of Oñate, Alcade, NM.

Mexico, sparking imaginative speculation over the foot thieves' identities. While some local arts leaders and historians responded in anger to the vandalism, other members of the public welcomed the opened dialogue about Oñate's legacy.[45] No medallions appeared publicly, and the centre moved quickly to erase visible evidence of the amputation. Within eight days, Rivera cast a new foot for Oñate (at a cost to taxpayers of $10,000) and welded it on, leaving a slight seam that is only noticeable upon close inspection.

Despite these efforts for immediate repair, in the statue's amputation, the celebratory narrative of the statue was complicated and extended to include Oñate's acts of violence. In an essay examining remembrance in Northern New Mexico, Michael Trujillo writes, "With cutting wit, the vandals ensured that the repressed memory of the Native Americans killed and oppressed in the process of colonization would return to haunt the monument."[46] In addition to broadening the remembrances made possible at the site, Trujillo argues that the act of amputation, and the vandals' proposed plans for the abducted foot, served to symbolically weaken the colonizer's stature. In echoing the act of punishment that Oñate inflicted on the men of Acoma four hundred years earlier, the strength and

---

[45] Doss, *Memorial Mania*, 314.
[46] Trujillo, "Oñate's Foot," 95.

survival of the people of Acoma is highlighted, serving as "a powerful counterpoint to positive assertions of colonization and progress."[47]

While the removal of Oñate's foot generated significant attention, it became evident over time that despite the successful funding to originally create and staff the visitor centre, there was not an adequate business plan to sustain it. A newly elected County Commission removed Naranjo from his role of County Manager soon after the dedication, and the centre only remained open a few years.[48] Though travellers on Highway 68 could see the statue from the road, a low wall and locked gate prevented visitors from approaching it. A variety of tenants, including a school, a flea market, and a yoga studio leased space in the complex.[49] Robert McGeagh, the Oñate Monument's first project director, calls the centre "a complete bust," that never fulfilled its intended mission.[50]

In 2017, the statue returned to public attention when another act of vandalism occurred – this time, Oñate's foot was painted red and the words "Remember 1680," invoking the year of the Pueblo Revolt, were written on the monument's wall.[51] Soon after, prompted by the national conversation about removing Confederate statues, the foot thief came forward to be anonymously interviewed in *New York Times*.[52] The same year, the former Oñate Monument Resource and Visitor Center became the headquarters of the Northern Rio Grande National Heritage Area. Established by Congress in 2006 and encompassing 10,000 square miles in North-central New Mexico, the Heritage Area's mission is to sustain the heritages, languages, traditions and environment of the region.

When the statue was ultimately removed in June 2020, strong emotions were unleashed. Art historian Erika Doss describes memorials as "archives of public affect, 'repositories of feelings and emotions' that are embodied in their material form and narrative content."[53] Controversial memorials like the statue of Oñate, she writes, "speak to the intersection of revisionist histories, origin myths, and feelings of anger in contemporary America."[54] In addition to intense feelings of joy, sorrow, fear, and anger, public response to the removal reflected very different understandings about the nature of history. Those who favoured the Oñate statue remaining in place tended to view history as something fixed in the past, as unalterable fact that must be recognized on its own terms. For instance, New Mexico's District 3 County Commissioner Danny Garcia did not understand the protests for removal, viewing the statue as a documentation of history rather than a glorification of the past. He said, "History happened, and we don't have control of what happened. It's not like we're repeating history just because we have the statue there."[55] Yet for some, this repetition of history is exactly what they saw happening. Elena Ortiz (Ohkay Owingeh), who serves as the chair of the Red Nation Santa Fe chapter (an activist group aiming to liberate Indigenous peoples from colonialism), claims that the statue removal is a reflection of "what is happening

[47] Ibid., 97.
[48] Barker, "State's $2M Visitor Center Oñate's Final Folly."
[49] Ibid.
[50] Ibid.
[51] Romero, "Statue's Stolen Foot Reflects Divisions Over Symbols of Conquest."
[52] Ibid.
[53] Doss, *Memorial Mania*, 13.
[54] Ibid., 14.
[55] Montgomery, "Hundreds Petition Country to Remove Oñate Monument."

now. We are the new ancestors, and this is the new revolt. This is sweeping the nation, and we want to be a part of it."[56] This perspective, aligned with broader movements for racial social justice, the eradication of symbols of historic violence is a necessary act of reclamation.

Santa Fe

From 3 August 2018 to 6 January 2019, at the contemporary art institution SITE Santa Fe, the biennial exhibition *Casa Tomada* centrally featured a cast of Oñate's missing right foot from the Alcade statue. The inclusion of the foot related to the exhibition's larger goal of questioning how history is told and remembered (Figure 2).[57] The biennial was the third in a three-part cycle beginning in 2014, titled "SITElines: New Perspectives on Art of the Americas." Intending to disrupt global trends, all three of SITElines exhibitions focused on the Americas, were collaboratively curated, and were inclusive of Indigenous art.[58] *Casa Tomada* was co-curated by Candice Hopkins, an independent curator based in Albuquerque, José Luis Blondet, Curator of Special Projects at the Los Angeles County Museum of Art, and Ruba Katrib, Curator at MoMA PS1 in New York City. Naomi Beckwith, Marilyn and Larry Fields, Curator at the Museum of Contemporary Art Chicago, served as the exhibition's curatorial advisor. While still responsive to an international audience, biennial organizers determined that "New Mexico, with its still dynamic layers of cultural histories dating back millennia, encompassing multiple pre-colonial and colonial pasts, must be foregrounded."[59]

   Casa Tomada (House Taken Over) was based on Argentine author Julio Cortázar's 1946 short story of the same name, about two elderly siblings who are forced from their ancestral home by a mysterious presence that gradually occupies more and more of their home. While the forces at first seem surreal, they are ultimately attributed to a "human and forcible act" of occupation in the Peronist era in Argentina.[60] An overview of the exhibition notes, "Questioning notions of private property—of the body, mind, land, and culture–the exhibition asks how boundaries are dissolved and/or violated."[61] Through this framework, the exhibition addresses issues of belonging, exclusion, displacement and resistance, and their connection to settler violence and colonialism.

   Oñate's foot came to be part of *Casa Tomada* through a chain of encounters. First, the foot abductor approached filmmaker Chris Eyre (Cheyenne-Arapaho), well known for such films as *Smoke Signals* and *Skins*, by delivering a note while Eyre was eating in a restaurant Santa Fe. While Eyre registered initial skepticism, he agreed to a meeting in September 2017 that resulted in a *New York Times* profile. After this meeting, he connected the foot thief with the biennial curators, who agreed to keep his anonymity. While the statute of limitations has since expired, the theft of the foot was considered a felony.[62]

---

[56] Ibid.
[57] Text panel, *Casa Tomada,* 2018.
[58] Karen Kramer, "SITElines 2018," *Afterimage* Vol. 45, No. 5, 1 March 2018, 7.
[59] Kramer, "SITElines 2018," 7.
[60] Ibid., 8.
[61] "Santa Fe SITElines: New Perspectives on Art of the Americas," https://sitesantafe.org/site-lines/ (accessed 25 March 2021).
[62] Ruby Woltring, "Belonging Together: Curator Candice Hopkins Discusses Threading the Narrative of the Exhibition," *Santa Fe Reporter,* 21–27 November 2018, 12.

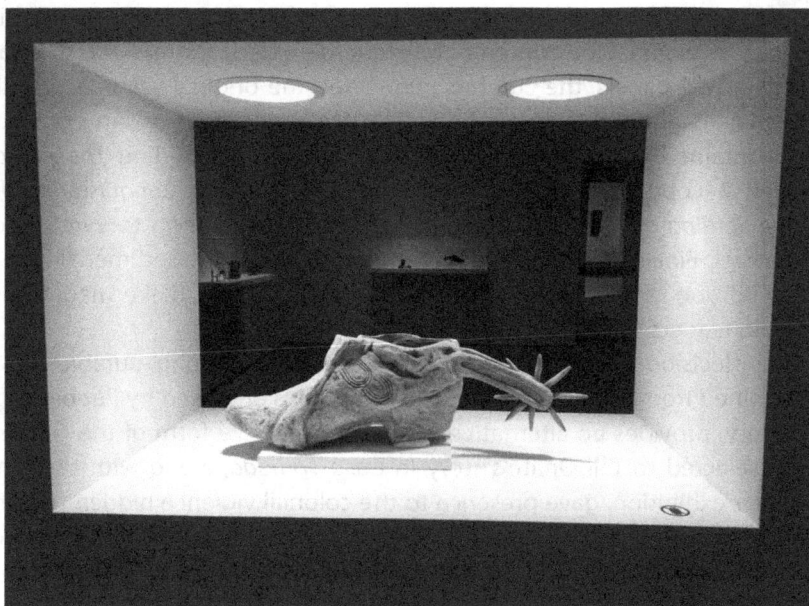

Figure 2. Oñate's boot in Casa Tomada exhibition, SITElines, Santa Fe, NM. Photograph by Alison Fields.

Together, the curators decided that the inclusion of the foot provided a "concrete example of the presence of historical context" that they wished to highlight in *Casa Tomada*. Hopkins saw the inclusion of the foot as "an act of historical reclamation," reflecting: "I thought the foot was an excellent object to speak on all of these complexities and I think it goes to show how something as simple as sculpture can actually be an incredibly resonant gesture, especially now."[63]

In an exhibition review, curator Karen Kramer points out that while *Casa Tomada* translates to "house taken over," the term has multiple implications – including "military seizure," "drunken house," and even "amputation."[64] While Oñate's foot helped to address the exhibition's serious concerns such as migration and displacement, Kramer points to a kind of play in the curator's approach – in both their curatorial roles and in creating dialogue between pieces in the exhibition. For instance, the curatorial team took an active role in creating exhibition content by commissioning a cast of the stolen foot in micaceous clay, displaying both the cast and the moulds in an alcove near the entrance of the exhibition. The foot served as an anchor and reference point for the rest of *Casa Tomada*. As the co-curators reached out to artists to participate, they shared their approach in including Oñate's foot. This led to a thematic and physical interplay between works in the exhibition. For instance, adjacent to Oñate's foot, Lutz Bacher's *Whiteboard*, a found school whiteboard demonstrating "the selectivity of American history," draws a connection between the "historical fallacy" present in the whiteboard's simplified characterization of historical events, and the celebratory narrative of the Oñate statue.[65]

---

[63] Woltring, "Belonging Together."
[64] Kramer, "SITElines 2018," 8.
[65] Woltring, "Belonging Together."

A display of supporting material, "more in line with the practices of national historical museums" than a biennial of contemporary art, provided context for the cast foot and moulds.[66] In text panels, the curators connected the original severance of the foot to current removals and protests over Confederate monuments.[67] An accompanying display case contained items reflecting the story of Oñate, including *The Albuquerque Journal* articles, a copy of historian Marc Simmons' *The Last Conquistador: Juan de Oñate and the Settling of the Far Southwest*, and materials relating to Eyre's encounter with the foot thief. Finally, the display features one of the promised medallions, noting "only the top portion of the foot's ankle was melted down to make medallions to be gifted to Pueblo leaders."

The curators' decision to cast the foot in micaceous clay, a strong, durable clay formed from mineral mined from the Sangre de Cristo mountains and used by Pueblo people for utilitarian pottery, provides an alternative to the fixed bronze form of the Oñate statue. The materials selected to tell Oñate's story in *Casa Tomada*, along with their interplay with the broader exhibition, gave presence to the colonial violence hidden from remembrance in Alcade. However, the curatorial team's strategy of posing open-ended questions, the temporary nature of the exhibition, and its placement in a contemporary art institution, made *Casa Tomada* function differently from the public statues of Oñate. While receiving acclaim from art critics, and considerable attention in local and national media, *Casa Tomada* drew a narrower audience than the public, freely accessible statues of Oñate. The statues, intended to honour Oñate's contributions to New Mexico in a fixed, unchanging form, stood in contrast to the more malleable and open form of *Casa Tomada*.

Albuquerque

In anticipation of the *Cuarto Centenario* celebration in Albuquerque, Millie Santillanes and Conchita Lucero, members of the city's Hispanic Culture Preservation League, proposed erecting a bust of Oñate in Old Town. The timing of this planning coincided with the amputation of the Alcade statue, as well as controversial plans for a massive equestrian statue of Oñate in El Paso, Texas.[68] From the outset, this context contributed to fierce public debate about the purpose and design of the *Cuarto Centenario* memorial. In response to public critique over celebrating Oñate, the city reframed the project as a tri-cultural endeavour that would represent multiple perspectives. The proposed bust quickly developed into much more expansive work of public art, with city taxpayers contributing $800,000. The memorial, which fractured into two parts after a contentious design process that involved a mediation process for the artists and hours of public hearings, was completed in 2005, seven years after the *Cuarto Centenario*. Installed in the Albuquerque Museum's sculpture garden, the memorial occupies 33,500 square feet at the intersection of Mountain Road NW and 19th Street NW. Created by Hispanic artist

---

[66] Kramer, "SITElines 2018," 9.
[67] Text panel, *Casa Tomada*, 2018.
[68] The statue of Oñate in El Paso took ten years to construct, and after its unveiling in 2007, was ultimately renamed "The Equestrian" to remove any reference to Oñate and reinstalled in a remote location near the El Paso airport. See Pérez and Ortega, *Deconstructing Eurocentric Tourism and Heritage in Mexican American Communities*, 92–105 for a detailed account.

Reynaldo "Sonny" Rivera (sculptor of Alcade's Oñate statue) and the late Anglo artist Betty Sabo, *La Jornada* is a bronze figurative grouping of statues representing Oñate's journey with soldiers and settlers along El Camino Real de Tierra Adentro. Adjacent to *La Jornada*, Santa Clara Pueblo artist Nora Naranjo Morse installed *Numbe Whageh*, a spiral earthwork reflecting an Indigenous approach to the landscape.

From the busy intersection, *La Jornada* is a highly visible grouping of sixteen bronze larger-than-life human figures, and a trail of animals, covering a ten by sixty-foot expanse.[69] Rivera placed Oñate as the lead figure on foot and wearing a helmet, facing North to San Gabriel, and flanked by two conquistadors and an Indian guide. In his vision for the memorial, Rivera wished to highlight the hardships, endurance, and honour in embarking on this difficult journey.[70] He emphasized the constant forward motion of the settler, depicting oxen pulling a *carreta*, or wagon, uphill while a man pushed from behind, along with horses carrying settlers. Sabo contributed figures of women, children, and a priest, some modeled after contemporary public figures in Albuquerque, and the smaller animals to the figurative grouping.

Next to the statues, a low wall lists the names of Spanish families that were part of the expedition. A stand-alone plaque narrates the scene, describing the group's journey through present day El Paso, Soccoro, and Albuquerque before reaching San Juan Pueblo, and ultimately establishing a new capital, concluding: "That summer, the first of many Hispanic settlements in New Mexico had been established. The heroic Jornada of 1598 to New Mexico is an important part of our national story." While *La Jornada* celebrates the difficult journey of the Spanish settlers and their ensuing contributions to the New World, like the site in Alcade, it hides Oñate's violent engagement with Native people. A security camera, trained on Oñate's feet, is the only visible reference to this history.

When Nora Naranjo-Morse was invited to join the *Cuarto Centenario* memorial project, Rivera and Sabo had already plans in place for *La Jornada*. As a conceptual artist who moves between media, her vision did not align with the proposed charette, and she turned her attention to the landscape. With *Numbe Whageh* ("Our Center Place"), Naranjo-Morse created a spiral earthwork that invites direct engagement. As visitors descend down the spiral path to a central point six and a half feet below sidewalk level, they are immersed in a landscape of indigenous plants, including shade trees, apache bloom, chamisa, yucca, and cactus, that pre-date Oñate's colonization.[71] Volcanic based rocks donated by Santa Clara Pueblo mark the descending path, and female Native artists have added etchings. Returning from the centre, a side path leads to a point Naranjo-Morse calls "Acoma Bluff," containing a large rock donated by the Pueblo, and facing in the direction of Acoma. Exiting the spiral, until its removal, the sculpture of Oñate was framed between two trees. The narrative of *Numbe Whageh* only engages Oñate, and his colonial force, in this subtle juxtaposition. Instead, the work's spiral form emphasizes a Native perspective on time, linking the past, present, and future. Organic materials stress a narrative of growth, survival, and continued presence, even in the face of colonization.

---

[69] Adult figures in La Jornada stand at least six and a half feet tall.
[70] Fields, "New Mexico's Cuarto Centenario," 58.
[71] Ibid., 62.

During the contentious design phase, the *Cuarto Centenario* memorial received more public response than any other work in Albuquerque's 1,100-piece public art collection. While emotions had flared in the years leading up to the memorial's installation, once completed, public dialogue surrounding the piece largely ceased. Naranjo-Morse reflected,

> After the physical pieces were in place and the project was 'closing down' with some finality to it, I think that people in the city and the Indigenous community, and maybe the Hispanic community, they were just tired. They wanted to move on. I always have maintained that this was just the beginning almost, in some ways, because, Ok, these pieces have gone through this whole period of ten years or so of trying to get born and say something with all of this really challenging dynamic that was taking place. And because everyone was exhausted from fighting and disagreeing, people wanted to just leave it, when to me it would have been a really opportune time to incorporate it into institutions even more.[72]

Following the installation, Naranjo-Morse made a couple of what she calls "futile" attempts to get the museum more actively engaged in dialogue about the controversial design process. She continued to periodically travel from Santa Clara to visit *Numbe Whageh*, maintaining stewardship to the land and removing trash from the site. After a long period of quiet, the site was significantly damaged in an incident when boys from a nearby school snuck down into the centre of *Numbe Whageh* to smoke in secret, and accidentally set the arid landscape on fire. While there was initial alarm that the site was intentionally vandalized, the fire was ultimately proven to be accidental. While Naranjo-Morse again saw an opportunity open dialogue between the school and the museum and expressed willingness to speak about the "real importance of this piece in relationship to La Jornada," the discussion never happened. After the fire, the city brought Naranjo-Morse and the project's landscape architect back to the *Numbe Whageh* to replant the trees and grasses that burnt down.[73] After this effort for rejuvenation, the landscape of *Numbe Whageh* is thriving again.

Removals

On 12 June 2020 the *Albuquerque Journal* ran the article "City faces new calls to remove the Oñate sculpture," reporting that the Albuquerque Museum Board of Trustees had made a request to Mayor Tim Keller to remove the multi-figure La Jornada sculpture from museum grounds, calling such action "overdue."[74] In the request, Pamela Weese Powell, the chair of the advisory board, wrote that *La Jornada* "has caused conflict, pain, and has divided our communities" since its inception.[75] The letter also included a statement from museum trustee Helen Atkins, who wrote that as a person of colour, she read the presence of Oñate at the museum as a sign that she is not welcome.[76] On June 15, shortly after the request on behalf of the museum was made, a prayer vigil was held in Tigeux Park to support the removal of the Oñate statue from the *La Jornada* sculptural grouping.

---

[72] Nora Naranjo-Morse, Interview with author, 23 March 2021.
[73] Ibid.
[74] Dyer and Rick Nathanson, "City faces new calls to remove Oñate sculpture."
[75] Ibid.
[76] Ibid.

Naranjo-Morse received an invitation from the director of the Albuquerque Museum to speak at the prayer vigil, but declined, wanting to learn more about the situation first. However, when she learned Rivera's statue was being taken down in Alcade, she drove the short distance to the site to film the removal, which she described as quick and peaceful. Naranjo-Morse spoke with an older Hispanic man who told her, "I feel sad because he was my hero." She also discussed with Native people who were thrilled with the removal, echoing the dual perspectives she had witnessed during the *Cuarto Centenario* memorial process.[77] As she left the site in Alcade, a light rain began to fall, and she reflected, "Pueblo people believe that rain is a very, very important thing, and I couldn't help but think that there was some cleansing that was happening for the people who had suffered and gone through the violent colonization."[78]

As Naranjo-Morse watched the news that evening, she saw that the prayer vigil in Albuquerque had escalated into a violent confrontation, and a shooting occurred, when five or six heavily armed members of the New Mexico Civil Guard, some dressed in military camouflage and tactical gear, positioned themselves around the statue in attempt to "defend" it. A self-described militia, with members including retired military and law enforcement personnel, the Civil Guard claims to defend the second amendment right to keep and bear arms.[79] Evading the Guard members, protestors brought out a pickax and chain to topple the statue, while Albuquerque police looked on at a distance. Other protestors carried the severed foot of the Oñate statue, again creating a link to events over time and space. During the standoff, Steven Baca, an armed counter protestor not affiliated with the Civil Guard, became engaged in a conflict with three female protesters. Baca drew his gun and fired four times, hitting one of the protestors, Scott Williams, who was taken to the hospital with critical injuries.[80] After the shooting, the Civil Guard formed a perimeter around Baca. Baca, along with members of the Civil Guard, were arrested and taken into custody. While the cause of the shooting was disputed, Baca, a conservative former city council candidate, was charged aggravated battery – a third-degree felony – and for use of a firearm in a felony. Baca's orginal charge was later reduced to "one count of unlawful carrying of a deadly weapon."[81] The police confiscated guns and ammunition from the Civil Guard members, who were released without charges.[82]

By the June 15 vigil, nationwide protests against policy brutality had entered their third week after George Floyd was murdered by a police officer in Minneapolis, and the Civil Guard was calling for new members. A June 8 post on the group's Facebook page claimed: "With police departments across the nation settling on the prospect of defunding or wholly disbanding their police departments it is going to be up to the Citizenry to

---

[77] Ibid.

[78] Ibid.

[79] Rachel Knapp, "New Mexico Civil Guard speaks out, governor and mayor condemn group," *KRQUE*, 16 June 2020, https://www.krqe.com/news/protests/new-mexico-civil-guard-speaks-out-governor-and-mayor-condemn-group/ (accessed 25 March 2021).

[80] John Burnett, "New Mexico Leaders To Militia: If You Want To Help Community, Stop Showing Up Armed," *NPR*, 7 July 2020, https://www.npr.org/2020/07/06/886586653/new-mexico-leaders-to-militia-if-you-want-to-help-community-stop-showing-up-arme (accessed 25 March 2021).

[81] "Suspect In Shooting At Albuquerque Statue Demonstration Faces New Charges," *NPR*, 17 June 2020, https://www.npr.org/sections/live-updates-protests-for-racial-justice/2020/06/17/879410425/man-charged-over-shooting-at-albuquerque-statue-protest#:~:text=Steven%20Ray%20Baca%20was%20initially%20arrested%20and%20charged, that%20also%20drew%20armed%20vigilantes%20to%20protect%20it (accessed 3 January 2022).

[82] Burnett, "New Mexico Leaders To Militia: If You Want To Help Community, Stop Showing Up Armed."

take up the slack and keep our cities and counties safe."[83] Like other recently formed militias, the group appeared at events where they expect to encounter leftists, such as Black Lives Matter protests and monument removals.[84] Led by a former member of a violent neo-Nazi gang, the Civil Guard claimed to have no position on the Oñate statue, and that they were present to serve as protectors of individual rights. However, Gilbert Gallegos, the APD spokesman, said they have told members of the group they "are not welcome" at public events. "The fact remains that the New Mexico Civil Guard has actively worked to intimidate peaceful protesters, make them fearful and raise tensions," Gallegos said.[85] After the shooting, the city responded by banning firearms in public parks. Like the statue in Alcade, the figure of Oñate was removed from *La Jornada* over concerns for public safety.

In viewing the news coverage of the protest, Naranjo-Morse found herself extremely bothered by the presence of militia in combat uniforms standing on the berm of *Numbe Whageh*, in an echo of colonial violence. In this stance, there was no recognition of *Numbe Whageh* as a sacred place, "blessed by people who understood that giving the land back to itself and following those Pueblo value systems is still a very important thing to do."[86] It was this information that Naranjo-Morse wished that she had been able to convey to the "naughty boys who burned down half of *Numbe Whageh*," to make a possible impact on how they viewed the land and its history. She continued, "But when I saw those guys standing with – they looked like very scary weapons – without too much respect but very willing to be part of this militia and this anger and this violence, again – different suits, same mentality."[87]

Conclusion

In response to the June 2020 violence at the *Cuarto Centenario* memorial and the removal of the Oñate statue, the city of Albuquerque launched the Race, Healing, and History Project, a series of public hearings and interviews meant to gauge public sentiment and develop a plan for the future of *La Jornada*. Rivera and Naranjo-Morse, the memorial's two living artists, have also been asked to share their perspectives. In an editorial written after his statues' removal, Rivera aligns himself with the racial justice movement against police brutality, but disagrees with the removal of controversial art. He writes that the removal of Spanish historical figures and symbols will only lead to "more retaliations, more destruction, and more violence."[88] Instead, Rivera suggests additional plaques be placed by his sculptures, allowing room for other perspectives.

Naranjo-Morse shared complex feelings about the future of *La Jornada*, and how to address the fear – of loss of identity, of having something to hold onto – that seemed to drive many discussions surrounding the *Cuarto Centenario*. She said,

---

[83] "Who are the New Mexico Civil Guard? All you need to know about militia group at center of Albuquerque shooting," *Meaww*, 16 June 2020, https://meaww.com/who-are-the-new-mexico-civil-gaurd-militia-group-center-albuquerque-shooting-statue-protests (accessed 25 March 2021).

[84] Matthew Reisen, "NM Civil Guard is marching forward, despite calls to stand down," *Albuquerque Journal*, 4 July 2020, https://www.abqjournal.com/1472698 (accessed 25 March 2021).

[85] Reisen, "NM Civil Guard is marching forward, despite calls to stand down."

[86] Interview with author, 23 March 2021.

[87] Ibid.

[88] Rivera, "Oñate sculptures need context, not banishment."

It's so deep and such a long history that to go back, especially with adults who have already been colonized and already been socialized to believe certain things about their neighbors or the pueblo next door … that this kind of teaching and understanding and listening and compassion has to start at a really early age.[89]

Like Rivera, Naranjo-Morse suggested that increased signage, along with more education experiences telling the story of the *Cuarto Centenario* would offer children to become aware of their own history.

What will happen with how the institutions, the city, the groups of people involved will decide what to do with Oñate, that is totally out of my control. But I can tell them what it was like for me and it profoundly changed me and actually made me a better artist, it made me a better human being.[90]

In October 2020, the Race, Healing, and History Project presented its report on *La Jornada* to the Albuquerque City Council, which concluded:

The takeaway from these responses is to balance two sets of needs. First are the needs to learn from history and to respect and honor all cultures. The second are the needs to stand in solidarity with groups that have been harmed and not glorify harmful actions.

While most participants in the project did not believe that the Oñate statue should not be returned to *La Jornada*, the city has not reached a final conclusion on its fate.[91]

It is evident that tracing the commemorative histories of Oñate remains an ongoing task. The events shaping remembrance of Oñate at sites in Alcade, Santa Fe, and Albuquerque, reinforce Kathy Friese's claim that "The most effective public memorials do not present a narrative as though it is complete. Instead, they point to the tension of the past that seeps into the present and taps into the instability of memory itself."[92] The multi-faceted exhibition of *Casa Tomada* and Naranjo-Morse's *Numbe Whageh* provide such open forms of remembrance. While Rivera's bronze, larger-than-life statues celebrated Oñate and his journey to New Mexico, their active histories revealed far more complex narratives. Through amputation and removal, representations of Oñate and his legacies of colonial violence, continue to resonate in the present day.

Disclosure Statement

No potential conflict of interest was reported by the author(s).

---

[89] Interview with author, 23 March 2021.
[90] Ibid.
[91] Jake Bullinger, "Building Better Monuments," 10 March 2021, *Bitterroot: The West's Magazine*, https://bitterrootmag.com/2021/03/10/building-better-monuments-albuquerque-onate-pueblo-new-mexico/ (accessed 25 March 2021).
[92] Kathy Freise, "Contesting Oñate: Sculpting the Shape of Memory," in *Expressing New Mexico*.

De-Colonizing Australia's Commemorative Landscape: "Truth-Telling," Contestation and the Dialogical Turn

Bruce Scates and Peter Yu

ABSTRACT
This article will explore the origins and afterlife of the Explorers' Memorial in Fremantle, Western Australia. Raised to commemorate the "murder" of white pioneers in the 1860s, the monument issued an explicit denial of Indigenous sovereignty and exonerated white violence on the frontier. In an instance of dialogical memorialization, an additional plaque was placed on the monument. It outlines the history of provocation that led to the explorers' deaths, acknowledges the right of Aboriginal people to defend their lands and commemorates those who died during the invasion of their country. The article will draw on community memory as well as white archival accounts. It will reveal the spaces counter-memorialization might offer for alternative readings of the past and explore the monument's transition from a symbol of racism and division to a platform for what is generally known in Australia as truth-telling and reconciliation.

To the European settler community, [Joe Edgar wrote] and [to] historians of the time, the explorers were "murdered" in cold blood in an unprovoked attack "at night by treacherous natives." To the Aboriginal community, the explorers were invaders. For the settler community the massacre at La Grange, was a "punitive" mission, the killing justified as punishment for the explorers' deaths. For the Aboriginal Community it was unjustified slaughter.[1]

In 2019, Joe Edgar's words became the focal point of an exhibition fielded by the Liyan Ngan Nyirrwa Cultural Centre in Broome, Western Australia. A direct descendent of a survivor of the La Grange Bay massacre of 1865, he recalled stories "handed down from his grandmother," relating the first fraught encounter between Karajarri people and white colonizers. Those forced incursions on Aboriginal lands set in train a catastrophic collision of cultures commonplace not just at La Grange but right across the Australian continent – all along the black/white frontier Aboriginal resistance met with brutal reprisal. For Joe Edgar, the massacre of 1865 was part of a historical continuum, "further genocidal acts

---

[1] Text of Budgerigars Nurani exhibition panel, Liyan-Ngan Nyirrwa Cultural Wellbeing Centre, Cable Beach, Broome, 2019. Text kindly provided by Sarah Yu. This paper emerged from a workshop convened in 2020 to consider the course of the statue wars. Thanks are due to the organizer Janne Lahti and Cynthia Culver Prescott, as well as Rae Frances, Bec Wheatley, and all involved in the project workshop. We also acknowledge the constructive critique offered by the readers and editors of the *Journal of Genocide Research*.

towards Aboriginal people," from "physical 'extermination'" to "the removal of children during the Stolen Generation period," visited immense trauma on families and communities, his own included. Like others at Bidyadanga (La Grange), he saw a need to give balance to "what had previously been a one-sided story," and challenge a (white) history that "in so many instances ignored Aboriginal perspectives."[2]

This article deals with one such interrogation of history. Its focus is on a memorial, the Explorers' Monument in Fremantle, Western Australia, raised to commemorate both the white explorers killed at La Grange and the "punitive expedition" that followed. We begin with a critical reassessment of claims made by "the settler community and white historians" of the time, outlining the history of provocation that led to explorers' deaths and revealing the scale of white retaliatory violence. We then consider attempts to raise a counter narrative alongside the original memorial, opening spaces for alternative interpretations of the past and acknowledging both the right of Aboriginal people to defend their lands and their unceded sovereignty over the same. We will argue that this process of "dialogical memorialisation" helps transform a symbol of racism and division into an active platform for what is often styled "truth telling and reconciliation." At a general level, (as Jeffrey Olick argues) all collective memory takes shape dialogically: social actors who rework images of the past do so in conversation with earlier narratives.[3] In this case, dialogical memorialization involves a "new and critical form of commemorative practice," namely the crafting of an alternative historical narrative that contests "the purpose and the design of a specific, existing monument, in an explicit, contrary and proximate pairing."[4]

The installation of this counter-monument was approved (in principle) by Fremantle City Council in November 1988. This was one of the first such interventions of its kind, and set an important precedent for subsequent commemorations of frontier violence.[5] The project is considered a landmark in Australia's "statue wars"[6] and it suggests ways "communities [might] deal with the symbols of violent and oppressive pasts whose legacies are still woven into both physical landscapes and social relations."[7] Such debates –

---

[2] Ibid.; Vanessa Mills and Ben Collins, "The Controversial Statue that was Added to, Not Torn Down or Vandalized," *ABC Kimberly*, https://www.abc.net.au/news/2017-08-29/explorers-monument-added-to-not-torn-down-or-vandalised/8853224 (accessed 10 March 2021).

[3] Jeffrey Olick, *The Politics of Regret: On Collective Memory and Historical Responsibility* (New York: Routledge, 2007), 106.

[4] Quentin Stevens, Karen A. Franck, and Ruth Fazakerley, "Counter-Monuments: The Anti-Monumental and the Dialogic," *The Journal of Architecture* 17, no. 6 (2012): 951–2.

[5] See, for instance, the memorials raised at Pinjarra and Ravensthorpe, WA. (2001 and 2015); Hospital Creek, Myall Creek and Appin, NSW (1995, 2000 and 2016) and Yarra Glen and Port Fairy, Victoria (2007 and 2011). Whilst each might be the subject of a separate article, all involve Indigenous communities contesting white narratives of "settlement" and dispossession. A useful survey of "public monuments and memorials which have been erected to commemorate the conflict between Indigenous Australians and immigrant settlers" is provided on the *Monument Australia* website, https://monumentaustralia.org.au/themes/conflict/indigenous (accessed 28 November 2021).

[6] Chilla Bulbeck, "Aborigines, Memorials and the History of the Frontier," *Australian Historical Studies* 24, no. 96 (April 1991): 168–78; Jenny Gregory, "Statue Wars: Collective Memory Reshaping the Past," *History Australia* 18, no. 3 (2021): 564–87; Bruce Scates, "Set in Stone? Dialogical Memorialisation and the Beginnings of Australia's Statue Wars," *Public History Review* 28 (2021): 1–12. "Statue Wars" involve the defacement, destruction, alteration or relocation of commemorative structures. They also encompass both the public debate and counter-memorialisation considered in this article. Gregory traces the course of the "Statue Wars" from the beginnings of the Rhodes Must Fall movement in 2014 through to Black Lives Matter protests of recent years, but also notes a much longer lineage. For a revealing history of what's been has called "iconoclasm," including the toppling of monuments in the former Soviet bloc see Dario Gamboni, *The Destruction of Art: Iconoclasm and Vandalism since the French Revolution* (London: Reaktion Books, 1997).

centred not just on this specific monument but what to do with contentious heritage generally – are canvassed in the article. We end by considering the "afterlife" of the Explorers' Memorial, and the role its remaking might play in the de-colonizing of commemorative landscapes.

The Making of a Monument

The Explorers' Monument was raised in Fremantle in 1913, almost half a century after that first violent encounter at La Grange. That in itself is significant. In the early years of the twentieth century white Australia was a newly federated nation, and, like most settler societies examined in this issue, intent on forging its own foundation narratives. The "pioneer myth"[8] served that purpose: a memorial raised to "intrepid" explorers "murdered by treacherous natives" recalled the dangers and privations faced by those who "opened up" the land, contrasted white valour and victimhood with "native savagery" and rationalized the dispossession of First Nations' Peoples. The same impulse (as one contemporary account put it) to "write history in stone" gave rise to a series of explorer monuments in all the states of the Commonwealth.[9] Many took the form of statues of "heroic size,"[10] some involved cairns retracing the explorers' routes,[11] all proclaimed – through text and statuary – white possession of Aboriginal lands.[12] Western Australia, in particular, was said to have "turned out her full share of brave and hardy pioneers," along with monumental tributes to the same, men who "carrying their lives in their hands … have gone forth into the wilderness."[13]

All those themes were taken up in earnest by Sir John Forrest, then the Premier of Western Australia and the principal speaker at the memorial's dedication ceremony. In his youth, Forrest had led a number of expeditions into what was often called the "hostile" interior acquiring first-hand knowledge of "the blacks."[14] In 1913, he spoke with conviction to the "large assembly of well-known citizens," relating the fate of the "murdered" men and exonerating those sent to avenge them. Forrest viewed the monument as a kind of bequest, "a way," as Benedict Anderson once observed, "of mediating between particular types of pasts and futures."[15]

---

[7] Christina Simko, David Cunningham, and Nicole Fox, "Contesting Commemorative Landscapes: Confederate Monuments and Trajectories of Change," *Social Problems* (2020): 1–21. The context is the commemorative landscape of the American south but the same observation applies to Australia and other white settler nations.

[8] Tom Stannage, *Western Australia's Heritage: The Pioneer Myth* (Nedlands: University Extension, University of Western Australia, 1985), 21–31.

[9] See the account of the monument erected to John McDouall Stuart (Maitland Brown's contemporary) who blazed a trail from Adelaide to the centre of the continent, *Advertiser*, 4 June 1904.

[10] This description applied to James Cook's memorial raised (in Melbourne) as Australians embarked for service in the Great War, *Argus*, 8 December 1914.

[11] Tom Griffiths, *Hunters and Collectors: The Antiquarian Imagination in Australia* (Cambridge: Cambridge University Press, 1996), 150.

[12] Many, though not all, of these monuments have been targeted in Australia's statue wars.

[13] *Eastern Districts Chronicle*, 5 May 1888.

[14] Elizabeth Goddard and Tom Stannage, "John Forrest and the Aborigines," *Studies in Western Australian History: European-Aboriginal Relations in Western Australian History*, eds. Bob Reece and C.T. Stannage, no. 8 (1984): 52–7. A decade after Panter, Harding, and Goldwyer's deaths Forrest trekked some two thousand miles across the West Australian interior. A statue raised in 1927 recounted that journey, as did a companion monument (sculpted by Peitro Porcelli) to the memory of his brother, see entries for Alexander Forrest and Lord Forrest on the *Monument Australia* website, https://monumentaustralia.org.au/search (accessed 28 November 2021).

[15] *Sunday Times*, 9 February 1913; Benedict Anderson, *Language and Power: Exploring Political Cultures in Indonesia* (Ithaca, NY; Cornell University Press, 1993), 174.

No doubt many of [you] remembered the story of the tragedy. At the time the three men Panter, Harding, and Goldwyer were engaged in exploration work to the south-west of Roebuck Bay. ... Some ... would remember how one night they were treacherously murdered by the natives, apparently while they were asleep. When no news had been received been received of the three men, the Government organised a search party and the command was given to Mr. Maitland Brown ... . It was now a matter of history how the remains had been discovered by the search party, and how later a ship was sent up north and the remains brought for burial. ... Regarding the statue they were unveiling that day, he thought that it would tend to remind the people of Western Australia of three things. It would serve to remind them of the terrible tragedy [that befell] Messrs. Panter, Harding, and Goldwyer. It would also be the means keeping green in the memory of them all the name of Julius Brockman, the generous donor, explorer, and son of the early colonist who was one of the founders of Western Australia. And it would serve to remind them of the able pioneer, that intrepid explorer, ... Maitland Brown, and the splendid services be had rendered his country.[16]

A few images of the dedication service survive. They show Forrest glancing hastily at his notes and Lady Forrest (who did not speak but played a ceremonial role) formally unveiling the monument. The photographs reveal a surprisingly large cross section of Western Australian society. The dedication of the Explorers' Monument was what historians would call "a ritual of social integration" – though one tightly structured in terms of class and gender.[17] Middle-aged men in black frock suits stand closest to the Premier, flanked by Fremantle's Mayor and Councillors. With the exception of Lady Forrest, women occupy an outer circle, dressed in voluminous skirts and sweltering beneath parasols. There are a large party of smart young men sporting boater hats, a man in a peaked clothed cap stands at the very edge of the crowd, straining (one suspects) to hear the words of his betters. In one photo taken that day, three children gaze curiously back at the camera – one appears to be smiling (Figure 1).

This was a ceremony set in what Joe Feagan would call a "white racial frame." It served to legitimize racial inequality and conceal the "bloody historical realities" of Indigenous People's dispossession.[18] By the early twentieth century, the Noonyar people of Perth were incarcerated on reserves and excluded from public places where such statues were raised. The Karajarri, descendants of those massacred at La Grange fifty years earlier, had been driven from their traditional lands and formed a vast pool of unpaid labour on northern pastoral stations, over 1,500 kilometres distant from Fremantle. Ironically, those who resisted the white occupation of their lands passed through the port city en-route to the island prison of Rottness. There dozens of Karajarri men succumbed to maltreatment and disease.

Some wondered at the time if the Explorers' Monument might have been better placed in Broome, the administrative centre of northern settlement and infinitely closer to where the tragedy unfolded.[19] But the frontier – as a white imaginary – seemed all the more compelling for distance; Fremantle was the place Maitland Brown had been born and the vibrant port stood at the centre of maritime links to the pastoral and pearling industries. The builders of the monument elected to place it on what is now the Esplanade

[16] *Western Mail*, 14 February 1913.
[17] E.J. Hobsbawm and Terence Ranger, *The Invention of Tradition* (Cambridge: Cambridge University Press, 1983), 263.
[18] Joe Feagin, *The White Racial Frame: Centuries of Racial Framing and Counter Framing* (New York: Routledge, 2013), 17.
[19] *Truth*, 16 March 1912.

Figure 1. "A ritual of social integration." The crowd relaxes after the formal dedication of the memorial. Note the Esplanade Hotel in the background. In 1913, the statue bordered the entrance to the Port City. Source: *Western Mail*, 14 February 1913.

Reserve but was then the busy entrance to the harbour. That place was chosen above a "prominent site" in the town and for one compelling reason. Within a stone's throw of the Reserve the first white settlers of Western Australia waded ashore almost a century earlier.[20]

A Sermon in Stone: The Meanings of the Monument

Contextualizing the Explorers' Monument is one task; visualizing it another. The memorial took the form of bronze bust, some five feet high, mounted on a granite pedestal. The former was "a wonderfully life-like representation" of Maitland Brown (though one contemporary complained that this "man of action" would never wear a necktie); the latter was ringed with "panel decorations." Their purpose is instructive – like Forrest's words that day, they tell a story and fashion a mythology. With a "fine disregard for punctuation,"[21] the monument's inscription outlines the multifaceted nature of remembrance:

> THIS MONUMENT WAS ERECTED BY
> G. J. BROCKMAN
> as a fellow bush wanderer's tribute to the memory of
> PANTER, HARDING and GOLDWYER

---

[20] *Daily News*, 3 September 1912.
[21] *Truth*, 16 March 1912; *Sunday Times*, 22 September 1916; see Healy's discussion of similar memorials, Chris Healy, *From the Ruins of Colonialism: History as Social Memory* (Cambridge: Cambridge University Press, 1997), 23.

> earliest explorers after Grey and Gregory of this
> "Terra Incognita", attacked at night by treachorous natives
> were murdered at Boola Boola near Le Grange Bay
> on the 13 November 1864.
> also as an appreciative token of remembrance of
> MAITLAND BROWN
> one of the pioneer pastoralists and premier politicians of this
> state, intrepid leader of the government search and punitive
> party. His remains together with the sad relics of the ill
> fated three recovered at great risk and danger from lone
> wilds repose under a public monument in the East Perth Cemetery
> "LEST WE FORGET."[22]

These words convey the mindset of white colonialism; they reinforce the binary division between colonizer and colonized, viewer and observed. Exploration, as historian Simon Ryan explains, is "constructed as a heroic practice, furthering the frontier of empire, penetrating and conquering unknown and unowned lands." One notes here the forceful exercise of political linguistics; blacks "murder" whites whilst the retaliatory violence of the punitive party passes quietly without mention. And the gendered nature of this discourse is striking – "a fellow bush wanderers' tribute" evokes the white masculine camaraderie of frontier society.[23]

The visual narrative provides a secondary "memory text."[24] Around the base of the monument the sculptor, Naples trained artist Pietro Porcelli, set three bas-reliefs. The first depicts the "ill-fated free": J. K. Panter, Inspector of Police and leader of the party; James Harding, manager of the Roebuck Bay Company and "in command of the commercial side of the expedition"; and William Henry Goldwyer, also seconded from the police and "a most experienced bushman." The purpose of their journey north was threefold. They would, as the Prospectus of the Company put it, "secure land" fit for pastoral purposes, identify harbours suitable for landing stock and "explore country southward ... with a view to ... occupation." This document made no mention of the prior occupation of the land by First Nations Peoples; nor did it suggest any need for negotiation or recompense. Rather, land would be granted to prospective settlers by white authorities in Perth, extending the boundaries of settlement and securing rich returns for private investment. The expedition of 1864 followed the pattern of almost a century of white exploration and occupation of the continent, a collusion of state and private interests predicated on the dispossession of Indigenous inhabitants.[25] For their part, Panter, Harding, and Goldwyer styled themselves adventurers, entrepreneurs who hoped to wrest "fabulous wealth" from the Nor'West. Panter had mastered the use of firearms policing the tense frontiers of Queensland, Harding married into the elite of West Australia's pastoral families, whilst Goldwyer had worked as a ship's mate and still wore seaman's earrings.[26] Porcelli's portraits in bronze reveal nothing of these men's colourful pasts, idealizing and ennobling them. Heroic statuary reduced complex and often contradictory historical actors to simplistic, one-dimension caricatures (Figure 2).

---

[22] Text of Bugarrigarra Nyurdany exhibition panel.
[23] Simon Ryan, *The Cartographic Eye: How Explorers Saw Australia* (Cambridge: Cambridge University Press, 1996), 1.
[24] Madge Dresser, "Set in Stone? Statues and Slavery in London," *History Workshop Journal* 64, no. 4 (2007): 167.
[25] *Perth Inquirer and Commercial News*, 3 August 1864.
[26] *Geraldton Express*, 24 September 1920 and 5 June 1937.

Figure 2. "Noble in Bearing." These studio portraits of the explorers provided the basis of Porcelli's bas relief. "In Memoriam" cards like this were another way the story of the explorers was circulated in the community. It also suggests the commercialization of their memory. Source: Battye Library, 225B.

The memorial also pays tribute to its sponsor. A second bas-relief depicts George Julius Brockman, dressed in a style that befits a public benefactor. Brockman would die six months before the monument was completed, but not before approving – at the cost of several hundred pounds – that finely sculpted image of himself. Power and privilege lie behind the building of every great memorial and this one is no exception. Brockman was a direct beneficiary of the explorers' "sacrifice." He made his fortune on pastoral stations they died to establish, working stolen Aboriginal lands with cheap (often unpaid) Aboriginal labour.[27] In that sense, the explorers' monument, raised, like much Confederate statuary, a generation after the events it commemorated, "can be understood less as arguments about battles fought long ago than as contestations for power rooted firmly in the here and now."[28]

A final plaque depicts Maitland Brown's discovery of the explorers' remains. Two bodies are framed by a makeshift tent, visual "confirmation" that these men were butchered in their sleep. A third body lays several feet distant, midst "broken spears and dowaks." Approaching the scene are two figures chained by the neck – these are the "native informants" Brown seized on landing at La Grange. For several hours these "unwilling guides" circled the camp, taking "roundabout routes" though dense bush, "endeavouring to escape" and infuriating their captors.[29] White men flanked by their horses complete the scene. Well-equipped and heavily armed, the punitive party takes on the appearance of a military expedition. And the figure of Brown himself commands this visual ensemble – one hand raised in the air, mounted tall on horseback. Regardless of "risk" to himself, he would bring black "murderers" to "justice."

That fourth plaque stopped history short. The bloody work of avenging the explorers' deaths is implied but never stated. To actually depict the "rough justice" of the frontier would have undermined the central narratives of "native savagery" and "white victimhood." Rather the whites presented themselves (as Joe Edgar's opening remarks observed) as "settlers" rather than "invaders." The only mention made of the punitive party emphasizes "risk and great danger" to the white men sent to avenge the explorers' deaths, overlooking the terror they unleashed on Aboriginal communities.

The killings in 1865 began with the prisoners, addressed only as "A" and "B" in Maitland Brown's journal. Both men "untied their ropes and bolted." They were pursued and gunned down by "Tommy," one of the "Native Trackers" recruited from further south to assist the punitive party. Shot through the heart "B" died "almost immediately." "A" lingered on for fifteen minutes, "he never uttered a groan," Brown's journal claimed, "but died as he had lived – a savage." "A" also confessed to both men's part in the murder – at least that is what Maitland Brown would tell the authorities back in Fremantle. Searching the bush in the hope of taking further prisoners, Brown encountered a group of hostile "natives." They were "ambushed," he told the Governor, yet another claim one must read with scepticism. That single "sharp encounter" alone cost the lives of around twenty Aboriginal people. None of the "ambushed" whites were killed or seriously wounded. Brown's account of the incident used a by now familiar narrative of white courage verses wanton savagery:

---

[27] *Sunday Times*, 5 February 1913; Mary Anne Jebb, *Blood, Sweat and Welfare: A History of White Bosses and Aboriginal Pastoral Workers* (Nedlands: University of Western Australia Press, 2002), chapter 1; Malcolm Allbrook, *Henry Prinsep's Empire: Framing a Distant Colony* (Canberra: ANU Press, 2014), 199–286.

[28] Alex W. Baker, "In Whose Honor/In Whose Time? Regimes of Historicity and the Debate over Confederate Monuments," *Museum Anthropology* 42, no. 2 (2018): 126.

[29] David Francisco, *The Panter-Harding-Goldwyer relief expedition of 1865 . . .* (Nedlands: Royal Western Australian Historical Society, 1928), 4 April 1865; *Eastern Districts Chronicle,* 19 May 1905.

... the natives stood their ground with the savage, though not cool, pluck of an Englishman, ... they disdained to throw down their arms, resisting savagely to the last. It was evident that this was the first lesson taught to the natives in this district of the superiority of civilised men and weapons over the savage ... they live only for the present these natives – strategy, cunning, lying and a thirst for blood are the first creeds taught to them.[30]

The "blood lust" of the "native" is a familiar trope in white colonial narratives. It served to justify savage reprisals by the punitive party. Under interrogation, two of the "natives" Brown had long held captive in the ship "confessed to having been engaged in the murder." It was Brown's intention these men be committed for trial but both "made their escape from the ship before daylight." Only of one of the "fugitives" reached the shore, the "other one was seen floating past the ship."[31] For each of the dead explorers, at least three Aboriginal people had been killed. Such was the arithmetic of white terror on the frontier.

Hidden Histories, Unstable Meanings

In early 1914, Perth's *Daily News* warned the Explorers' Monument was "in dangerous disrepair." The sculptor confirmed the foundations were "insecure" and warned Fremantle City Council of "the present danger which threatens both the statue and the public." The paper urged the authorities to "make the memorial safe without delay."[32] At the time this warning was made, the *Daily News'* recommendation was simple and straightforward. The Explorers' Monument was in need of repair. No-one (or at least no-one in the largely white community of Fremantle) called for its removal or destruction. Even so, the observation that the memorial's foundations were "unstable" presented an unintended irony. In the first instance, the monument faced what scholars have termed an unintended "oblivion," its presence eclipsed by the changing civic landscape around it.[33] When the monument came again into public focus, in the late twentieth century, its original meanings would be assailed and discredited, and a new memorial – embodying a very different reading of history – set at its foundation.

Robert Musil once remarked that it was the fate of most monuments to become invisible.[34] Initially that adage rang true for the Explorers' Monument. As the century moved on, it became less and less celebrated a feature of the civic landscape but arguably, from the moment the monument had been raised, it had neared the effective end of what Jay Winter would call its "shelf life."[35] Fremantle's "founding fathers" (Maitland Brown and G. J. Brockman included) were dead by 1913, the explorers themselves had been killed half a century earlier. By the mid-twentieth century, with the occupation of the Nor'West largely complete, their heroic narrative of white pioneering had lost something of its urgency. Changes to the layout of Fremantle hastened that slippage from collective memory. The Inner Harbour was opened up, shipping and commercial activities diverted from the area, and Esplanade Reserve, formally the frontage of a busy coastal port, cut off

---

[30] Maitland Brown, *Journal of an Expedition in the Roebuck Bay District* ... (Perth, 1865), 17–20; *Western Mail*, 4 April 1908.

[31] *Francisco Diary*, 10, 11 April 1865.

[32] *Daily News*, 19 May 1914.

[33] See, for example, Adrian Forty and Susanne Küchler, *The Art of Forgetting* (Oxford: Berg, 1999).

[34] Werner Fenz, "The Monument is Invisible, the Sign Visible," *October* 48 (1989): 75.

[35] Jay Winter and Emmanuel Sivan, *War and Remembrance* (Cambridge: Cambridge University Press, 2000), 16.

in a kind of "backwater."[36] By 1949, the *West Australian* described the monument as the city's "forgotten memorial," standing "quiet and almost forlorn" in the shade of "lofty" pine trees. Nor did Porcelli's work age particularly well. The brisk salt air of Fremantle weathered several of the plagues and to all but a determined eye, parts of the inscription became almost illegible.[37] The statue stood there, "on the edge of awareness, waiting to come to life." It would "regain visibility" (as David Morgan observed of Confederate memorials) "in episodes of crisis" when even aged monuments can still polarize public life and serve as "lightning rods … of social conflict."[38]

The arrival of white Australia's bicentennial year in 1988 provided just such a moment of crisis. Two hundred years of European settlement sparked a series of protests across the entire nation. Indigenous and non-Indigenous Australians marched beneath banners reading "White Australia Has A Black History"; there was a new willingness to acknowledge and embrace Indigenous readings of the past, and the term "invasion" abruptly supplanted that of "settlement."[39]

So far as the monument was concerned, Australia's bicentennial year would mark a reversal of over a century of white scholarship, fresh academic inquiry, and a reassessment of the cause and significance of frontier violence in Western Australia reflected a much wider process underway in Australian society to grapple with difficult colonial legacies.[40] Generations of white historians had exonerated the explorers as innocent men. "Nothing had been taken from the camp," J. S. Battye's foundational history of the state in 1924 declared, "showing the act to have been one of brutal murder to satisfy the natives lust for blood." Over sixty years later Peter Cowan still subscribed to the fiction of men murdered "as they slept." "[They] were lying in their beds as they were made," he wrote "it was clear there had been no fight."[41] Both accounts suggest uncritical acceptance of the explorers' partial and partisan record, those "thrilling stories of pluck and adventure"[42] that formed the fabric of pioneer mythology. A more nuanced reading of contemporary accounts, engagement with an emerging scholarship on frontier violence[43] and an acknowledgement of what Joe Edgar called an "Aboriginal perspective," suggested a very different story. In many ways what happened around Lake Boola Boola over 1864/65 proved a paradigm for much of Australia. Though the pattern of encounter differed varied over time and place there was often conflict over the occupation of Aboriginal land, often a clash of cultures, often same brutal spiral of violence and retaliation.[44]

---

[36] *Western Australian*, 16 February 1949.

[37] *Daily News*, 19 May 1914; *Western Australian*, 16 February 1949.

[38] David Morgan, "Soldier Statues and Empty Pedestals: Public Memory in the Wake of the Confederacy," *Material Religion*, 4, no. 1 (2018): 156–7.

[39] Kim Anderson, Jacqueline Kent, and Clare Crag, eds., *Australians 1988* (Willoughby: Fairfax, Syme and Weldon Associates, 1989).

[40] *Fremantle Focus*, November 1988; Bruce Scates, "A Monument to Murder: Celebrating the Conquest of Aboriginal Australia," *Studies in Western Australian History* 10 (April 1989): 21–32.

[41] J.S. Battye, *Western Australia: A History from Its Discovery to the Inauguration of the Commonwealth* (Oxford: Oxford University Press, 1924), 200; Peter Cowen, *Maitland Brown* (Fremantle: Fremantle Arts Centre Press, 1988), chapter 4.

[42] L.C. Burgess, *Pioneers of Nor'West Australia* (Geraldton: Constantine and Gardner, 1905); *Eastern Districts Chronicle*, 5 May 1888.

[43] See, for example, Stannage, *The Pioneer Myth*, 21–31; Henry Reynolds, *The Other Side of the Frontier: An Interpretation of the Aboriginal Response to the Invasion and Settlement of Australia* (Townsville: James Cook University Press, 1981).

[44] Lake Boola Boola is also referred to as Ingedana in documentary records and known as Injitana by Karajarri people today. For a summary of the patterns of frontier violence see Henry Reynolds, *Forgotten War* (Sydney: New South Publishing, 2013).

Panter, Harding, and Goldwyer were killed after months of provocation. Their journals describe the way they exhausted "native wells," draining them of the water for their horses and disturbing the fragile ecology that delineated fresh water springs from salt water intrusion.[45] Finding that water was as great a source of conflict as stealing it. A diary entry in May 1864 relates the way they captured and interrogated a "native woman" dragging her back to the stronghold of their camp as she spat and scratched at them.[46] These men made little attempt to negotiate the complex protocols that guided any passage across Aboriginal lands. Nor were they unaware of such protocols. Panter's previous dealings with diverse Indigenous communities in both Queensland and Western Australia suggests considerable prior knowledge of cultural practice in regard to country. Rather, the party assumed they had a right to explore, occupy and develop territory they "discovered." As Panter acknowledged, this clash of interest between colonizer and colonized meant that conflict was virtually inevitable: "before the next ship arrives [he told his superiors in Perth] some of these niggers (sic) will get a pass to kingdom come." Finally, there is some evidence to suggest the explorers may have trespassed (albeit unwittingly) on sites sacred to Karajarri people. The last entry in Panter's diary, made on the evening of his death, describes how during the day a sizable number of "natives" regaled his party. "They kept whispering" he wrote "and making signs we could not understand." The explorers had journeyed to the juncture of Karajarri and Yawuru lands, intertwining stories of immense cultural significance ran across this country. As Indigenous communities remember it, white intruders had camped without permission beside a waterhole, traditionally a gathering place, and often a site of trade, initiation and ceremony.[47] White accounts describe heated exchanges with an "insolent and aggressive" crowd, the "natives" dispersing only when revolvers were "fired over their heads." They moved "sullenly away," [that narrative continues] still bearing spears and "still intent on mischief."[48]

Panter's action leads us to question the most potent of the myths embodied in the monument: that the explorers were murdered in their sleep. Harding, Panter, and Goldwyer were all experienced bushmen. Two of the party were trained as policemen and would no doubt follow the standard police procedure of mounting a guard. The records of the inquest and the grisly testimony of the men who found them suggest that Goldwyer stood guard while Panter and Harding rested. Four shots were fired from Goldwyer's revolver before he was killed, suggesting something very quite different to the commonly accepted narrative of the deaths of sleeping innocents. Maitland Brown crafted a tale of men butchered in their beds to present Aboriginal resistance as a criminal rather than a political act and justify his actions. In this discursive framework, the explorers were not killed in a frontier war, (with acts of violence and retaliation on both sides) but slaughtered, as one typical account put it, "under circumstances of

---

[45] Journal extract 9 November 1864, *Perth Gazette and WA Times,* 12 May 1865; for the role water plays in both a physical and metaphysical landscape see Sarah Yu, "Ngapa Kunangkul (Living Water): An Indigenous View of Goundwater," in *Country: Visions of Land and People in Western Australia,* ed. Andrea Gainor, Matt Trinca, and Anna Haebich (Perth: Western Australian Museum, 2002), 32–55.

[46] Journal dated 19 May 1864, CSR Acc 36, vol 538, 283–5, State Record Office, Western Australia.

[47] Fiona Skyring and Sara Yu with the Karajarri Native Title Holders, "Strange Strangers: First Contact between Europeans and Karajarri People on the Kimberley Coast of Western Australia," in *Strangers on the Shore: Early Coastal Contacts in Australia,* ed. Peter Veth, Peter Sutton, and Margo Neale (Canberra: National Museum of Australia, 2008), 60–1.

[48] *Perth Gazette and WA Times,* 12 May 1864; *Western Mail,* 4 April 1908.

revolting barbarity."[49] It seems Brown told a rather different story in private circles. "In his narration of the affair," an associate later reported, "Mr. Brown mentioned to me that … four chambers of Constable Goldwyer's revolver had been discharged, the assumption being that he was on the *qui vive*, and discharged the shots at his assailants."[50] In the end, the monument betrayed its own sorry secret. A weathered plaque shows Goldwyer's body several feet away from that of his comrades. Near his outstretched hand lies a revolver (Figure 3).

We have dealt with the "ambush" of the punitive party and what was often called the "dispersal" of the "natives".[51] But these particular killings were only part of a much wider culture of white violence. "The government search party" led by Brown was actually a series of separate raids on diverse Aboriginal communities. The vessel that carried the expedition north was laden with a cargo of guns, horses, men and provisions. It anchored at several points along the coast, ranging between Lagrange Bay and Roebuck Bay further north. Brown and his men usually rode their horses through surf or mangroves to the shore, each expedition would last several days with regular signals to and from the boat connecting sea and shore parties. For several weeks, the *Clarence Packet* served as a supply ship and a prison. As many as a dozen "natives" would be captured in a single raid, chained together, ferried to the vessel and crowded onto the deck. Conditions became so intolerable that the ship's master refused to take on further prisoners. The kidnapping and detention of such large numbers of men had a devasting impact on communities scattered through the district. The traumatic memory of men charging on horseback through "native camps" prevails to this day at Bidyadanga. On one occasion (a pioneer's reminiscence reported),

> The party [Brown] was leading dropped right into an encampment of blacks who had apparently never seen either white men or horses … They were mostly women and children, and there was an instantaneous screaming stampede. An invasion from Mars could hardly have scared mere earth-dwellers more.[52]

Equally terrifying was the arsenal of weaponry Brown had at his disposal. Brown noted the effect of "emptying revolvers" into "natives" at close quarters, describing the roar of gunfire and its devasting effect on human bodies. In many cases, his victims "did not seem to know the power of our arms,"[53] but an attempt by one group to escape provided the opportunity to show them.

> Karima persuaded the natives to rise in the body and to try to make their escape … . Toovey clutched five or six and threw them sprawling on their faces, while William dealt the leader, Karima, a severe blow in the head with his gun-barrel and shot one of their dogs in front of them to show its power. This had the desired effect of stopping them.[54]

Exemplary punishment became the *modus operandi* of the punitive expedition. Finding fences "broken to pieces by natives for the sake of the nails" Brown instructed his men

---

[49] *Eastern Districts Chronicle*, 13 May 1905.
[50] *Western Mail*, 4 April 1908.
[51] Chilla Bulbeck, "Aborigines, Memorials and the History of the Frontier," *Australian Historical Studies* 24, no. 96 (April 1991): 168–78.
[52] *Sunday Times*, 24 September 1916.
[53] *Fremantle Times*, 14 November 1919.
[54] Maitland Brown, *Journal of an Expedition*, 11.

Figure 3. "Murdered in their Sleep?" A contemporary engraving of the discovery of Panter, Harding, and Goldwyer's remains. Published in the heart of the Imperial metropolis, this image confirms the global reach of the Explorers' story. Note the portrayal of the hostages, their bowed heads suggesting complicity in the killings. Source: *Illustrated London News*, 7 October 1865.

to "take the first opportunity of punishing them ... catching and thrashing a native [any native] for every nail stolen." Exasperated by early failures to find the missing men, Brown vowed to hang his prisoners, one each day until those "unwilling guides" lead them to the explorers. How many of these threats were actually carried out is difficult to determine. Brown knew authorities in London were mindful of the brazen abuse of white authority on the fringes of the British Empire (Western Australia would not be granted self-government until 1890) and no doubt modified reports accordingly. He became an authority unto himself, acting well beyond any legal sanction and resolved to "treat the natives according to circumstances."

> If they resist us in examining their camps or themselves, I am determined to teach them a lesson. If from any articles in their keeping, or from any other circumstances I imagine them guilty, and can capture them without resistance, I shall put them on board ship, and send them to Roebuck Bay ... But ... throughout the whole trip there will be no necessity of capture ... the guilty natives, if such there are, will either attack or resist us in exterminating them.[55]

This detailed reconstruction of the violence in the "NorWest" is not an attempt to demonize white settlers or substitute one simple model of right and wrong, victim and innocent with another. It is done with a view to contesting a pioneer mythology writ deep in the

---

[55] *Fremantle Times*, 14 November 1919.

psyche of white settler society and set down in stone, bronze and print in monument and history book. The most recent scholarship on the frontier has presented it as a liminal space, a series of zones rather than a rigid black/white divide and a site of compromise, negotiation and alliance.[56] But such dialogue was less in evidence in this first catastrophic collision of cultures, characterized (as it was) by conflict, misunderstanding and miscommunication. Rather the explorers, and the Indigenous men, women and children killed in subsequent punitive expeditions, were caught up in a maelstrom of violence, a conflict that generated traumatic and contested memories for all the communities concerned.[57]

Dialogical Memorialization: The Remaking of a Monument

Re-evaluation of the meanings of a monument is one matter, altering and amending that commemorative structure another. Accordingly, this article will now shift focus, away from what Maria Nugent called the "the history told on [a] memorial," to "the history *of* the memorial itself."[58] From 1988, that first inquiry into the making of the Explorers' Monument, to 1994, and the placement of what might be called a counter-memorial, there was a protracted period of debate, lobbying and negotiation. It involved a complex array of government agencies, communities and individuals and raised challenging issues regarding local heritage, Indigenous knowledge and national history. Not all the citizens of Fremantle supported the call for a counter-monument. Some questioned the extent of white violence on the frontier, labouring to defend the tarnished reputation of West Australia's pioneers. Some believed historians and Indigenous communities urged "a sense of guilt on the white community."[59]

Throughout that protracted process of community debate there was a steady shift of focus. First came the reckoning with the dominant white narrative, reassessment of that first violent encounter between First Nations peoples and European "settlers" in the far north west. This involved the assembly of a vast evidential archive: the explorers' original accounts and the records of the punitive party sent to avenge them, Colonial Secretary's reports, police files, coronial inquests, press reports, historical accounts and private reminiscences. The careful re-assessment of sources was a task largely undertaken by staff and students at Murdoch University, but involved from the outset a much wider frame of reference. This work culminated in a successful submission to the local government calling for the corrective plaque to be placed on the memorial, a call endorsed by the elders of Perth's Indigenous communities.[60]

By far the most important element of that campaign was the involvement of descendants of the massacre itself. This was led by Ray Minniecon, now a revered elder within Sydney's First Nations communities, then a young Aboriginal theology student at Murdoch University. A descendent of the Kabi Kabi Nation and the Gurang Gurang Nation in South East Queensland, Minniecon travelled to Bidyadanga and gathered stories from the vibrant oral culture of the Karajarri people. There, as Joe Edgar's

---

[56] Grace Karskens, *People of the River: Lost Worlds of Early Australia* (Sydney: Allen and Unwin, 2020).

[57] Skyring and Yu, "Strange Strangers," 60–1.

[58] Maria Nugent, "Historical Encounters: Aboriginal Testimony and Colonial Forms of Commemoration," *Aboriginal History* 30 (2006): 36.

[59] See, for example, *Fremantle Gazatte*, 1 November 1988; *West Australian*, 19 and 24 October 1988.

[60] Bruce Scates, "Remaking Out History," *Labour History* 67 (November 1994): 164–5; SJ Monti (City Architect) to Bruce Scates, 29 November 1988, City of Fremantle 1.4.6/1.6.14/SJM/SR.

opening reminiscence suggest, people still remembered the massacre, "legacies of historical unresolved grief" affect this First Nation's Community as they do many others.[61] Ray Minniecon would continue to work with both the Baldja network in Perth and Karajarri people up north – in 1994, he would speak at the installation of the counter-memorial, in a ceremony "initiated and controlled by Aboriginal people."[62] Therein lay the shift of emphasis. A story that had privileged a white archival history and powerful white actors in the past gave way to Indigenous forms of knowledge and empowered Indigenous voices.[63]

In 1994, the United Nations Year of Indigenous peoples, a fifth plaque was laid at the memorial's base. It acknowledged "the right of Aboriginal people to defend *their* land," outlined "the history of provocation that ended in the explorers' deaths" and commemorated "all ... Aboriginal people who died during the invasion of their country." This is a striking instance of what historians have called dialogical memorialization. From its opening line, "This plaque was placed here by people who found the monument before you offensive," to its closing statement in (Indigenous) language – *Mapa Jarriya-Nyalaku* – this counter monument decries a history "from one perspective only." It displaces the colonizers' narrative and offers a different reading of violence on the frontier.[64]

This is a powerful statement today but even more so when it was first made. Today, it is accepted protocol to acknowledge Country – "invasion" rather than "settlement" is often used to describe white colonization. That was not the case in 1988. The text of the counter-memorial in Fremantle was approved four years before the Mabo judgement (unseating the legal fiction of Terra Nullius and recognizing that "native title" existed within the common law), two decades before the First Nations Constitutional Convention at Uluru (calling for an Indigenous voice to the Australian parliament), and long before the Black Lives Matter movement took to our streets. The First Report of the Council for Aboriginal Reconciliation styled this the "re-writing of history."

> An important aspect of the whole recognition was the participation of all parties – the Baldja Network, City of Fremantle, the historians, and in particular the people of La Grange, whose history they were commemorating. "We wanted the interpretation that murderers were justifiably punished amended to show Aborigines died defending the country from white invaders," Glad Milroy of the Baldja Network said, "and it was important that it be done with the support, approval and involvement of people from La Grange."[65]

Baldja is a Noonyar word meaning "coming together." It suggested the meeting of diverse communities.

In many ways, the counter monument, and the complex debates leading up it, anticipated what the Uluru convention called "truth telling." The convention (held in May

---

[61] Amy Lonetree, *Decolonising Museums: Representing Native Americans in National and Tribal Museums* (Chapel Hill: University of North Carolina Press, 2012), 5.

[62] "History Re-Written: City of Fremantle Monument," Council for Aboriginal Reconciliation, *Walking Together: The First Steps, Report of the Council for Aboriginal Reconciliation to Federal Parliament, 1991–94* (Canberra: Australian Government Printing Service, 1994), 203. Robyn Ninyette and Peter Scott also facilitated liaison between Noonyar people in Perth and Bidyadanga.

[63] "Aboriginal Legend Tells Other Side of Massacre," *West Australian*, 9 April 1994; Bill and Jenny Bunbury, *Many Maps: Charting Two Cultures: First Nations and Europeans in Western Australia* (Crawley: UWA Publishing, 2020), 168–71.

[64] Text taken from the counter-memorial.

[65] "History Re-Written," 202–3.

2017 and involving Indigenous leaders from across the right across the country) considered constitutional reforms to ensure Aboriginal and Torres Strait Islander peoples were formally consulted on policy and legislation affecting their communities. In doing so, it envisaged a process of "Truth-telling," an attempt at dialogue between Indigenous and non-Indigenous Australia whereby "the true history of colonisation [would] be told: the genocides, the massacres, the wars and the ongoing injustices and discrimination."[66]

"Truth" was much-disputed on the frontier. As the former narrative suggests, understandings of the causes and consequences of conflict differed between different protagonists and across different generations. Nor was the Convention very specific about the form "truth-telling" might take. Delegates conceded "Truth-telling" would unfold unevenly over time and envisaged very different conservations across local, state, and national forums. In that regard, the Uluru proposal is quite different to the Truth and Reconciliation Commission (TRC) founded in South Africa in the wake of apartheid, a court-like body charged with healing past wrongs. What it shares with the TRC is a belief in reparative rather than retributive justice. Reparative justice, as scholars have noted, places great store on symbolic measures, such as apologies and commemorations or the recognition of Indigenous place names and language. Public memorialization is particularly important in the process: it "teaches citizens about injustices of their history [and] it is supposed to help survivors and relatives of victims to live with their trauma by honouring those who suffered."[67] Therein lies the significance of the counter plaque in Fremantle; it transforms a powerful symbol of a racist past into a platform for reconciliation, and offers "an opportunity for Aboriginal and Torres Strait Islander peoples to record evidence about past actions and share their culture, heritage and history with the broader community."[68] First Nations people have styled this a "Makarrata," a complex Yolngu word signifying conflict resolution, peacemaking and justice.[69]

At the height of the recent statue wars, the Australian Heritage Council also cited the "memory-work"[70] around the Explorers Monument as a chance to "amend" a "one-sided history."[71] It noted that the intervention in Fremantle was not an attempt to "edit history," but rather "added to the story": "It is a striking example of how a dialogue can occur in memorialisation where one view of the past takes issue with another and history is seen, not as some final statement, but a contingent and contested narrative." The Council's report was solicited by the federal government to ensure that "legal protections for places and monuments that relate to Australia's early colonial history and interactions between European explorers and settlers and Australia's Indigenous peoples" were "adequate." It concluded they were but also acknowledged that racist colonial monuments

[66] James Haughton and Apolline Kohen, "Indigenous Constitutional Recognition and Representation," https://www.aph.gov.au/About_Parliament/Parliamentary_Departments/Parliamentary_Library/pubs/BriefingBook46p/IndigenousRecognition (accessed 28 November 2021).

[67] Klaus Newmann and Janna Thompson, eds., *Historical Justice and Memory* (Maddison: University of Wisconsin Press, 2015), 9; Shireen Morris, *A First Nations Voice in the Australian Constitution* (Oxford: Hart Publishing, 2020).

[68] Haughton and Kohen, "Indigenous Constitutional Recognition and Representation."

[69] The First Nations National Constitutional Convention 2017, "Uluru Statement from the Heart," https://fromtheheart.com.au/uluru-statement/the-statement/ (accessed 19 September 2020).

[70] To borrow James Young's phrase, "The Counter-Monument: Memory against itself in Germany today," *Critical Inquiry* 18, no. 2 (Winter 1992): 272.

[71] Text of Bugarrigarra Nyurdany exhibition panel.

would remain a controversial feature of Australia's commemorative landscape. Its final recommendation called for the "addition of Indigenous stories." Such "expansion" could "see colonial monuments turned into points of reflection and tools for education, instead of attempts to 'tidy up the past' by their removal."[72]

Fremantle, for many, seems to signal "a way forward."[73] That said, there is no one solution to the decolonization of Australia's commemorative landscape – and the history of the monument did not end with the placement of a plaque.

Monumental Errors: Dealing with Difficult Heritage

There are several ways to deal with what's been called "difficult" heritage.[74] The following options were flagged by the authors during the collaborative process of writing this article. We have assessed each strategy both in the light of what actually transpired in Fremantle but also comparable interventions in both Australia and overseas. We would stress (from the outset) that any future redevelopment should only take part after extended negotiation with Indigenous stakeholders, at Bidyadanga and elsewhere.

The most obvious alternative to a "additional" plaque is the relocation of monuments themselves. The removal of contentious memorials from civic landscapes has been widely practised overseas, especially in recent times. With the rise of the Black Lives Matter movement (triggered by the murder of George Floyd in June 2021) a host of series of Confederate memorials were ousted from parklands, city streets and university grounds throughout the United States.[75] Before that, statues to Cecil Rhodes, (the imperialist and white supremacist seen by many as the architect of apartheid) had been toppled by decolonization movements across Africa and beyond. In Eastern Europe, the collapse of the communism prompted the purging of monumental effigies to Stalin, Lenin, and other symbols of the Soviet regime. Some were placed in local museums, others (in a brilliant parody of what's been called "socialist giantism") displayed in what's been styled Tyranny Statue Theme Parks.[76] Like these other monuments to oppressive regimes, the Explorers' memorial was raised as a statement of power and privilege. Depicting Aboriginal people clad in chains, and openly condoning white violence, it is a haunting reminder of the pain and injustices suffered by First Nations' Peoples. By occupying civic space, it serves to legitimize narratives of conquest and dispossession, arguably colonizing minds in the same ways white "settlers" seized vast tracts of territory.

---

[72] Australian Heritage Council, *Protection of Australia's Commemorative Places and Monuments* (Canberra: Commonwealth of Australia 2018) (PDF), https://www.awe.gov.au/sites/default/files/documents/protection-australia-commemorative-places-monuments.pdf (accessed 28 November 2021).

[73] Bruce Scates, "Monumental Errors: How Australia Can Fix Its Racist Colonial Statues", *The Conversation*, 28 August 2017, https://theconversation.com/monumental-errors-how-australia-can-fix-its-racist-colonial-statues-82980 (accessed 9 March 2021).

[74] Sharon Macdonald, *Difficult Heritage: Negotiating the Nazi Past in Nuremberg and Beyond* (London: Routledge, 2009).

[75] Simko, Cunningham, and Fox, "Contesting Commemorative Landscapes"; for earlier reckonings with confederate legacies see Patrick Slattery, "Deconstructing Racism One Statue at a Time: Visual Culture Wars at Texas A & M University and the University of Texas at Austin," *Visual Arts Research* 32, no.1 2 (2006): 28–31 (we thank Frank Bongiorno for this reference); also Kirk Savage, *Standing Soldiers, Kneeling Slaves: Race, War and Monument in Nineteenth Century America* (Princeton, NJ: Princeton University Press, 1997).

[76] David Lowe and Tony Joel, *Remembering the Cold War: Global Contest and National Stories* (Abingdon: Taylor and Francis, 2013), 103–12. We thank Iva Glisac for drawing our attention to the work of Mischa Gabowitsch in this field.

Having said that, we see three main failings with any proposal for relocation. In the first place, it assumes that museums (usually the preferred destination for what been called "orphaned" statuary[77]) are neutral spaces where unfettered debate and contextualization can be freely practiced. They are not. As vexed discussion over the fate of Confederate memorials suggests, museums "are inherently imbued with their own politics and ideologies." Corralling a memorial in an exhibition space does not necessarily diminish its power to "normalise racism."[78] Secondly, we believe that public spaces *are* the appropriate place for civic discourse, municipal landscapes constituting "a kind of museum without walls."[79] In this approach white memorial precincts can and must be read through another gaze, affirming Indigenous perspectives. Finally, and to our minds most importantly, the removal of this particular monument was never countenanced by Indigenous communities, not in Fremantle, greater Perth or Bidyadanga. Rather, as Mariko Smith aptly put it in the course of Sydney's recent statue wars, the task was to "re-signify monuments," bending cold stone to accommodate multiple and complex narratives.[80] In that light, to simply remove the monument risked inducing a kind of historical amnesia. What would generations hence read into the empty space left by a banished memorial, why squander this opportunity – as Joe Edgar put it – to contest colonizer history?

A second approach we've identified is to assail the physical fabric of the memorial itself. Again this has been commonplace through recent statue wars. Great white men have been literally and figuratively unseated from their pedestals, "rolled into harbours, set aflame on their plinths, defaced with graffiti, hung with signs."[81] The memorial in Fremantle did not escape that same "iconoclastic" impulse.[82] On more than one occasion the original plaques have been deliberately damaged or "stolen."[83] As late as June 1990, in that protracted period between the discrediting of the Explorers' Monument and the construction of a counter-memorial, Maitland Brown's bust was "chiselled" from its granite pedestal and carried off in the night.[84] Some have viewed this as a wilfully destructive act, an erasure of history. But we would suggest another reading. The severing of Aboriginal heads was not uncommon in the eighteenth and nineteenth centuries. Sometimes this was done in the name of white science. In the case of the resistance leader Yagan, beheading was a ghoulish instance of trophy hunting on the frontier.[85] In that light, the decapitation of a statue had enormous symbolic power. An instance of what Britta Knudsen and Casper Anderson have called "affective politics,"[86] it subverts the colonial past. A powerful protest to be sure, but also, as one historian has observed, an "essentially

[77] Richard M Lowenthal and Brian I. Daniels, "'Orphaned Objects', Ethical Standards, and the Acquisition of Antiquities," *DePaul Journal of Art, Technology and Intellectual Property Law* 23, no. 2 (2013): 339–61.

[78] Gwendolyn W. Saul and Diana E. Marsh, "Extended Commentary: In Whose Honor? On Monuments, Public Spaces, Historical Narratives, and Memory," *Museum Anthropology* 42, no. 2 (2018): 17–20.

[79] Morgan, "Soldier Statues," 157.

[80] Mariko Smith, "Tear It Down," *Australian Museum*, 25 August 2021, https://australian.museum/learn/first-nations/tear-it-down/ (accessed 19 September 2020).

[81] Julia Baird, "The Toppling of Statues Is Enriching Not Erasing History and It Has Thrilled My Heart," *The Sydney Morning Herald*, 13 June 2020, https://www.smh.com.au/national/the-toppling-of-statues-is-enriching-not-erasing-history-and-it-has-thrilled-my-heart-20200612-p5523r.html (accessed 28 November 2021).

[82] Gamboni, *Destruction of Art*, 67.

[83] *The Australian*, 31 August 2017.

[84] *Fremantle Herald*, 14 June 1990.

[85] Neville Green, *Broken Spears: Aborigines and Europeans in the southwest of Australia* (Perth: Focus Education, 1984), 88.

[86] Britta Timm Knudsen and Casper Anderson, "Affective Politics and Colonial Heritage: Rhodes Must Fall at UCT and Oxford," *International Journal of Heritage Studies* 25, no. 3 (2019): 239–58.

ephemeral one."[87] A replica of Brown's bust was quickly reinstated. In that light, we would argue that the success of the counter monument can be measured partly by its permanence, one narrative in bronze continuously contesting another.

A third response involves the creation of a dissenting commemorative complex. Grappling with what's been called "undesired monuments"[88] has given rise to a new and subversive memorial culture. These have often been styled *Gegendenkmal* by German-language scholars: the "counter-monument." Such objects and structures are raised in intentional juxtaposition "to another, pre-existing monument located nearby and ... critically questions the values the pre-existing monument expresses." An early example of this, and the first to be addressed as *Gegendenkmal*, was Alfred Hrdlicka's 1985/86 memorial against War and Fascism in Hamburg, itself designed as a direct counter to Richard Kuöhl's Monument to the Fallen of Infantry Regiment No 76. Kuöhl's massive cubic structure carried a bar relief of marching soldiers, critics claimed it glorified war and condoned German militarism. Hrdlicka's response was to recreate these soldiers in three-dimensional form. They would step out from the memorial and into the monument's surrounds. Reminiscent of gravestones, rows of marching men progressively sink into the ground, eventually transforming into slabs in the adjacent pavement.[89] A still more radical example of *Gegendenkmal* is Martin Broszat's "vanishing" counter-moment raised in Harburg in 1986. A memorial to the victims of the Holocaust openly sceptical of traditional memorial forms, it took the form of a pillar that was progressively lowered into the earth, burying both itself and the graffitied messages of Harburg's citizens. This was a memorial space, as James Young explains it, "conceived to challenge the very premise of its being ... For once we assign monumental form to memory, we have to some degree divested ourselves of the obligation to remember."[90]

Intentionally taking issue with a re-existing commemorative structure, the new memorial plaque embedded in the base of the Explorers' Monument in 1994 must also be considered a "counter-monument." Its sparse but compelling account of the violence visited on Indigenous communities is also "a necessary breach in the conventional memorial code."[91] And in the deliberations surrounding its installation, additional counter-monuments were also considered. Encouraged by the project's initial success, Ray Minniecon proposed a second memorial. Its frame of reference was ironic. Minniecon suggested a stylized water hole, sharing the very resource explorers had killed and died for. The original monument was designed by Pietro Porcelli, an Italian sculptor long celebrated in this city of immigrants. The new monument was designed by Ronny Cameron, an Aboriginal artist then imprisoned in Fremantle jail. The Explorers' Monument is an incitement to racial hatred – in its place, Minniecon proposed a gesture of reconciliation. "Let us all sit down together in Peace" was to be inscribed in language at the base of the memorial.[92] In structure as well as content, this new memorial issued an explicit challenge. The Explorers' Monument, like most traditional commemorative pieces, stood alone,

---

[87] Graeme Davison, "The Use and Abuse of Australian History," in *Making the Bicentenary*, ed. Sue Janson and Stuart Macintyre (Melbourne: Australian Historical Studies, 1988), 55–76.

[88] The phrase is drawn from Walter Grasskamp, Gamboni, *Destruction of Art*, 133.

[89] Stevens, Franck, and Fazakerley, "Counter-Monuments," 962–3.

[90] Young, "The Counter Monument," 271–9.

[91] Ibid., 271.

[92] R.J. Cameron, "Plan of the Proposed Memorial in Remembrance of the Aboriginals that Died at the Injudinah Swamp Massacre," June 1989, copy kindly provided by Ray Minniecon.

"isolated in urban space," a "single impenetrable object." Cameron's design, by contrast, invited the visitor into a commemorative complex, signalling a shift from "viewing to engaging."[93] The Council – long divided over the question of the monument[94] – had no funding line for so ambitious a project. Nor did the proposal gain much traction at the time within Indigenous communities. Under the pretext that a water hole in a public park pre-empted Council planning for the entire precinct, the suggestion was shelved. This suggestion for an additional layer of interpretation remains, as we see it, as unfinished business. The counter plaque was never intended as a substitute to other memorials raised by Aboriginal communities and these reworkings of the commemorative landscape can and should continue.

That leads us to a fourth option, a hybrid solution which (we would suggest) addresses many of the concerns flagged above. There may come a time when the monument is removed, signalling the community will no longer tolerate so offensive a statement in its midst. Replacing it could be a new but very different kind of memorial, one focused not just on the events of 1864 and 1865 but also the shifting history of the monument itself. This new installation could relate the evolving story of how and why frontier violence came to commemorated and chart the learning process that has involved. Such a story must be told in a different way, on the basis of equal participation in the process of truth telling and cognisant of what all who own the story wish to say. This new memorial space would take on a creative life of its own, inviting all who view it into a conversation about a shared yet divided past. Such a reckoning with difficult heritage might well offer "a better way." To succeed it requires patience, good will and a far more robust commitment to truth telling and reconciliation than the current government is prepared to contemplate.

Walking Together: Afterlives and Re-Imaginings

The plaque installed in Fremantle offered a compelling critique to lies writ deep in Australia's history, but challenging the history books, the memory texts, the "brass dogma,"[95] clearly isn't enough. Decolonizing the commemorative landscape, and centring Indigenous narratives, takes us on a far more demanding and more rewarding journey and one that transcends the monument's physical and temporal dimensions. That was seen on the day of the counter plaque's dedication. No white politicians, officials, or historians spoke on 9 April 1994. In a dramatic reversal of the monument's inauguration, white dignitaries watched on from an outer circle where representatives of state, local and national government, and the historical profession gathered silently and respectfully. It was Indigenous speakers who stepped up to the podium. Charlie and Everett Kickett (from the Balja network) examined the history of frontier, focusing first on Bidyadanga then ranging across the country. Behind them an Aboriginal flag draped the base of the Explorers' Memorial, at once an act of healing and appropriation. Ray Minniecon spoke of the project's beginnings, Joe Roe (a Karajarri man) appealed for remembrance and understanding. They wanted to put this "bloody episode" behind

---

[93] Quentin Stevens and Karen A. Franck, *Memorials as Spaces of Engagement: Design, Use and Meaning* (Abingdon: Taylor and Francis, 2015), 11–12.
[94] *Fremantle Gazette*, 25 October 1988.
[95] Healy, *From the Ruins of Colonialism*, 23.

them, he said. "Let's not keep the hatred in our hearts because that will destroy us." Joe Roe spoke for the Karajarri community but his moving appeal to "be in peace" was equally directed at white Australians.[96] Reconciliation was the key note of the ceremony – a monument that had long sanctioned division serving a new and therapeutic purpose. The hum of didgeridoos echoed from those lofty Norfolk Pines and a performance by Aboriginal dancers from Pinjarra kept the culture alive and vibrant and strong. Then, under bright West Australian skies, Doris Edgar and John Dodo, elders from Bidyadanga, unveiled a plaque in commemoration of their people. The ceremony ended as Aboriginal people scattered dust from the site of the massacre and two white children laid wreaths of flowers decked in Aboriginal colours. Bottom up rather than top down, creative and participatory, the ceremony was of itself a remaking of history. As Bailey J. Duhé has observed of comparable ceremonies elsewhere, it "push[ed] the conversation beyond just a question of physical markers, centring it instead towards actual community healing and tangible, recognised reparations ... [it] challenged who gets to tell the stories."[97]

Remaking history also takes us well beyond the immediate province of an aging monument (Figure 4). What, as Madge Dresser asked in the context of London's slavery statues, is "the subsequent 'social life' of these memorials. ... What impact have they had on the public consciousness."[98] "Public consciousness" is a notoriously difficult thing to gauge but a shift in Australia's national curricula might provide a useful barometer. Through much of the twentieth century, the first primers in Australian history lauded the feats of the country's white explorers. A long and costly battle against "the bush" and "the blacks" provided the stuff of a heroic national narrative. By 2002, the National Museum of Australia shifted the focus to the other side of the frontier, a series of curriculum resources, co-created with community and the Museum's Indigenous Education Officers, revisiting the controversies surrounding the explorers' deaths and the long campaign to alter the monument. Students were invited to "experience how history 'hears' and 'silences' voices" and consider "how people use the past in the present." All these projects reproduced archival sources gathered for the first submission to Fremantle City Council, they actively questioned the "reliability of evidence" and challenged old historical understandings. Most important of all students were encouraged to "invite Aboriginal speakers into the classroom," fostering respect for Indigenous knowledge.[99] More recently, the monument featured in the Museum's digital classroom, an initiative aligned to the national curricula and again highlighting Indigenous testimony.[100] It was also the subject of a freestanding documentary series co-commissioned by the Museum, the Australian National University, and Monash University, exploring the story of Australia through objects.[101] It may well be that these digital renderings of the

---

[96] Joe Roe, recorded by Bill Bunbury for the Australian Broadcasting Commission, 9 April 1994, cited in Bunbury, *Many Maps*, 171.

[97] Duhé, "Decentering Whiteness and Refocusing on the Local," 121.

[98] Dresser, "Set in Stone?" 165.

[99] Robert Lewis et al., *Australian History Mysteries: Investigating Five Case Studies in Australian History* (Brunswick: National Museum of Australia and Ryebuck Media, 2002), 81–100; Trish Albert, *Making a Difference* (Melbourne: Pearson, 2009).

[100] Explorers' Monument in Esplanade Park, Fremantle, Western Australia, National Museum of Australia – Australia's Defining Moments Digital Classroom, https://digital-classroom.nma.gov.au/images/explorers-monument-esplanade-park-fremantle-western-australia (accessed 28 November 2021); The Australian National University, National Museum, and Monash University, "Australian Journey: The Story of a Nation in 12 Objects," https://www.nma.gov.au/learn/classroom-resources/australian-journey (accessed 28 November 2021).

Figure 4. "Challenging who gets to tell the stories": Noonyar dancers from Pinjarra circle the monument during the installation of the counter-memorial. Dance offered an entirely different commemorative vocabulary to that of 1913. Source: Bruce Scates.

monument extend the shelf-life of a memorial, invite its scrutiny by future generations, and carry its stories further than corroding testimony in bronze.

Whilst the Museum's focus was national in its scope, equally important work has been done at a local level. In 1911, the makers of the memorial debated if their tribute to Maitland Brown's punitive expedition should be raised on the lands white men invaded. A century later, an exhibition at the Liyan-Ngan Nyirrwa Cultural Wellbeing Centre, where Joe Edgar's opening words in this article were featured, restored an Indigenous perspective to that white colonizer's history. It empowered Indigenous people through the telling of their stories.

Set in stone has long been a cliché associated with what Graeme Davison termed "the heroic age" of colonial statuary. What the case of the Explorers' Monument shows is that far from being static and unchanging memorials provide an arena of open possibilities, affirming James E. Young's observation that "new generations visit memorials under new circumstances and invest them with new meanings."[102] In that light, Australia's long and challenging progress towards national reconciliation

---

[101] The Australian National University, National Museum, and Monash University, "Australian Journey: The Story of a Nation in 12 Objects," https://www.nma.gov.au/learn/classroom-resources/australian-journey (accessed 28 November 2021); The Australian National University, National Museum, and Monash University, "Encounters" in "Australian Journey: The Story of a Nation in 12 Objects," https://australianjourney.anu.edu.au/episodes/nation/encounters (accessed 28 November 2021).

[102] Graeme Davison, *The Use and Abuse of Australian History* (Sydney: Allen and Unwin, 2000), 37; James E. Young, *The Texture of Memory: Holocaust Memorials and Meaning* (New Haven, CT: Yale University Press, 1993), 3, 208.

will continue to open new and necessary conversations. This reflective piece is a part of that process.

Disclosure Statement

No potential conflict of interest was reported by the author(s).

The Pinjarra Massacre in the Age of the Statue Wars

Ann Curthoys and Shino Konishi ⓘ

ABSTRACT

The Pinjarra Massacre of 1834 was a large-scale colonial attack on Aboriginal people in Western Australia. Led by Governor James Stirling, a party of British police, soldiers and settlers ambushed a group of Bindjareb Noongar, killing of at least 15 Bindjareb Noongar men by Stirling's reckoning, and as many as 80 men, women, and children by other accounts. Though the event was widely recorded in the nineteenth-century, this massacre was effaced in the commemoration of its leader – Governor Stirling. This article will trace the history of the massacre and how it has been remembered, the troubled history of a statue of Stirling which still stands in the city of Perth, and the fight by Bindjareb Noongar to establish a memorial to the victims.

Historians of genocide seek to understand how genocides are remembered by perpetrators, victims, descendants, and subsequent generations. Such understanding involves tracing how events that may be considered genocidal are conceptualized and named, who among the victims and the perpetrators are remembered and memorialized, and what forms these memories and memorials take. While the case of Turkish remembrance of the Armenian genocide is perhaps the most outstanding example of disputed naming and historical memory, settler colonial societies such as the United States, South Africa, Australia, Canada, and New Zealand have also produced highly contested memories of their violent past. Indigenous peoples have remembered and honoured their ancestors as victims of a brutal process of invasion and dispossession, while dominant populations have frequently honoured those who oversaw, conducted, and benefited from that same process. These contests over the history of colonization have occurred in many cultural sites, such as school textbooks, academic texts, national public holidays, museums, and monuments. In these counterposed historical memories, a major point of contention has been the idea that colonization could become, and often was, a genocidal process. This was especially true in Australia's "history wars" of the early 2000s, as A. Dirk Moses has pointed out, and such differences continue still.[1]

In recent years, especially in the wake of the Black Lives Matter movement and its reverberations around the world, statues have become an important site of contestation and struggle for decolonization. In this essay we explore the controversy surrounding the

---

[1] A. Dirk Moses, "Moving the Genocide Debate beyond the History Wars," *Australian Journal of Politics and History* 54, no. 2 (2008): 248–70.

statue of Governor James Stirling, from 1829 to 1839 the founding governor of the colony of Western Australia, now Australia's largest state. We begin with the attacks on and calls for removal of the Stirling statue from public display in Perth, the state's capital city, in the context of the statue wars emerging from the Black Lives Matter movement in 2020. The statue's opponents argued that Stirling should not be honoured as a hero because, on 28 October 1834, he led a massacre of between 15 and 80 Bindjareb Noongar people at Pinjarra, a site ninety kilometres south of Perth.[2] We then examine in detail what happened at Pinjarra in 1834, examining the uncharacteristically detailed perpetrator accounts and drawing on the significant existing historical literature on these events.[3] Next we trace the history of the statue from early proposals in the 1920s to its eventual erection over fifty years later and its subsequent intermittent display. We conclude with the creation by Bindjareb Noongar of a Pinjarra massacre memorial on site and the unfinished business still surrounding memorialization of this troubled period in Australia's history. This is a complex story of historical consciousness demonstrating that colonizer statues may in fact mean very little to the people who are meant to revere them, and that criticism of them is far from new.

Controversy over James Stirling's statue

Following the murder of George Floyd by Minneapolis police on 25 May 2020, protestors held a series of rallies across the globe to demonstrate their solidarity with the Black Lives Matter (BLM) movement and protest against police brutality. "I can't breathe," the words Floyd cried out as one officer knelt on his neck during his arrest, became the rallying cry for the movement. Floyd's words had particular resonance in Australia, recalling the 2015 death of Dunghutti man David Dungay Jr in similar circumstances at Sydney's Long Bay Gaol. Despite the COVID-19 restrictions demanding social distancing and banning protest marches, thousands signed up online to join BLM protests in Australia's capital cities. Their aim was not just to support the global BLM movement, but also highlight Australia's appalling Indigenous deaths in custody record, and memorialize the 470 Aboriginal and Torres Strait Islander people who, like Dungay Jr, had died in police custody since the Australian Government's Royal Commission into Aboriginal Deaths in Custody in 1991.[4]

The BLM movement's focus is not only contemporary racism but also symbols of white supremacy, not least statues and monuments glorifying historical "figures whose reputations (and fortunes) were built on the crushing of peoples of colour and the stifling of

---

[2] For another consideration of the Stirling statue and its critics, see Jenny Gregory, "Dark Pasts in the Landscape: Statue Wars in Western Australia," *Public History Review* 28 (2021): 1–9. Note also that alternative spellings for Bindjareb include Pindjarup and Pinjareb.

[3] The main accounts are Ronald Richards, *The Murray District of Western Australia: a history* (Pinjarra: Shire of Murray, 1978), chapters 5 and 6; Neville Green, *Broken Spears: Aboriginals and Europeans in the southwest of Australia* (Perth: Focus Education Services, 1984), 99–106; John Mulvaney, *Encounters in Place: Outsiders and Aboriginal Australians 1606–1985* (St. Lucia: University of Queensland Press, 1989), 168–71; Natalie Contos, Theo A. Kearing, the Murray Districts Aboriginal Association, Len Collard, and Dave Palmer, *Pinjarra Massacre Site Research and Development Project Report for State 1* (Pinjarra: Murray Districts Aboriginal Association, June 1998); Pamela Statham-Drew, *James Stirling: admiral and founding governor of Western Australia* (Crawley: University of Western Australia Press, 2003), 260–71; and Pamela Statham-Drew, "Stirling and Pinjarra: a battle in more ways than one," *Studies in Western Australian History* 23 (2003): 167–94.

[4] Maani Truu, "George Floyd: How a nine minute video reignited a decades-old civil rights movement in Australia," *SBS News*, 21 April 2021, https://www.sbs.com.au/news/george-floyd-how-a-nine-minute-video-reignited-a-decades-old-civil-rights-movement-in-australia

indigenous cultures."[5] Debates which began with the Rhodes Must Fall movement in 2015, focussing on Cecil Rhodes, an architect of British imperialism in southern Africa, were reignited by Floyd's murder. Across the United States, statues of confederates were toppled, defaced, or removed, and elsewhere in the world imperial and colonial figures, especially those implicated in slavery, were similarly dispatched. A significant moment for the statue wars in Western Australia happened in the United Kingdom: on 7 June 2020 the statue of seventeenth-century slaver Edward Colston was toppled into the Bristol harbour.

Upon seeing images of this, Western Australian Greens senator Jordan Steele-John tweeted "[i]t's great to see these symbols of white supremacy being torn down." Reflecting on Western Australia's monuments, he felt that it was "[t]ime to stop celebrating these men and hold them accountable for the roles they played in WA's history of First Nations Genecide [sic]." Steele-John refuted criticisms that his tweets were an "incitement to criminal behaviour, anarchy and vandalism," insisting he was compelled to reflect on local "place names and statues" commemorating men who "engaged in, perpetrated or normalised horrific violence against First Nations peoples." He singled out the colony's founder James Stirling and surveyor-general John Septimus Roe, asserting "they are the perpetrators of a significant massacre."[6]

Arguments like Steele-John's are often criticized by opponents as a "left sort of fringe" preoccupation with "trying to edit our history," as former Australian Prime Minister Malcolm Turnbull argued in 2017. "We can't get into this sort of Stalinist exercise of trying to white out or obliterate or blank out parts of our history," he exclaimed, because "[a]ll of those statues, all of those monuments, are part of our history and we should respect them and preserve them."[7] Yet, rather than seeking to obliterate a respected history, proponents like Steele-John advocate creating "a space for truth to be told," by uncovering or acknowledging an unspoken history of colonial violence left silent by these mute statues.[8]

Within days, Steele-John's speculations were realized. On 12 June 2020, the day before the planned BLM rally in Perth, Western Australia, local musician Malachy John O'Connor was arrested for vandalizing the central business district's bronze statue of Captain James Stirling. That afternoon he sprayed the statue's hands and neck red and painted an Aboriginal flag over its plaque. Although the paint was quickly removed, images were published online and remain in circulation. (See Figure 1a and b). O'Connor did not target Stirling's statue simply because it was "a figure from Australia's colonial era."[9] He specifically defaced it because of Stirling's active involvement in the 1834 Pinjarra massacre; in his words, because "the man behind the likeness of that statue murdered up to about 150 Indigenous people." O'Connor had a history of agitating for the statue's removal, having previously written to the City of Perth arguing it is "culturally insensitive that [Stirling's

[5] Kelly Grovier, "Black Lives Matter Protests: Why are statues so powerful?," *BBC Online*, 10 June 2020, https://www.bbc.com/culture/article/20200612-black-lives-matter-protests-why-are-statues-so-powerful

[6] Nathan Hondros, "WA Greens senator cops spray for inciting 'anarchy and vandalism' in historical statue tweets," *WA Today*, 10 June 2020, https://www.watoday.com.au/national/western-australia/wa-greens-senator-cops-spray-for-inciting-anarchy-and-vandalism-in-historical-statue-tweets-20200610-p5518a.html

[7] Alison Bevage, "Australia's PM says changing statues, rewriting history is 'Stalinist,'" Reuters APAC, 25 August 2017, https://www.reuters.com/article/us-australia-statue-idUSKCN1B50OY

[8] Hondros, "WA Greens senator cops spray."

[9] "Perth man charged after statue vandalised," *Australian Associated Press*, 15 June 2020.

Figure 1. (a and b) Sir James Stirling statue. Credit: Images from the City of Perth Cultural Collections.

statue] stands outside the City of Perth Library containing works about those murders he committed." Moreover, the statue was only "200 m from the District Court of Western Australia," highlighting for him, and others, the direct connection between past colonial atrocities and contemporary deaths in custody.[10]

This was not the only defacement of Stirling's statue. Three months later, on 13 September 2020, the HEAVY DUTY artist collective initiated "The Statue Review," replacing the statue's inscription which read "Founder Governor of Western Australia" with a new magnetized plaque stating:

Captain James Stirling

Governor of Western Australia

On 28 October 1834 Captain Stirling led the Pinjarra Massacre, an attack on the Binjareb Noongar camp that killed up to 80 Noongar men, women, and children.

He belongs in a museum, not on our streets.

The Statue Review.

See figure 2a and 2b HEAVY DUTY member Chris explained that their aim was to highlight that the statue's commemoration of Stirling as a "founder" masked the "shocking side of history that wasn't being told," the Pinjarra massacre. He observed that "we need to be really wary of First Nations' peoples and their feelings towards these statues."[11] In many

---

[10] Shannon Hampton, "Vandal faces the music," *The West Australian,* 27 June 2020.

[11] "Perth artists replace plaques on CBD statues to tell the 'whole story' of WA's complex history," Breakfast with Russell Woolfe, *ABC Radio Perth*, 16 September 2020, https://www.abc.net.au/radio/perth/programs/breakfast/plaques-covered-on-perth-statues/12668894 They added an identical plaque with the same description of the Pinjarra massacre on the statue of fellow perpetrator John Septimus Roe, located nearby on the corner of Victoria Avenue and

Figure 2. (a and b) Sir James Stirling Statue. Credit: HEAVY DUTY, by permission.

ways, his sentiments reflect views expressed by many Indigenous commentators in the wake of the toppling of Colston's statue. For example, in describing the statue of South Australia's Charles Cameron Kingston, acknowledged as an "originator of the White Australia policy," Natasha Wanganeen commented that, '[l]ooking at that statue every day as an Aboriginal woman, walking out of my house, it is a mental health trigger."[12]

Stirling and the Pinjarra Massacre

When Stirling gathered together a party of police, soldiers, and settlers and led them to Pinjarra to quell Bindjareb resistance to the spread of settlement, it was only five years after the process of colonization had begun. In June 1829, ships began arriving from Britain bringing settlers and their servants to what was at first called the Swan River Colony. Almost immediately beset by failed farms, intra-colonial squabbles, financial failures, and inadequate supplies of labour, the colony quickly developed a reputation in England as a failure.[13] At the same time, the colonizers faced strong resistance from local Noongar people, and as Ann Hunter shows, the legal position on how the government and settlers ought to respond to Noongar resistance was unclear. Stirling's detailed instructions, received in April 1832, were a contradictory mix, mandating the legal protection of Aboriginal people under British law, but at the same time authorizing the use of force to quell resistance and protect settlers and their property.[14] The British

---

Adelaide Terrace, Perth. This statue was sculpted by Greg James in 1990 and donated to the City of Perth in 2007 by MacCormac Architects.

[12] Cameron Slessor and Eugene Boisvert, "Black Lives Matter protest renew push to remove 'racist' monuments to colonial figures," *ABC News*, 10 June 2020.

[13] For the most detailed biography of James Stirling, see Statham-Drew, *James Stirling*.

[14] Ann Hunter, *A Different Kind of Subject: Colonial Law in Aboriginal-European Relations in Nineteenth Century Western Australia 1829–61* (Melbourne: Australian Scholarly Publishing, 2012), 6–7.

government's inconsistent instructions left the governor with considerable discretion; one solution Stirling adopted in May 1832 was to declare Aboriginal leaders as outlaws, and thus not deserving of legal protection.[15]

After a troubled first three years, Stirling took a two-year leave of absence in England from August 1832, during which time he was knighted. In the interim, the colony was governed by a succession of military men – Captain Frederick Irwin, Captain Richard Daniell, and Captain Picton Beete. Under their leadership, conflict in the Perth district with the local Whadjuk Noongar peaked in 1833 resulting in the deaths of key Aboriginal leaders. Colonial authorities outlawed and in May 1833 executed an elder named Midgegooroo, and two months later outlawed his son, Yagan, resulting in Yagan's execution by two youths enticed by the promise of a bounty.[16] The shock to Whadjuk Noongar of losing two of its most important leaders was exacerbated by the desecration of Yagan's body; his distinguishing scarification marks were flayed and his body decapitated, with his head taken to England where it was displayed in a museum.[17] The killing of such leaders meant that by 1834, with Stirling still away, conflict with Whadjuk Noongar clans in the Perth district was waning.

Attacks, however, by other Noongar dialectal groups to the north, east, and south of the settlement continued, to which authorities responded with flogging and imprisonment at Fremantle Gaol.[18] Calyute, a leader of the Bindjareb Noongar to the south of the settlement, who had led a raid on a leading settler's flour mill, was held in confinement and twice flogged with sixty lashes. After his release, he and several others on 15 July 1834 attacked two settlers at Mandurah, a coastal settlement south of Perth, killing a young servant named Hugh Nesbitt.[19] Calling on a long British imperial tradition, settlers immediately demanded a punitive expedition not only to kill the perpetrators but also to collectively punish their families in an attempt to terrorize the Bindjareb into submission. In the colonization of Australia, such expeditions were sometimes settler-initiated and sometimes government-initiated, sometimes reactive and sometimes pre-emptive, but always designed to terrorize Indigenous peoples against further resistance to British settlement.

Stirling arrived back in the colony, at King George's Sound, on 19 June 1834 and immediately resumed duty as governor. However, it would be seven weeks before he was able to reach the seat of government in Perth, finally arriving there on 19 August.[20] He became increasingly concerned that the colony was in a weak position, destined to be overrun and destroyed. With only 1,800 settlers, including officials and the military, it was still a tiny settlement. Noongar responses were sporadic and appeared uncoordinated, but Stirling feared the different Aboriginal groups would unite and threaten the colony's future. As he put it in a letter to the Secretary of State in Britain after the massacre had occurred, "There was danger, that their success in this species of warfare might tempt other tribes to pursue the same course, and eventually combine together for the extermination of the whites."[21] Barry Morris has pointed out in relation to New

---

[15] Hunter, *A Different Kind of Subject*, 18.

[16] "Yagan and Heegan, Two Natives Shot. William Keats, A Youth, speared," *Perth Gazette*, 13 July 1833, and Green, *Broken Spears*, 87.

[17] Cressida Fforde, "Yagan," in *The dead and their possessions: repatriation in principle, policy and practice*, ed. Cressida Fforde, Jane Hubert, Paul Turnbull (New York: Routledge, 2002), 229–41.

[18] Green, *Broken Spears*, 92.

[19] *Perth Gazette*, 26 July 1834, 326–7.

[20] *Perth Gazette*, 19 July 1834, 321 and *Perth Gazette*, 23 August 1834, 342.

[21] Stirling to Stanley, letter no 14, 1 November 1834, cited in Contos et al, *Pinjarra Massacre Site*, 146–7.

South Wales, and we can see it here in Stirling, the "spectre of an 'Aboriginal rising' gave expression to the fears that haunted the colonial project, that is, that a collective and sustained Aboriginal resistance could menace and potentially overturn colonial occupation."[22]

Stirling then ceased declaring Noongar leaders outlaws and turned to a military solution.[23] To protect settler expansion southwards, where he had already selected land for himself, it became clear that a military garrison would be needed at or near Pinjarra. He re-established the Mounted Police Corps, selecting three experienced officers and seven privates, in readiness for a direct attack on Calyute and his warriors.[24] With the killing of Nesbitt providing an excuse for action, he organized the punitive expedition to the Pinjarra area that local settlers wanted. Roe joined the expedition party in order to inspect the country and to plan the military garrison and future settlement. Like Stirling, Roe had a naval education and experience, though he was from a modest clerical background in contrast to Stirling's wealthy extended family, which had made a fortune from unfree labour and slavery in the Caribbean.[25] Roe's journal entries concerning the Pinjarra expedition are now amongst the most detailed accounts we have.[26] They describe the separate departures and gathering together of the various members of the party over three days as it travelled south to Pinjarra. Having camped overnight, he noted, the expedition party reached a large group of Bindjareb at Pinjarra at 8.35 am on 28 October. On arrival, Captain Ellis, Captain Norcott, and three mounted police approached the group to determine if this was, indeed, the tribe of Calyute. They saw that it was, though Calyute himself was probably not present. None of the reports mention sighting him specifically, and several captured Bindjareb women later reported that he was away in another part of the country.[27] Stirling's party decided to attack, surrounding the group from three different vantage points in such a way that they would be trapped.

The eyewitness accounts from the members of the punitive expedition emphasise that at first the Bindjareb resisted. According to an anonymous account by a member of the party, published in the *Perth Gazette* three days later, as soon as they saw the police, the Bindjareb men "seized their numerous and recently made spears, and showed a formidable front."[28] When this did not stop the police advance, they "sullenly retreated."[29] The Binjareb continued to throw spears as they "retreated to the river" and the military continued to fire.[30] Their retreat was blocked by a second contingent, this one headed by Stirling, prompting those under attack to hide in the water and among the riverbank bushes and logs, where, in Roe's words, they were "picked off by the party on either

---

[22] Barry Morris, "Frontier colonialism as a culture of terror," *Journal of Australian Studies* 16, no. 35 (2009): 76.

[23] Hunter, *A Different Kind of Subject*, 25.

[24] Green, *Broken Spears*, 97.

[25] Georgina Arnott, "WA's first governor James Stirling had links to slavery, as well as directing a massacre. Should he be honoured?," *The Conversation*, 8 June 2021.

[26] See 'Extract from Capt. J.S. Roe's Registered Fieldbook #3: 25th – 28th October 1834', in the appendix to Contos et al, *Pinjarra Massacre Site*, 148–50, hereafter cited as Roe Journal. The original diaries are held by the State Library of Western Australia.

[27] Anonymous, "Encounter with the natives in the Pinjarra District on the banks of the Murray," *Perth Gazette*, 1 November 1834, 383.

[28] Anon, "Encounter with the Natives in the Pinjarra District," 383.

[29] For the suggestion that the anonymous author of this report was probably Captain Norcott, see Statham-Drew, "Stirling and Pinjarra," 177.

[30] Anon, "Encounter with the Natives in the Pinjarra District," 383.

shore."[31] Roe, who was unarmed, had taken up a position with four soldiers further south along the river; from there he could hear the firing and the voices of the retreating Bindjareb "for upwards of an hour." Roe emphasised that the natives resisted; despite being "crouched in very small and scarcely discernible holes and places, and in many instances had immersed themselves in water, having only their nose and mouth above water, nevertheless threw numerous spears with amazing precision and force." It was not enough, however, and the shooting continued unabated. "In this way," records Roe, "between 15 and 20 were shot dead, very few of the wounded being suffered to escape," until the party considered that the punishment had been "sufficiently exemplary."[32]

The *Perth Gazette* participant observer thought the number killed was higher, saying that "the cross fire from both banks" continued "until between 25 and 30 were left dead on the field and in the river." He thought also that it was "very probable that more men were killed in the river and floated down with the stream," to the extent that about half of the Binjareb's male population had been killed. On the question of who was killed, the *Perth Gazette* says it was mainly men but also included one woman and several children, and one of the eight women taken prisoners had been injured. Natalie Contos *et al* question this report, suggesting the victims were mainly women and children.[33] Their view reflects the testimony of Yaburgurt (also known as George Winjan), a child survivor of the massacre and later Bindjareb leader: "They rush camp. They shoot-em man, shoot-em gin [women], shoot-em picaninnies [children], and they shoot-em dogs too."[34] In any case, some women were detained for a period and then released, after being told that "if they again offered to spear white men or their cattle, or to revenge in any way the punishment which had just been inflicted on them for their numerous murders and outrages, *four times the present number of men would proceed amongst them and destroy every man, woman and child.*"[35] In his report to the Secretary of State for the Colonies four days later, Governor Stirling gives a similar account of the threat to the women. The women, he says, were informed that.

> ... the punishment had been inflicted because of the misconduct of the tribe; that the white men never forgot to punish murder; that on this occasion the women and children had been spared; but if any other person should be killed by them, not one would be allowed to remain alive on this side of the mountains.[36]

The estimate of the numbers killed has been the subject of dispute, as it has for many such punitive expeditions, where figures vary according to the allegiances and the proximity in time and space of those making the estimate.[37] Further complicating the figures in the contemporary records is a relatively little-known 1927 article by Jane Elizabeth Grose,

---

[31] Roe Journal, 149.
[32] Roe Journal, 150.
[33] Contos et al, *Pinjarra Massacre Site*, 37–41.
[34] Ronald Richards, *Murray and Mandurah: A sequel history of the Old Murray District of Western Australia* (Pinjarra: Shire of Murray and City of Mandurah, 1993), 8, cited in Jennifer Harris, "Memorials and Trauma: Pinjarra 1834," in *Trauma, Media, Art: New Perspectives*, ed. Mick Broderick and Antonio Traverso (Newcastle-upon-tyne: Cambridge Scholars Publisher, 2010), 47.
[35] Our emphasis. Anon, "Encounter with the Natives in the Pinjarra District," 383.
[36] Stirling to Stanley, 1 November 1834, 147.
[37] Morris, "Frontier Colonialism as a Culture of Terror," 76–7.

citing her settler grandfather's journal: "About 80 blacks were killed and ... about 50 natives were buried in one great hole."[38] Further, Noongar oral histories collected in 1973 asserted that 750 people were killed, an "impossible" figure which John Mulvaney suggests is not necessarily an actual death toll, but instead indicates the degree of trauma suffered by the Bindjareb, not just physically, but also politically, socially and culturally.[39] Perhaps we will never know the number of Bindjareb people who died at the site or later from injuries.

Whatever the number killed, this was undoubtedly a massacre. In their discussion of massacres, archaeologists Mirani Litster and Lynley Wallis, describe the dynamic between the two groups involved in terms that fit the events at Pinjarra very well:

> Victims – a group comprising more than one person, typically possessing inferior weaponry with which to defend themselves; and,

> Perpetrators – another group, who distinguish themselves from their victims by having the power to kill without substantial risk of physically injuring themselves, and who might generally be considered to have instigated the event.[40]

When Pamela Statham-Drew, Stirling's biographer, approached the controversial question of whether these events are best described as a battle or a massacre, she favoured the term *battle* on the grounds that even when surrounded and overpowered, the surprised and trapped Bindjareb people had "bravely fought an unwinnable contest."[41] Yet armed and resistant people can still be subject to massacre; the victims' resistance does not mean a massacre did not occur.

No other punitive expedition in the Australian colonies was, or would be, led by a governor. To his surprise, Stirling found that while local press and settlers praised him for his decisive action, there were dissenting voices. The British authorities were far from pleased. A new British government was elected in April 1835, in which evangelical influence was strong, affecting Aboriginal policy. Lord Glenelg, as Secretary of State for the Colonies, was shocked when he learned that Stirling himself had led a military action against Aboriginal people and censured him in a despatch on 23 July 1835.[42] The House of Commons Select Committee on Aborigines in British Settlements in 1837 commented that Stirling's party had failed to confine "their vengeance to the actual murderers," and condemned acts of "indiscriminate punishment" and "threats extending to the destruction of women and children."[43] Similar acts of collective punishment were deemed criminal in 1838, when an unofficial settler party attacked a group of Wirrayaraay Kamilaroi at Myall Creek in New South Wales. The change in British government policy meant that Governor George Gipps oversaw and supported a legal process which ultimately led to the conviction and execution of the perpetrators.[44]

---

[38] Chris Owen, "The Pinjarra massacre: it's time to speak the truth of this terrible slaughter," *The Guardian*, 17 November 2019. Grose's article was recently brought to light by historian Chris Owen, and perhaps influenced HEAVY DUTY's plaque.

[39] John Mulvaney, *Encounters in Place: Outsider and Aboriginal Australians, 1606–1985* (St Lucia: University of Queensland Press, 1989), 170.

[40] Mirani Litster and Lynley A. Wallis, "Looking for the proverbial needle? The archaeology of Australian colonial frontier massacres," *Archaeology in Oceania* 46, no. 3 (2011): 106.

[41] Statham-Drew, "Stirling and Pinjarra," 192; Statham-Drew, *Stirling*, 270.

[42] Extracts quoted in the *Perth Gazette*, 30 July 1836, 736 and in Paul Hasluck, *Black Australians: A Survey of Native Policy in Western Australia, 1829–1897* (Melbourne: Melbourne University Press, 1970 [1942]), 50.

[43] Quoted in Hunter, *A Different Kind of Subject*, 74.

[44] See Jane Lydon and Lyndall Ryan, eds., *Remembering the Myall Creek Massacre* (Sydney: NewSouth, 2018).

Bindjareb people survived the massacre and continued to live on their own country, as they do today. Stirling had, though, seriously damaged their capacity for resistance, and the survivors were forced to find new ways, such as working for settlers and protecting their families, to maintain their community in the face of colonization. Furthermore, for decades the Pinjarra massacre continued to reverberate through settler-Indigenous relations in Western Australia. As colonizers encroached further into Noongar land, the pattern of Noongar resistance and punitive expeditions would continue, first in Ballardong Noongar Country in the Avon Valley and subsequently further north and east. The Pinjarra massacre was frequently referred to when authorities, wishing to deter Aboriginal groups from resisting settlement, threatened another "Pinjarra style" action, or a "second Pinjarra."[45] Thus Pinjarra became synonymous with an exemplary form of colonial violence, acting as a deterrent against Aboriginal people questioning or disrupting settler rule. Further massacres did occur, but the details were usually hidden from public view in order not to attract British government censure.

Other forms of punishment and deterrence were also vigorously pursued. From 1838 in Western Australia, Indigenous men convicted of stealing or committing *inter se* crimes such as payback killings were often sent to an island off the coast of Perth that Noongar knew as Wadjemup and settlers called Rottnest Island, which became an especially feared and hated site of punishment. Given the difficulty in taking arrested people to court over vast distances, local authorities often preferred a policy of summary trial and punishment on the spot (which usually meant whipping) of Aboriginal offenders.[46] Inherited from both the British convict system and from Caribbean slavery, whipping would persist in Western Australian practice and legislation for decades to come. Capital punishment was another weapon in the colony's arsenal against Indigenous opponents; men found guilty in court of the murder of settlers were hung from 1840 onward.[47] Even with all these techniques at the disposal of the colonial authorities, massacres perpetrated by settlers and police would continue as settlement expanded, rising to a peak in the Kimberley region in the late nineteenth century – a period remembered by Aboriginal people as "the killing time" – and extending, in the case of the Forrest River massacre in 1926, into the twentieth.[48]

Contested statues of Stirling and Yagan

The creation and erection of a statue commemorating Stirling was not a product of settler society enthusiasm and patriotism, as might be assumed, but instead reflected the endeavour of a select few "privileged" individuals.[49] As the centenary of the founding of the colony of Western Australia loomed in the 1920s, a group of history-minded citizens including journalist and university student, Paul Hasluck, were prompted to form the

---

[45] An early example of newspaper commentary is "Robbery committed by the York natives, and seizure of two of the party," *Perth Gazette*, 1 April 1837, 876: with response by L. Giustiniani, *Swan River Guardian*, 27 April 1837, 108.

[46] Hunter, *A Different Kind of Subject*, 201–20.

[47] Hunter, *A Different Kind of Subject*, 118–9.

[48] Chris Owen, *Every Mother's Son is Guilty: Policing the Kimberley Frontier of Western Australia 1882–1905* (Crawley: UWA Publishing, 2016). For the Forrest River Massacre of 1926, which has been the subject of historiographical dispute, see Neville Green, *The Forrest River Massacre* (Fremantle: Fremantle Arts Centre Press, 1995); Noel Loos, *White Christ, Black Cross*, (Canberra: Aboriginal Studies Press, 2007), 100–16, and notes on 193–4.

[49] For a broader discussion see Richard Drayton, "Rhodes Must Not Fall?," *Third Text* 33, no. 4–5 (2019): 553.

Royal Western Australian Historical Society (RWAHS) in September 1926.[50] To celebrate the state's centenary in 1929, the RWAHS decided it was "time to erect a statue of the state's founder." The Society may have been encouraged by the success of the shilling fund for a memorial to mark the Jubilee of former premier, John Forrest, which successfully raised £1800, and resulted in the unveiling of his statue in King's Park's prestigious memorial row in 1927.[51] Forrest was well remembered (having only died in 1918) and appealed to the public's liking for "bush pioneer" figures, and as the colony's first premier represented the state's political autonomy.[52]

The story of Stirling's statue presented a stark contrast. The RWAHS devoted £25, equivalent to a little over $2000 today, and requested subscriptions from "the public who will," they believed, "welcome the opportunity to give honour where honour is due."[53] The state government pledged £50 to stimulate public donations, with Premier Philip Collier predicting that "the citizens of Perth" will give Stirling "a fitting memorial."[54] Yet after two months, only "£8 to £10" was donated, a far cry from the £1000 anticipated by the RWAHS. The Society's president Sir James Mitchell blamed the government, complaining that it should fully "bear the cost," but as this was unlikely, the RWAHS instead launched a "state-wide appeal."[55] Paul Hasluck, the honorary secretary, reminded the public that the state's foundation was thanks to Stirling's "own energy in promoting colonisation."[56] But the people remained unmoved, and after eight years only £150 had been collected. Insufficient funds forced the Society to shelve its plans.[57] While the Great Depression probably inhibited donations, economic hardship was never explicitly cited as cause for the moribund fundraising. Low public interest in a Stirling statue probably stemmed from the fact he was not well remembered, and associated with the trouble-stricken early colonial period.

While interest in a Stirling statue languished, less expensive forms of official remembrance were adopted.[58] The Stirling name, already ascribed to a number of places including the Stirling Range in 1835, was also given to a major highway in 1932, a dam in 1947, a town in 1959, and a municipal council in 1971.

For some, naming was not enough. As the sesquicentenary approached, Hasluck remained committed to the idea of a statue. Since the state's Centenary he had forged an illustrious career as a historian, journalist, federal government minister, and governor-general of Australia (1969–1974). He was also an architect of Aboriginal assimilation. In the 1930s, he toured the Kimberley, reporting on the Moseley Royal Commission's

---

[50] "A Brief History," Royal Western Australian Historical Society, https://www.histwest.org.au/brief-history (accessed 21 December 2021), Anne Porter, 'Birtwhistle, Ivor Treharne (1892–1976)' and Malcolm Allbrook, "Hasluck, Sir Paul Meernaa (1905–1993)," *Australian Dictionary of Biography*, https://adb.anu.edu.au/biography/hasluck-sir-paul-meernaa-18555 (accessed 21 December 2021).

[51] "Sir John Forrest's Jubilee: Proposal for a statue," *Sun*, 15 August 1915, and "Statue of Lord Forrest," *Sydney Morning Herald*, 26 June 1923.

[52] Governor William Campion cited in "Governor's Holiday: Visit to England: Admiration for Pioneers," *The West Australian*, 7 January 1929.

[53] "State Centenary: Sir James Stirling," *West Australian*, 3 July 1929.

[54] "Stirling Memorial: Government Supports Fund," *West Australian*, 9 October 1929.

[55] "Stirling Memorial: Appeal Meets with Poor Response," *West Australian*, 2 December 1929.

[56] "Memorial to Sir James Stirling," *Great Southern Leader*, 13 June 1930.

[57] F. I. Bray, Chairman, Memorials Committee, W.A. Historical Society to A. Berkeley, Under Treasurer, The Treasury, 5 May 1937, WA State Records Office, Premier's Department: WA Historical Society, 433/29; A. Berkeley, Under Treasurer, The Treasury to Chairman, Memorials Committee, W.A. Historical Society, 18 June 1937, WA State Records Office, Premier's Department: WA Historical Society, 433/29.

[58] "State News Summary," *Western Mail*, 24 November 1949, 14.

investigation of the condition and treatment of Aboriginal people.[59] This experience shaped his belief that Aboriginal people could only advance as individuals by relinquishing their group identity and distinct culture. He tried to implement this policy of cultural genocide as the federal Minister for Territories (1951 to 1963) advocating cultural assimilation, and the need for a "single British Australian society."[60] Hasluck attributed the strengths of Australia's heritage to its inherited British culture, traditions, religious faith, and civilization that the "first settlers brought to this land," and which linked it to a wider Anglo world. For Hasluck, an opportunity to celebrate this "national heritage" arose in the lead up to Western Australia's sesquicentenary.[61]

In 1978 the Western Australian government called for ideas to celebrate the upcoming sesquicentenary, prompting Noongar leader Ken Colbung to suggest the government fund a commemorative statue of Yagan. Quoting the 1833 *Perth Gazette's* description of Yagan as "a patriot and a warrior ... the Wallace of the age," Colbung argued that "[t]here is no doubt that Yagan is part of this State's history and that his memory is venerated by Aborigines." This was a revolutionary proposal, as there were no other bronze sculptures memorializing an Aboriginal person at that time in Australia.[62] Confident that he would receive a positive response, Colbung commissioned sculptor Robert Hitchcock to produce a maquette, and when the proposed 3.6 m bronze statue was costed at $30,000, suggesting that the Aboriginal Lands Trust could contribute $10,000 if the government paid the balance.[63]

Concerned that Yagan was "something of an outlaw," Premier Charles Court sought the confidential advice of Hasluck and his wife Alexandra, a freelance historian who had researched Yagan.[64] Hasluck argued that if there were to be a statue of an Aboriginal it should not be Yagan, who "seems not a leader of his people but rather a tragic individual figure." He warned Court that many would think it strange to commemorate the founding of Western Australia "by a statue to Yagan and not to Stirling, who had much more to do with the founding than Yagan had."[65] Court invited Hasluck to suggest another suitable "Aboriginal personality," but he was unlikely to do so.[66] While Hasluck claimed to "respect" stories about Aboriginal "warriors" and "faithful helpers [to] the heroic pioneers," he did not perceive Aboriginal people as a "different group of Australians" with a separate history. Nor did he believe an Aboriginal historical figure should be singled out in the Sesquicentenary commemorations: he assumed Aboriginal people would follow the path of "minority groups" elsewhere, by "gradually chang[ing] their customs, los[ing] their

---

[59] Anna Haebich, "The Formative Years: Paul Hasluck and Aboriginal Issues During the 1930s," in *Paul Hasluck in Australian History: civic personality and public life,* ed. Tom Stannage, Kay Saunders and Richard Nile (St Lucia: University of Queensland Press, 1998), 93–8.

[60] Anthony Moran, "White Australia, Settler Nationalism and Aboriginal Assimilation," *Australian Journal of Politics and History* 51, no. 2 (2005): 186–7.

[61] Paul Hasluck, *Light that Time Has Made* (Canberra: National Library of Australia, 1995), 53–4, and 56.

[62] Bronwen Batten and Paul Batten, "Memorialising the Past: Is there an Aboriginal way?," *Public History Review* 15 (2008): 98. For details on specific memorials to Aboriginal individuals see "Indigenous," Monuments Australia, https://monumentaustralia.org.au/themes/people/indigenous (accessed 21 December 2021).

[63] Ken Colbung to Charles Court, 28 July 1978, in "Yagan" Memorial, SRO 165/78, and David Pougher, "Yagan 'not worth a tribute'," *West Australian*, 20 September 1978.

[64] Premier Charles Court to The Rt. Hon. Sir Paul Hasluck, 1 August 1978, in "Yagan" Memorial, SRO 165/78.

[65] Rt. Hon. Sir Paul Hasluck to Premier Charles Court, 4 August 1978, in "Yagan" Memorial, SRO 165/78 and reproduced in Paul Hasluck, "Yagan Statue Opposed," *West Australian*, 19 October 1978.

[66] Premier Charles Court to The Rt. Hon. Sir Paul Hasluck, 1 August 1978, in "Yagan" Memorial, SRO 165/78.

identity and either disappear[ing] by merging with" the Anglo-Australian "majority or accommodate[ing] themselves" to that "larger community."[67]

When Court accepted the Haslucks' advice not to proceed with a Yagan statue, he was strongly criticized by many, including the editor of the West Australian who wrote: "Yagan was respected by the first white settlers and his name still means much to the Aboriginal members of the community. His commemoration would be eminently appropriate to next year's occasion."[68] Realizing that the statue had become a controversial issue, Court announced that the government was now considering a mural instead. A furious Colbung responded that a "mural of a large bloodstain," would be an "apt memorial to show that Aboriginal people have been continually knocking their heads against a brick wall for 150 years and looked like doing it for the next 150."[69]

As it turned out, neither a statue nor mural commemorating Aboriginal people was erected for the sesquicentenary. Seven years later, however, a three-metre-tall bronze sculpture of Yagan was unveiled on Matagarup (Heirrison Island), a significant Whadjuk meeting place, Colbung having succeeded in raising funds from other sources.[70]

A statue of James Stirling was also erected for the sesquicentenary, but without government funding. After the imbroglio over the Yagan statue, Court could not allocate public funds to a statue of Governor Stirling, but private donors came to the rescue, very likely encouraged by the Premier.[71] Local media organizations Channel 9 and Radio 6KY funded a bronze statue of Stirling designed by Clement P. Somers, most likely to the tune of $22,000, while mining company Hamersley Iron provided a four tonne block of iron ore for the base.[72] Thus, fifty years after first being proposed by Hasluck and the RWAHS, a statue of Stirling was finally erected in front of the R & I Bank in Barrack Street, Perth, the site where Stirling had staged the colony's ceremonial founding on 12 August 1829 by felling a tree. Prince Charles, formally unveiled the statue on 10 March 1979, after attending a re-enactment of Stirling's first landing. Foreshadowing the controversy that erupted in 2020, this unveiling ceremony was conducted amidst Aboriginal protestors demanding Land Rights (see Figure 3). Rallied by the Black Action Movement, protestors attempted to petition Charles to advocate on their behalf for land rights and better conditions, but unable to approach, they chanted during the ceremony.[73]

The statue's existence was just as ignominious as its inception. When the bank building was demolished in 1996, Stirling's statue was stored at the Midland Railway Workshops and soon forgotten. It was not until prompting by the West Australian that the statue was found six years later, and moved to the Treasury Building. Then in 2012 when the building was redeveloped, Stirling's statue was again removed, and left in "limbo" for

---

[67] Hasluck, Light that Time Has Made, 47, 50, 171, 172.
[68] Pougher, "Yagan 'not worth a tribute'"; "Yagan Statue," West Australian, 17 October 1978.
[69] Premier's Department, Perth WA, "News Release," 17 October 1978, in "Yagan" Memorial, SRO 165/78; "Colbung hits at Yagan decision," Daily News, 19 October 1978.
[70] Bronwyn Batten and Paul Batten, "Memorialising the Past: Is There an Aboriginal Way?," 98 and 100. Yagan's statue suffered defacement on multiple occasions, including decapitation by vandals in September 1997.
[71] Premier Charles Court to Under Secretary, 17th October 1978, in "Yagan" Memorial, SRO 165/78.
[72] Swan Television and Radio Broadcasters Perth, Western Australia, State Library of Western Australia, available at https://purl.slwa.wa.gov.au/slwa_b3654898_35.pdf; W. F. Ellis, Director, to G. C. MacKinnon, Minister for Tourism, 27 October 1978, in SRO 150th Anniversary, "Aboriginal Groups," SRO 150.5.8.
[73] "Senator Chaney says: WA Aborigines have a point ... ," Daily News, 3 March 1979 and "Charles misses the Aboriginal protestors," Daily News, 10 March 1979.

Figure 3. Prince Charles walks towards Stirling statue to perform the unveiling with Aboriginal protestors in the background. Credit: Sourced from the collections of the State Library of Western Australia and reproduced with the permission of the Library Board of Western Australia.

three years. Claiming that it took time to find a suitable location which adequately reflected Stirling's role as the "city's founding father," the Council finally placed the statue in its current location in front of the City of Perth Library in 2015.[74] Soon after Noongar demanded the statue be removed altogether because of Stirling's role in the Pinjarra massacre, which was supported by City of Fremantle councillor, Sam Wainwright in 2017.[75] No action was taken, however, and the statue remained where it was until the events of 2020. Rather than merely copying a "left sort of fringe" zeitgeist,[76] the statue challengers of 2020 were, in fact, expressing a persistent and growing concern at the insufficient official recognition of a history of frontier violence and genocidal colonization.

Stirling's statue, the Pinjarra Massacre Memorial, and public memory

One of the obstacles to resolving conflict over the Stirling statue has been the profound disagreement about what had happened at Pinjarra and therefore how both Governor Stirling and those killed ought to be remembered. Stirling and other eyewitnesses initially described the Pinjarra massacre as a "skirmish," a "rencontre," an "encounter," a

---

[74] Bronwyn Pearce, "Stirling Statue Found," *West Australian*, 2 November 2002, Malcolm Queckett, "City Plan for Stirling site still in limbo," *West Australian*, 25 May 2015, and "No to Stirling offer for Stirling statue," *Guardian Express*, 7 July 2015.
[75] Kate Campbell, "Calls for statues of key figures in WA history to be removed," *Perth Now*, 27 August 2017. See also "Stirling statue protest," *Fremantle Herald Interactive*, 27 October 2017.
[76] Grovier, "Black Lives Matter Protests."

"chastisement," and an "affray," but the term "the Battle of Pinjarra," which appears to have been coined by Stirling himself, was soon adopted.[77] It was used two years after the event by the colony's interpreter, Francis Armstrong, when describing a throwing stick decorated by a Bindjareb artist. It depicted, he said, the "battle of Pinjarra" in a drawing of a river along whose banks were the "outlines of human and horses' feet, and the graves of the slain."[78] Naming the event as a battle fostered an image of two equal sides at war, and for a century and a half it was widely known as such. It would take time for *massacre*, a politically charged term that derives etymologically from the Old French for "butchery" or "slaughterhouse" and that draws attention to the cold-blooded exertion of power, to be accepted in relation to Pinjarra.

A push within the Murray Shire in which Pinjarra is located for a formal memorial to the victims began in the 1970s, when the Federal government finally began taking heed of Indigenous calls for self-determination. As Noongar elders note, it was not until this time that they felt sufficiently empowered to voice their interests without "fear of jeopardizing their jobs and personal safety."[79] Shortly after the establishment of the Murray Districts Aboriginal Association (MDAA) in 1973, a wooden plaque was placed on a large jarrah tree as the first memorial. By 1985 it had been destroyed in a bushfire, so the MDAA, led firstly by President Oscar Little and later by coordinator Theo Kearing, began campaigning for a more enduring monument.

They did so in a context where public understanding was beginning to shift towards recognizing the Pinjarra event as a massacre. Neville Green's detailed study in 1984 argued that although it was "glorified as the Battle of Pinjarra," the "event" was in fact a massacre.[80] Green's work was part of a wider recognition of the role of massacres in Australia's colonizing history. As genocide scholar Colin Tatz has pointed out, in the 1980s and 1990s, before Australian historians turned to the question of genocide, "the developing preoccupation was with massacre. Myall Creek, Waterloo Creek, Forrest River, Bathurst, Orara River, Gippsland, Palmer River, Pinjarra, and Alice Springs became more familiar as sites of killing."[81] Slowly, during the 1990s public awareness that what happened at Pinjarra might be better described as the Pinjarra Massacre grew. For Bindjareb Noongar, these new studies of Pinjarra reinforced what they already knew.[82] Influenced by Green and by John Mulvaney's similar account in *Encounters in Place*, and with the approval of Bindjareb elders in Pinjarra, Noongar actors and writers Geoff Kelso, Kelton Pell, and Phil Thomson, began working in the early 1990s on a play about the massacre.[83] *Bindjareb Pinjarra* was first presented in Perth in September 1994 and was a huge success, performed in regional southwest Australia, including at Pinjarra, and later in other states.[84]

---

[77] George Fletcher Moore, in his diary entry for 1 November 1834, records Stirling's own account of what happened, using the phrase "Battle of Pinjarra": *Diary of ten years eventful life of an early settler in Western Australia, and also A descriptive vocabulary of the language of the Aborigines* (Nedlands: UWA Press, 1978 [1842]), 10. See Statham-Drew, "Stirling and Pinjarra," 184.

[78] "Manners and Habits of the Aborigines of Western Australia. From information collected by Mr F. Armstrong, Interpreter," *Perth Gazette*, 5 November 1836, 793, cited in Neville Green, "Aborigines and White Settlers in the Nineteenth Century," in *A New History of Western Australia*, ed. Tom Stannage (Nedlands: UWA Press, 1981), 86.

[79] Contos et al, *Pinjarra Massacre Site*, 66.

[80] Green, *Broken Spears*, 99, 105

[81] Colin Tatz, "Confronting Australian Genocide," *Aboriginal History* 25 (2001): 18.

[82] See Anna Haebich, *Dancing in Shadows: Histories of Nyungar Performance* (Perth: UWA Publishing, 2018) 56.

[83] Mulvaney, *Encounters in Place*, 168–71. See also Lois Tilbrook, *Nyungar tradition: glimpses of Aborigines of South-Western Australia 1829–1914* (Nedlands: University of Western Australia Press, 1983).

[84] Haebich, *Dancing in Shadows*, 275–99.

Even as public understanding began to shift, recognition of the events as a massacre continued to be highly contested, with serious consequences for the memorialization of its victims. An opportunity to gain funding soon arose as part of Australia's Bicentenary commemoration, but was missed when the Murray Shire Council refused to provide essential support.[85] When the Australian Heritage Commission took steps to enter the site of the massacre on the Register of the National Estate, some members of the council protested. Eventually, a compromise was reached, and the Pinjarra Battle Memorial Area was registered in June 1992.[86] But resistance to the term massacre remained in December 1998, when the Murray Shire council refused to formally recognise the word "massacre."[87]

In 2001, after a ten-year campaign, a permanent memorial was finally erected on the site. This was a large boulder surrounded by a circular paved area with mosaic medallions depicting black and white figures and handprints. The conflict over nomenclature, however, meant there was no inscription explaining what was being memorialized. As Jennifer Harris comments, the absence of any explanatory sign made "the site mysterious and incomplete" so that it became a place of double trauma, not only for the descendants of the massacre but also for the non-Indigenous population for whom it means "having to contemplate the revision of their history and of all of the values associated with it." The struggle over naming continued. In 2007 the Shire of Murray installed a plaque on the memorial commemorating the Battle of Pinjarra, a move criticized by the WA Heritage Council which recognized it as a massacre; it seems that a member of the public agreed with the Council, for the plaque soon disappeared.[88] On the massacre's 176th anniversary in 2010, after a long campaign by Binjareb representative Kerrie-Anne Kearing-Salmon, the WA Police Service erected a new plaque as "an act of reconciliation." It omitted both contentious words and instead commemorated the "memory of the men, women and children of the Bindjareb Noongar people and a Colonial Officer" who died "as part of confrontations in the early days of the Swan River Colony." Illustrating the ongoing tensions concerning how the memorial should be framed, this plaque too was stolen.[89] When it was eventually replaced, the text remained the same, but was now in both Noongar and English (see Figure 4a and b).

Since 2007 the "Pinjarra Massacre Site" has been listed on the Heritage Council of Western Australia's heritage register. In November 2018, after decades of opposition, the Shire of Murray council finally acceded to defining the 1834 events as a massacre and voted in favour of providing in-principle support for a new memorial which, as we write, is still in the early stages of planning.[90] The implications of this formal recognition of the Pinjarra massacre for the Stirling Statue, which still sits outside the City of Perth Library, remain to be seen.

---

[85] Contos et al, *Pinjarra Massacre Site*, 114 and Harris, "Memorials and Trauma," 48.

[86] Fay Gale, *Shared Space – Divided Cultures: Australia Today,* Cunningham Lecture (Canberra: Academic of Social Sciences, 1998), 4.

[87] Harris, "Memorials and Trauma," 49.

[88] Harris, "Memorials and Trauma," 48–9.

[89] "Memorial plaque stolen after a month," *Weekend Courier*, 3 December 2010.

[90] The Pinjarra massacre is also listed on the University of Newcastle's Colonial Frontier Massacre Map. "Pinjarra," Colonial Frontier Massacres, Australia, 1780 to 1930, https://c21ch.newcastle.edu.au/colonialmassacres/detail.php?r=887 (accessed 21 May 2021).

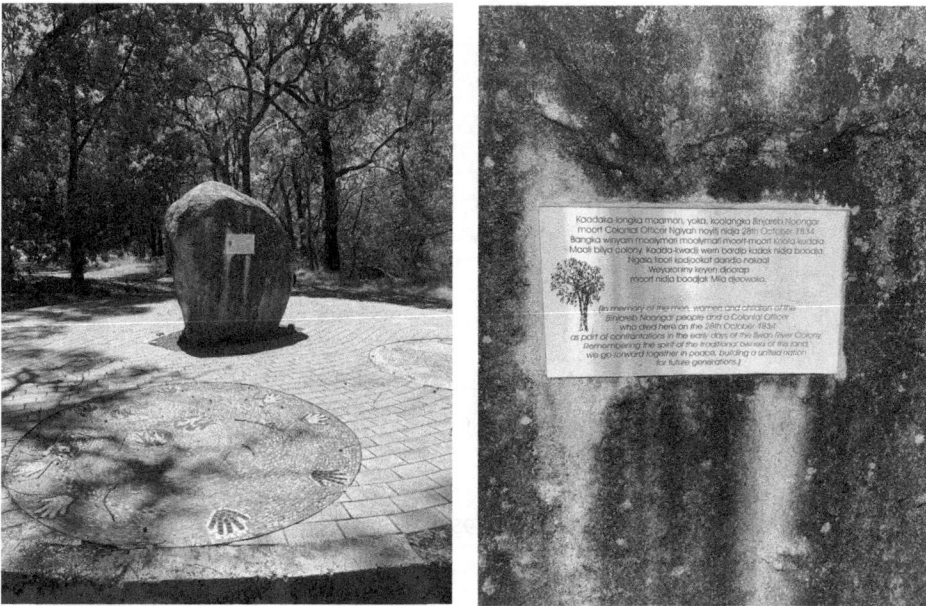

Figure 4. (a and b) Pinjarra Massacre Memorial. Credit: authors.

Conclusion

For genocide and massacre studies, the debates over the Stirling statue are significant for drawing attention to a massacre that provides us with unusually explicit statements of the aims of the perpetrators. The question of intent has been a difficult one for historians of massacre and genocide, in part because of difficulties in ascribing intention to what some suggest is best understood as a "structure of power" and in part because perpetrators rarely provide clear documentary evidence of their genocidal intentions.[91] In the case of the Pinjarra massacre, however, we have unusually clear expressions of genocidal intent by the perpetrators – the reports that Stirling's party considered punishment to have been "sufficiently exemplary" and that surviving Bindjareb women were warned any retaliation would be met by a military expedition determined to "destroy every man, woman and child" are unusually clear statements of genocidal intention.[92] That this genocidal action was led by a governor representing British imperial power in the colonies makes it all the more striking.

It is time for Stirling's statue to be removed, as so many other statues around the world have been both now and in the past. It is time, also, for full acknowledgement of the genocidal dimension of the Pinjarra massacre and, most importantly of all, for proper memorialization of its victims.

Disclosure statement

No potential conflict of interest was reported by the author(s).

---

[91] Jacques Semelin, "Towards a vocabulary of massacre and genocide," *Journal of Genocide Research* 5, no. 2 (2003): 193–210, esp. 198.

[92] Anon, "Encounter with the Natives in the Pinjarra District," 383.

ORCID

Shino Konishi ⓘ http://orcid.org/0000-0002-2771-9555

Südwester Reiter: Fear, Belonging, and Settler Colonial Violence in Namibia

Janne Lahti ⓘD

ABSTRACT
This article examines the continuities between the Herero and Nama genocide and the history of the *Reiterdenkmal* statue in Windhoek, Namibia. It interprets the statue as an extension of the lived experience of the genocide and a contested symbol of settler belonging. The *Reiterdenkmal* reformulated colonial violence as white victimhood and black savagery, and advanced German settler claims over African soil. Violence and the "rider" together remade black African space into white settler space. Yet, this settler belonging was and remains grounded on fears. Uncertainty over belonging and fear of the Natives had driven the killing and exploitation of black Africans in the first place, and settler identities remain uncertain as the legacies and reckonings of past violence continue unresolved in independent Namibia.

Windhoek, Namibia, 24 December 2013. It is the night of Christmas Eve and the nation's capitol is enjoying the holiday spirit. Yet, the city centre is buzzing with nervous commotion, taken over by a large police operation. The target: the *Reiterdenkmal*, also known as the *Südwester Reiter*, or in common parlance simply as the "rider." Standing at the heart of the city, near the preeminent Lutheran church, the *Christuskirche*, and the old German garrison, now a museum, *Alte Feste*, this equestrian statue dates back to the German colonial era and for many it signifies white settler power over black Africans. The monument depicts a white German soldier-settler, *Schutztruppe*, a common man on horseback with a rifle in hand, looking assertive, masculine, and triumphant. But now, as Namibia's German-language newspaper *Allgemeine Zeitung* alarmingly reports, the police have sealed off the "rider" from any curious bystanders, kept out the press, and offered no answers to inquiries as workers cut off the statue from its pedestal and haul it away. There, the paper suggests, was no information of who had ordered the removal and where the statue was going.[1] What looked certain was that the nation was

---

[1] "Eilmeldung: Reiterdenkmal is abgesägt," *Allgemeine Zeitung*, 24 December 2013.

Figure 1. The "rider" after 2013, in the courtyard of the Alte Feste, twice-removed, stocked away from public spotlight but still standing, though supported and without a pedestal. Less forceful, less commanding than before. Photo Wikimedia Commons.

making a strong symbolic reckoning with its colonial past, interrupting the narrative of settler triumph, and that this raised fears among the German-speaking minority (Figures 1 and 2).[2]

Set up in 1912 to commemorate the German victims of the "Herero uprising" of 1904 and German mastery over the land, the "rider" was first removed in 2009 for a short distance from a hill overlooking the *Christuskirche* to the front of the *Alte Feste* museum. It

---

[2] The heated commentary in the Namibian press – including white fears as well as views of the statue as an insult to black Namibians that needs to be moved – surrounding the "rider's" removal is voluminous. See, for instance, Tuyeimo Haidula, "Battle over Statues," *The Namibian*, 24 March 2014; Filemon Iiyambo, "The Horse, the Past, and Hypocrisy," *The Namibian*, 7 January 2014; Pendapala Hangala, "The Reiterdenkmal Must be Trashed," *New Era*, 8 November 2013.

Figure 2. The "rider" before, looking at the *Christuskirche*, assertive and powerful. Photo Wikimedia Commons.

moved again in 2013, as described above, this time to the inner courtyard of the said museum. The story of the "rider" is a battle over narratives, mastery over the past and the present in Namibia's identity-politics. It is about the remembrance of the colonial era, the calls for genocide repercussions from Germany, and the ongoing tensions between different ethnic groups in the country.[3] Through its removal, the Swapo-led government, dominated by the northern Ovambo majority, created a break from the colonial past. And by erecting on the rider's place a Genocide Memorial and a statue of Sam Nujoma, a revolutionary hero and the first president of Namibia, it advanced the prominence of the anticolonial liberation struggle.[4]

Yet, by substituting the "rider" with these new statues, the government also provided a reinterpretation of the nation's past that not only repositioned black Africans as heroes, but both sidelined whites from the national narrative and recast them as perpetrators of colonial aggression. The removal interrupted the narrative of the "rider" also on

---

[3] The descendants of the most affected groups, Herero and Nama, have been shut out by the Ovambo government from the still ongoing bilateral negotiations between Namibia and Germany over the acknowledgement of the 1904–08 genocide and possible restitution. See Henning Melber, "Colonial Genocide and the German-Namibian 'Reconciliation Agreement'," *The Round Table* 110, no. 4 (2021): 510–1; Henning Melber, "Why Reconciliation Agreement Between Germany and Namibia Has Hit the Buffers," *The Conversation*, 9 January 2022, https://theconversation.com/why-reconciliation-agreement-between-germany-and-namibia-has-hit-the-buffers-173452 (accessed 10 January 2022). On German memory politics, see Franziska Boehme, "Reactive Remembrance: The Political Struggle over Apologies and Reparations Between Germany and Namibia for the Herero Genocide," *Journal of Human Rights* 19, no. 2 (2020): 238–55.

[4] Elke Zuern, "Memorial Politics: Challenging the Dominant Party's Narrative in Namibia," *Journal of Modern African Studies* 50, no. 3 (2012): 495–7.

another level. While settler colonialism relies on the replacement of Indigenous peoples by the incoming, conquering, settlers, now it looks as if the settlers are the ones facing displacement when the "rider" was substituted. Out of public view, its pedestal destroyed, supported by steel poles, the "rider" today looks feeble and handicapped, increasingly irrelevant, as if its present condition is marking an end to the period of settler belonging in the Namibian society.

German colonial history comes with a paradoxical relationship to monuments. At least since the Cold War and the removal of the Herman von Wissman (colonial administrator in German East Africa) statue in Hamburg in 1967 after student protests, there has existed anticolonial activity in Germany targeting public monuments and spaces. Colonial monuments have been toppled and defaced and their histories questioned. But there also exists a widespread notion that Germans suffer from colonial amnesia and ignorance as colonial histories are hidden and marginalized in school curriculums and public discussions. Yet, there currently exists numerous active grass-root movements, calling for the decolonization of public spaces and return of stolen artefacts, coupled with ongoing negotiations between Germany and Namibia over recognition and compensation of the Herero geno- cide. Thus, the discussion on colonialism and colonial legacies today is very active.[5]

If situated in this bigger picture the "rider" reflects overlapping international and internal renegotiations and battles over who owns the past, what kind of histories we tell, and the difficulties in moving to the next step of decolonization, to reconciliation, for- giveness, equality, living together. It epitomizes disputes over ethnic and national iden- tity, land distribution, and racial inequality, all linked to the fraught interpretations and bloodied past of settler colonialism and its ongoing heritage and durabilities.

This article looks specifically at the origins and life of the *Reiterdenkmal* statue in Wind- hoek, in order to examine the continuities and connections between the Herero and Nama genocide and the history of this monument. It interprets the statue as an extension of the lived experience of the genocide and a contested symbol of settler belonging up to the twenty-first century. It sees colonial violence and the "rider" as inseparable, part of the same historical and narrative processes. First, from its initiation, the "rider" underlined German prominence over the land in Southwest Africa acquired through colonial violence against the Herero and Nama in 1904–08. It promoted white victimhood and black sava- gery while camouflaging and repackaging genocidal violence as a triumphant white sacrifice, a symbolic birthing of a German settler society through "blood and soil." In doing so, it sought to affirm settler belonging, that the land now belonged to the settlers for good. In a sense, genocidal violence and the "rider" together remade black African space into white settler space. Violence had cleared the land, bringing it to German settler hands and the "rider" affirmed this new order, this settler triumph.

Yet, second, the "rider" also acts as an indicator on how fragile and uncertain this settler belonging was in the past and remains such in the present. Uncertainty over belonging and fear of the local Herero and Nama had driven the killing and exploitation in the first place, and settler identities remain uncertain as the legacies and reckonings of

---

[5] Among the oldest groups are Arbeitskreis Hamburg Postkolonial (2004), freiburg-postkolonial (2005), Köln postkolo- nial/KopfWelten (started preparations for their exhibition as early as 2000). There are also Germany-wide initiatives like the touring exhibition "freedom roads" or the NGO-alliance "No amnesty on genocide." For an extensive list of organ- izations and initiatives, see https://www.kolonialismus.uni-hamburg.de/2015/09/10/postkoloniale-initiativen-in- deutschland-2/.

past violence continue unresolved in independent Namibia.[6] After the end of formal German colonialization in 1915, the settlers remained and so did the "rider." The statue stood at the heart of the capitol as an effort to control the past in the present, quelling settler uncertainties, while echoing the ongoing power and relevance of the settlers in a changing world. But in the twenty-first century independent Namibia, the "rider" has been pushed aside and replaced by new monuments to black Africans. The settler colonial narrative of belonging has come full circle as settler fears and insecurities have resurfaced.

This article combines what historian Maria Nugent called the "history *of* the memorial" with "history told *on* the memorial."[7] It starts by discussing the initiation of the "rider," the character of the settler colonial narratives of belonging it conveys, and the question of settler colonial endings. Then it goes back in time to describe the "rider's" origins in German violence against the Herero and Nama, a settler genocide driven by fear with staggering human cost. Finally, it moves to highlight how the "rider's" repackaging of violence as settler triumph and innocence stood changing times and decolonization, until it did no more.

A Monument for Settler Belonging

Windhoek, German Southwest Africa, 27 January 1912. The town woke to a festive mood abuzz with patriotic fervour. The red, white, and black flag of the *Kaiserreich* was visible everywhere and a large white crowd wearing their best gathered on the hill where the German garrison, *Alte Feste*, stood. People made their way along Kaiser Wilhelm Strasse, Garten Strasse, and numerous others in a town that by now looked like Germany in miniature. The main cause of festivities was the unveiling of a 16-foot bronze statue, the *Reiterdenkmal*, "a monument of victory" for Germans over black Africans, as historian Reinhart Kössler asserts.[8]

The choice of an equestrian figure in itself reflects a tradition in the German-speaking cultures of making statements about triumph and rule. During the *Kaiserreich* equestrian monuments, such as the gigantic *Deutsches Eck* (German corner), a rider figure of Kaiser Wilhelm erected in Koblenz near the French border in 1897, commemorated German victories, in this case the wars of unification. The "rider" in Windhoek came to existence via a public fundraising campaign conducted in Germany and through an artistic competition announced in Berlin. Yet, local authorities and settlers in German Southwest Africa initiated the process, petitioning the Colonial Office in Berlin already in 1907. Thus, resources were involved from both the colony and the metropole. Adolf Kürle designed the monument in Berlin, from where it travelled via Hamburg to Swakopmund on the coast of Southwest Africa. Changing from boat to rails, it arrived in Windhoek a few weeks before its inauguration.[9]

---

[6] On the close association between fear and colonial violence, Richard N. Price, "The Psychology of Colonial Violence," in *Violence, Colonialism, and Empire in the Modern World*, eds. Philip Dwyer and Amanda Nettelbeck (New York: Palgrave Macmillan, 2017), 30–7; Kim A. Wagner, *Amritsar 1919: An Empire of Fear and the Making of a Massacre* (New Haven, CT: Yale University Press, 2019); Matthias Häussler, *The Herero Genocide: War, Emotion, and Extreme Violence in Colonial Namibia* (New York: Berghahn Books, 2021).

[7] Maria Nugent, "Historical Encounters: Aboriginal Testimony and Colonial Forms of Commemoration," *Aboriginal History* 30 (2006): 36.

[8] Reinhart Kössler, *Namibia and Germany: Negotiating the Past* (Windhoek: University of Namibia Press, 2015), 148.

[9] "Chronology of the Monument," in *The Equestrian Monument (Reiterdenkmal) 1912–2014: A Chronological Documentation of Reports, Newspaper Clippings, and Photos/Illustrations* (Windhoek: Kuiseb Verlag, 2014), 7.

Figure 3. The "rider" as it stood after its inauguration, with Windhoek's settler community in audience. Bildarchiv der Deutschen Kolonialgesellschaft, Universitätsbibliothek Frankfurt am Main, urn:nbn:de: hebis:30:2-993395.

There is a movement forward mimicking settler advance in the statue's travelogue: it arrived on Southwestern soil from Germany, via the global shipping nexus Hamburg and the local port town of Swakopmund, much as the bulk of the settlers did. This is only fitting for a monument interpreted at the time as a symbol of German belonging in Africa. That the unveiling took place on the birthday of Kaiser Wilhelm II drove home the point more powerfully: the "rider" epitomized the rise of German power that had materialized through German blood connected with German soil. This land now had a prosperous German future ahead. At the inauguration ceremony, Governor Theodor Seitz proclaimed this message to all when stating that the German soldier depicted in the statue was "on the look-out ... over the land, proclaims to the world that we are the masters here and shall remain so" (Figure 3).[10]

The bronze equestrian figure at Windhoek rode on a base made of granite blocks. In front of this base stood a dedication plaque with an inscription that lists the white victims of the colonial war by their rank, profession, and gender. The text reads:

> In honor of the brave German warriors who lost their lives for the emperor and empire to save and preserve this country during the Herero and Hottentot [Nama] uprisings from 1903 to 1907 and during the Kalahari expedition in 1908. In honor of the German citizens who fell victim to the natives in the uprising. Fallen, lost, killed in an accident, killed [due to] their wounds and dead of diseases, from the Schutztruppe: officers 100, NCOs 254, riders 1180,

---

[10] Seitz quoted in Joachim Zeller, *Kolonialdenkmäler und Geschichtsbewusstsein: Eine Untersuchung der kolonialduetschen Erinnerungskultur* (Frankfurt am Main; Iko Verlag, 2000), 120.

from the Navy: officers 7, NCOs 13, crew 72. Slain in the uprising: men 119, women 4 children 1.[11]

While this plaque commemorates those Germans who had died, it can be read as an effort to reinforce the German settler colonial rule. First, it stressed German sacrifice as it repackaged German colonial violence against the Herero and Nama as white innocence. The statue explicitly and exclusively commemorates fallen German soldiers killed by aggressive black Africans. White Germans gave their lives both for the empire, the larger whole of Germanness stretching across the world and personified in the *Kaiser*, and to this particular land. They spilled blood for the sake of this land, which affirmed their belonging to it. Second, none of the dead were named. Not even the highest-ranking officers. They were all part of the settler project not as individuals but as part of a collective. They had made an individual sacrifice for the good of all the white settlers, saving the colony from savage danger and for the prosperous future of the settler community. It is this collective ethos that enforces the notion that the "rider" is meant to stand for the white settler community as a whole, in 1912 and in the future. It has been a symbol of the settler collective from its initiation.

Thirdly, the text makes no mention of black African dead in this colonial conflict. It gives no indication to their suffering, but instead dismisses it completely. Indeed, like Winfried Speitkamp has noted, as colonial rulers occupied African space through monuments they at the same time subjugated African history.[12] The sole role black Africans have here is that of the aggressors. The plaque casts the blame for the violence on the Herero and Nama, making them instigators of killings and Germans the victims of their bloodthirstiness. This regardless that the "rider" stands at the site of a former concentration camp for the Herero and Nama, a site where numerous black Africans perished in German hands. The plaque casts the Herero and Nama as a threat that the Germans have managed to check, in the process "preserving" the country for the settlers and their future generations. In this manner, the Herero and Nama get written out of the futures of this land. Here the "rider" mirrors what was de facto already taking place in the society as Germans ousted the Herero and Nama survivors from the land, used them as forced labour, and quelled their sovereignty, making the survivors servants to the whites.[13]

As the "rider" stood for German victory and for the presence and permanence of Germans in Africa, it carried high hopes, potentially signifying the birth of what the German settler Clara Brockman at the time called "new Germany on African soil."[14] Settlers like Brockman had reasons for optimism with the mining rush around Lüderitz Bay finally booming the colony's economy from 1908 onward. Combination of mineral riches and visions of family farmers and ranchers dominated the future-oriented settler minds. People like Brockman or the geographer and publicist Paul Rohrbach, tasked to

---

[11] Translated from German by author. Image of the plaque at Joachim Zeller, "Das Reiterdenkmal in Windhoek (Namibia) – Die Geschichte eines deutschen Kolonialdenkmals," https://www.freiburg-postkolonial.de/Seiten/Zeller-Reiterdenkmal-1912.htm (accessed 27 April 2021).

[12] Winfried Speitkamp, "Kolonialherrschaft und Denkmal: Afrikanische und deutsche Erinnerungskultur im Konflikt," in *Architektur und Erinnerung*, ed. Wolfram Martini (Göttingen: Vandenhoek & Ruprecht, 2000), 166.

[13] On the post-genocide social order in Southwest Africa, see Daniel J. Walther, *Creating Germans Abroad: Cultural Policies and National Identity in Namibia* (Athens: Ohio University Press, 2002).

[14] Clara Brockman, *Die deutsche Frau in Südwestafrika. Ein Beitrag zur Frauenfrage in unseren Kolonien* (Berlin: E. S. Mittler & Sohn, 1910), iv.

promote German immigration to Southwest Africa, envisioned a colony that would rein-vigorate *Deutschtum* (Germanness), producing a purer German space, a counterpoint to the modernizing, industrial, and politically divided metropole *Kaiserreich* in Europe. As Rohrbach envisioned that over 2 million Germans would settle in Africa in the twentieth century, both he and Brockman championed German families, while denigrating local Africans as incapable of self-rule.[15]

The "rider" celebrates this vision of the ordinary settler. He is a cavalryman dressed in *Schutztruppe* uniform and holding a rifle upright. His posture is erect and assertive, his uniform spotless. He is a proud conqueror, both looking over the country as it was his, but also prepared for war and violence, for any further trouble from the belligerent Afri-cans. While assertive, the statue nevertheless symbolized ongoing German insecurities. It marked incipient, not yet fully consolidated rule, promising security to the settlers, while serving as a warning and a threat to potential insurgents. Thus, the "rider" is both convey-ing a message of power but reflecting underlying German fears toward the natives; the notion that further uprisings may happen at any moment and that the settlers' position remains uncertain. While the plague painted the Germans as victims and stressed their sacrifice in cementing the connection to the land, the "rider's" posture projects both mas-culine strength and that the settler needs to remain vigilant and willing to fight if he is to remain in this land permanently. It is this double message, of power and frailty, that the "rider" would carry post-German colonial rule.

A typical colonial narrative has a circular form with a clear return, while a settler colo-nial narrative differs from this as it moves forward without a return.[16] The key ingredient of this kind of narrative structure is the settlers' quest to indigenize themselves. They transform space, by replacing the natives, by carrying their lifestyles with them and making the place their own, and by renewing the settler to suit the land. They make claims that the land and the sacrifice and work the settler has put into this land have made them belong. As Mahmood Mamdani suggests, both initial replacement and ongoing dominance require and rest on violence, physical and discursive. Settlers remain settlers through continuous privilege and difference between them and the natives.[17] Central here is the idea of permanence and belonging to the land. It is the settler who is at home and who makes the future. Until that is, the settler is kicked out. While settler rule remains firmly fixed in North America and Australia, for example, it has officially at least been overturned in Africa.

In settler colonies, ending, meaning decolonization, usually takes the form of settler exodus, settlers leaving the land, and the repression of the settler colonial narrative. This was the case in French Algeria, where forced settler departure after World War II created bitterness, longing, and nostalgia. But much of this took place in France, the des-tination of the settler diaspora, not in the former settler colony itself.[18] When departing

---

[15] Mark T. Kettler, "What did Paul Rohrbach Actually Learn in Africa? The Influence of Colonial Experience on a Publicist's Imperial Fantasies in Eastern Europe," *German History* 38, no. 2 (2020): 243–5; Paul Rohrbach, *Deutsche Kolonial-wirtschaft- 1 Band: Südwest Afrika* (Berlin: Buchverlag der Hilfe, 1907); Lora Wildenthal, *German Women for Empire* (Durham, NC: Duke University Press, 2001).

[16] My text here is inspired by Lorenco Veracini's thoughts. See Veracini, *Settler Colonialism: A Theoretical Overview* (London: Palgrave, 2010), especially 21–3, 96–8, 113–4.

[17] On settler colonial identity and replacement, see Mahmood Mamdani, "Settler Colonialism: Then and Now," *Critical Inquiry* 41, no. 3 (2015): 596–614; Patrick Wolfe, "Settler Colonialism and the Elimination of the Native," *Journal of Gen-ocide Research* 8, no. 4 (2006): 387–409.

French Algeria, settlers also took many of their statues with them, while others were demolished soon afterwards by the new regime. Repatriated to France, some of these monuments were re-erected in key public spaces. For instance, the statue of Marshall Thomas Robert Bugeaud, known for his merciless "razzia" tactics in colonial warfare, was originally erected in Algiers in 1852. Much like the "rider," it stood as a symbol of settler power and victory over the natives, originating from extreme violence and openly celebrating settler conquest and erasure of Africans. But as Algeria struggled for independence, Bugeaud's monument needed to go in 1962. This French settler hero was erased from the Algerian public space and he no longer belonged to the narrative the decolonizing nation wanted to elaborate as its heroes. Yet, Bugeaud found a new home in Excideuil, France, where he still stands.[19]

In German Southwest Africa, this kind of process never happened. The "rider" did not go to Germany when Germany lost Southwest Africa to the British during World War I. The area became subject to a South African "mandate" rule and many of the white settlers – some 15,000–20,000 in all, of whom approximately half were Germans, the rest British and Boers – stayed. Some Germans – officials and soldiers – the new regime deported, but new white settlers also continued to arrive, including Germans. German culture and presence remained strong, whether it was imports of goods, street names, architecture and design of public spaces, food, holidays, festivals, or language and customs.[20] So stood the "rider," becoming a focal point for the emerging identity of the German-speaking populace. Affirming the German settlers' ongoing standing, the apartheid regime even declared the "rider" a national monument in 1969.

Conquest of Fear

Okahandja, German Southwest Africa, 12 January 1904. News of fighting in the streets and Herero siege of the German fort alerted the settlers, quickly spreading panic among them. After the initial chaos, German Governor Theodor Leutwein still saw it as a local trouble. He was sure that if he would personally meet the Herero leader Samuel Maharero, things would calm down quickly and cooler heads prevail. But they never did. Leutwein never got his chance for developing a diplomatic compromise, as Berlin hurried reinforcements to Southwest Africa so that soldiers soon outnumbered settlers. Pointing out that this "genocide arose from failures in planning and became the tragic climax in a campaign of disappointments," historian Matthias Häussler has recently emphasized racism and emotionality in explaining the conflict. Failure and frustration, shame and fear fuelled the violence.[21] Violence stemmed from and brought to the fore the tensions between fear and belonging; the gaps between settler aspirations for land and often disappointing realities. German doubts and weaknesses on the ground clashed with their claims for superiority over supposedly savage foes. The Germans saw the natives as expendable,

[18] Amy L. Hubbard, *Remembering French Algeria: Pieds-Noir, Identity, and Exile* (Lincoln: University of Nebraska Press, 2015); Fiona Barclay, "Remembering Algeria: Melancholy, Depression and the Colonising of the Pieds-Noirs," *Settler Colonial Studies* 8, no. 2 (2018): 244–61.

[19] Zeynep Celik, "Colonial Statues and their Afterlives," *Journal of North African Studies* 25, no. 5 (2020): 716–7.

[20] On the identity-building of the German settler community, see Walther, *Creating Germans Abroad*, especially 112–9 on the post-World War I situation.

[21] Häussler, *Herero Genocide*, 3–18 (quote 3). See also Jeremy Sarkin, *Germany's Genocide of the Herero: Kaiser Wilhelm II, His General, His Settlers, His Soldiers* (New York: Boydell & Brewer, 2011), especially 8.

inferior obstacles to be ridden over when fulfilling the goals of a higher European settler civilization looking for land and prosperous futures. What was at stake was much more than German pride among empires. German settler futures in Africa stood on the line.

To understand this vortex of fear, one can start with how many in Germany worried over mass flight to the Americas, fearing it would sap the young nation of its energy and talent, necessary for industrial growth and world-power status. Seeking to divert these emigrant flows to German colonies, Southwest Africa became the only even remotely suitable option for large numbers of Germans to live in. But it proved a disappointing failure. Acquired as a protectorate in 1884, the German sphere of influence in Southwest Africa rested on a series of protection treaties with local communities, and only gradually advanced inland from the coastal area. Flanked by the Namib and Kalahari deserts in the west and east, the central highland plateau held the potential for low-density cattle ranching and possibly even some farming with irrigation.[22] It provided just enough water for imagining settler futures there. But the plateau was a highly contested ground and German presence was weak. There were few traders, some missionaries, and limited government presence in the form of an imperial commissioner (governor after 1898) and a handful of soldiers. Crucially, very few Germans actually wanted to start a new life there, and by 1902 only 2,500 had done so. This was a pitiful figure compared to the hundreds of thousands of Germans who relocated to the Americas.[23]

As settler colonization teetered on the brink of failure, the official rhetoric promoted German mastery over the country. This had been the case since the German Chancellor Leo von Caprivi declared to the *Reichstag* in March 1893: "We possess South-West Africa once and for all; it is German territory and must be preserved as such."[24] Although its value as a settler destination remained questionable, Southwest Africa had already aroused feelings of national pride and stirred imaginations of German destiny. In order to attract white settlers to realize an agrarian settler society, which many Germans advocated as ideal, vast tracts of cheap land needed to be available. Yet, in the eyes of settlers and German officials, strong native tribes stood in the way, forming a major obstacle for German settler futures.

The Herero and Nama were cattle-raisers, traders, and raiders. They were also expansionists and rivals for grazing lands and trade control, and as such active participants in the contested and dynamic borderlands exchanges and networks that linked Portuguese Angola and the Cape Frontier through modern Namibia. The Herero occupied the northern ends of the central highlands, but slowly migrated to the south, while the Nama were part of the northward expanding peoples from the Cape. In the mix were also the missions of the Rhenish Mission Society, highly influential in the economic and political issues in times of periodic drought and ongoing intertribal wars.[25] When the Germans arrived to

---

[22] With their irrigation projects in Southwest Africa, the Germans sought practical advice from the United States and its conquest of the arid deserts and plains in the trans-Mississippi West. See Jeannette Eileen Jones, "How the Südwest Was Won: Transnational Currents of American Agriculture and Land Colonization in German Southwest Africa," in *German and United States Colonialism in a Connected World: Entangled Empires*, ed. Janne Lahti (London: Palgrave, 2021), 153–76.

[23] Stefan Manz, *Constructing a German Diaspora: The "Greater German Empire", 1871–1914* (London: Routledge, 2014); Dirk Hoerder and Jörg Nagel, eds., *People in Transit: German Migrations in Comparative Perspective, 1820–1930* (Cambridge: Cambridge University Press, 1995).

[24] Von Caprivi quoted in Helmut Bley, *South-West Africa under German Rule, 1894–1914* (London: Heinemann, 1971), 3.

[25] For a more detailed analysis of the Herero-Nama relations, see Jan-Bart Gewald, *Herero Heroes: A Socio-Political History of the Herero of Namibia, 1890–1923* (Athens: Ohio University Press 1999), 10–28; Bley, *South-West Africa*, xxi–xxvi;

this already contested borderland, they were a new player hardly worth Herero and Nama attention. Soon the Germans also realized how the locals refused to accept German authority. This, as historian Adam Blackler notes, "shattered the illusion of German cultural superiority."[26]

Emphasizing an increasingly militant approach, the Germans tried to advance their power by sending in the colonial army, the *Schutztruppe* and Captain Curt von Francois to subdue competition. Von Francois openly advocated violence against the Africans as a way to establish German rule. He fought against and established treaties with the Herero, set up a base at Windhoek, and campaigned against Nama sovereignty in the early 1890s.[27] In the late 1890s further interpersonal violence, of beatings, rapes, and murders by settlers against black Africans, coexisted with the Rinderpest (cattle plague) epidemic that killed most of the Herero stock.[28]

Still, the native respect for the Germany military remained, in Leutwein's words, "zero."[29] Germans became increasingly marred by self-doubts and frustrated by their inability to dictate their will on the natives. This feeling of insecurity fuelled self-doubts and racial animosities. Since the beginning of German presence, there had existed a matrix of concerns over what Africa and Africans would do to the settlers psyche. One strand of these narratives focused on the apparent futility of civilizing and ruling over Africans. These notions claimed that black Africans, inherently ignorant and child-like, lacked the mental capacities to work as Germans expected, to understand Christianity, or to follow European social mores and use of domestic goods. Teaching them amounted to a loss of time.[30] Furthermore, there existed concerns that colonial terrain and the environment corrupted and decivilized the white settler, altered and spoiled the German character. This happened as the settler succumbs to savage violence that was purportedly needed to control the unruly natives and resorts to sexual predation when lured by hypersexual and seductive Indigenous women. The real fear was that the settler imports these traits to his home, to Germany proper and to the domestic sphere.[31]

From the instant violence erupted in January 1904, various types of fears guided German military actions; fears over what the natives would do to the settlers and fears that the Germans would not effectively manage to prove their superiority in the field and crush the enemy. At the first moments in Okahandja, Germans clustered to the fort, overcome with fear. One settler caught in the turmoil painted the Herero as wicked murderers who had planned the attack weeks ahead. He noted how "farms were attacked everywhere in the country and the owners murdered," while the settlement at Okahandja, he continued, "looked devastated, all the private houses looted

---

Gesine Krüger, "The Golden Age of the Pastoralists," in *Genocide in German South-West Africa: The Colonial War (1904–1908) in Namibia and Its Aftermath*, eds. Jürgen Zimmerer and Joachim Zeller (Monmouth: Merlin Press, 2008), 8–14.

[26] Adam Blackler, "From Boondoggle to Settlement Colony: Hendrik Witbooi and the Evolution of Germany's Imperial Project in Southwest Africa, 1884–1894," *Central European History* 50, no. 4 (2017): 454. On German weakness in relation to Herero and Nama, see Häussler, *Herero Genocide*; David Olusoga and Casper W. Erichsen, *The Kaiser's Holocaust: Germany's Forgotten Genocide* (London: Faber & Faber, 2010), esp. 50–5.

[27] Olusoga and Erichsen, *Kaiser's Holocaust*, 56–69, 76–8; Gewald, *Herero Heroes*.

[28] On the Rinderpest, see Bley, *South-West Africa*, 124–9.

[29] Theodore Leutwein, *Elf Jahre Gouverneur in Deutsch-Südwestafrika* (Berlin: Mittler und Son, 1908), 19.

[30] Paul J. Edwards, "'Bury the Gold Again Before the Europeans Bring Us Their Culture': Witzblätter and the Paradox of German Anticolonialism," *German Studies Review* 44, no. 1 (2021): 5–7.

[31] Suggesting that something had gone awry in German Southwest Africa, commentaries were made in popular German satirical magazines such as *Simplicissimus*. See Edwards, "Bury the Gold Again," 12–13.

and badly burned."[32] As the Herero raided German settlements, German reports and newspapers feasted on alleged reports of Herero raping and killing German settler women and children. In reality, this was not the case. Yet stories did not die down, and the official General Staff account repeated these rumours of Herero savagery.[33] Interestingly, the "rider" does not advance this colonial myth. While promoting German blood sacrifice, the plague lists only four German women and one child killed.

As German reinforcements poured into Southwest Africa, fear metamorphosed into revenge. Fear grew into a doctrine that first mixed exemplary violence with the search for a standing battle, and as the latter proved humiliating for the Germans at Waterberg in August 1904, evolved into a dictum of punishment and annihilation. Punishment was what even the more moderate Germans on the ground called for. They saw that the natives needed to be taught a lesson, punished for their transgressions so that they would learn never again to rise against the settlers. This, in turn, would guarantee peace and Herero submission to German rule.[34]

Yet, what constituted punishment in the field was usually the death sentence. It had few or no alternatives at first. Writing in May 1904, Leutwein made it known to his superiors that in the field "nonwounded Herero have not been taken at all" and only few wounded had been captured before court-martialed to death.[35] Killing had become the norm, an everyday occurrence as a settler diary remark from 3 February seems to attest: "On the way to Waldau we caught two Hereros with rifles, whom we simply hung on to the next tree."[36] Local units and junior officers had great latitude to punish any Herero without authorization from their superiors. Thus, the German military campaign took the appearance of summary proceedings followed by summary executions in the bush. Some patrols made of deputized settlers shot at any Africans they viewed as the enemy, or suspected as thieves.[37]

Fear of the colonized Africans and a sense of privilege resulted in the pedagogy of punishment, to a situation where executions formed the standard conduct of war expected and even demanded of the German troops. This method was carried over to Summer and Fall of 1904. Replacing the more diplomatic Leutwein, General Lothar von Trotha advocated a race war, envisioning a showdown at Waterberg against the Herero in August. As that failed to produce a triumphant victory, he issued a proclamation to the Herero on 2 October 1904, with a core message that "every Herero, whether found armed or unarmed ... will be shot." Concerned over German performance, Trotha explained his de facto extermination order to his superiors by arguing that the African "negroes will yield only to brute force, whereas negotiations are quite pointless" and that there could be "no question of negotiations" unless the Germans wanted to "betray our impotence and confusion."[38] For Trotha, violence

---

[32] Eugen Mansfeld, *The Autobiography of Eugen Mansfeld: A Settler's Life in Colonial Namibia*, trans. Will Sellick (London: Jeppestown Press, 2017), 45, see also 46–51.

[33] General Staff, *Die Kämpfe der Deutschen Truppen in Sudwestafrika* (Berlin: Mittler und Son, 1907), 24–6.

[34] Isabel V. Hull, *Absolute Destruction: Military Culture and the Practices of War in Imperial Germany* (London: Cornell University Press, 2006), 18–19.

[35] Leutwein to Colonial Department, Nr. 395, Windhuk, 17 May 1904, Bundesarchiv-Berlin, R 1001M Nr. 2115, 68.

[36] Mansfeld, *Autobiography*, 53.

[37] Hull, *Absolute Destruction*, 18–20; Viktor Franke Diary, Bundesarchiv-Koblenz, N1 Franke.

[38] Von Trotha quoted in Horst Drechsler, *"Let Us Die Fighting": The Struggle of the Herero and Nama Against German Imperialism* (London: Zed Press, 1980), 156–7, 160–1.

was about hiding the doubts of German weakness and assuring German futures in Africa, a means for ensuring German settler rule over the land.

At the time Trotha delivered his proclamation the conflict spread to include Hendrik Witbooi's Nama, horrified of what the Germans were doing. The *Kaiser* in turn apparently did not know of Trotha's proclamation beforehand, but delayed rescinding the order and ultimately sanctioned its methods. Driven to the deserts, chased and annihilated when met, the Herero and Nama faced a disaster, although some managed to escape the German reach into neighbouring British territories. Soon the Germans cleared space by gathering the survivors into camps where the death toll rose to staggering figures. In 1908, the final days of the genocidal violence bled into the early days of the diamond boom around Lüderitz, contributing to mass death of African workers in the diamond fields. The doctrine of punishment was again prevalent as former military men supervised the African labour that was treated "as all-but-formal slaves."[39]

While we will never know exactly how many died, even the general estimates reveal the shocking human cost. There were only an estimated 15,000 Herero and 11,000 Nama left by "rider's" inauguration, compared to the 70,000–90,000 Herero and 20,000 Nama before the violence.[40] Today, a majority of scholars treat the conflict as the first genocide of the twentieth century. Many argue that it was a significant precedent for the Nazis and the Holocaust, in championing mentalities, honing techniques, and nurturing personal connections that culminated in the mass killings of European Jews.[41] In the present, Germany and Namibia also engage in tardy negotiations over official recognition of the genocide as well as possible monetary compensation and the return of looted colonial artefacts.

But in the early twentieth century, violence had "opened" the land for the settlers. As Matthias Leanza recently pointed out it was not truly until after the genocidal violence that German settler colonization gained momentum.[42] Germans had taken Herero and Nama lands, subjected the survivors to servile labour and to reservations where they were forbidden to practice their own religion and culture. Native lives were controlled by three ordinances set in 1907: among other things these established a native register, mandatory pass-badge and travel permits. They also denied native ownership of livestock without white permission. Germans had also issued legislation banning interracial marriages (effective retrospectively) and instigated biological racial designations. In 1912, settler futures looked brighter than they ever had before. Yet, they continued to rest on multiple doubts and fears, even after being cemented by an impressive new monument at the heart of the capitol.

---

[39] Steven Press, *Blood and Diamonds: Germany's Imperial Ambitions in Africa* (Cambridge, MA: Harvard University Press, 2021), 124–5. On the camps, see Jonas Kreienbaum, *A Sad Fiasco: Colonial Concentration Camps in Southern Africa, 1900–1908* (New York: Berghahn Books, 2019).

[40] For population estimates, see Drechsler, *Let Us Die Fighting*, 214, 229; Olusoga and Erichsen, *Kaiser's Holocaust*, 229–30; Leutwein, *Elf Jahre*, 11.

[41] See, for example, Jürgen Zimmerer, *Von Windhuk nach Auschwitz?: Beiträge zum Verhältnis von Kolonialismus und Holocaust* (Münster: Lit Verlag, 2011); Jürgen Zimmerer, "Colonialism and the Holocaust: Towards an Archeology of Genocide," in *Genocide and Settler Society: Frontier Violence and Stolen Indigenous Children in Australian History*, ed. Dirk A. Moses (New York: Berghahn Books, 2004); Matthew P. Fitzpatrick, "The Pre-History of the Holocaust? The Sonderweg and Historikerstreit Debates and the Abject Colonial Past," *Central European History* 41, no. 3 (2008): 477–503; Benjamin Madley, "From Africa to Auschwitz: How German South West Africa Incubated Ideas and Methods Adopted and Developed by the Nazis in Eastern Europe," *European History Quarterly* 35, no. 3 (2005): 429–64.

[42] Matthias Leanza, "Colonial Trajectories: On the Evolution of the German Protectorate of Southwest Africa," *Comparativ* 30, no. 3–4 (2020): 376.

From Settler Innocence to Settler Replacement

Windhoek, Namibia, 27 January 2012. An anxious crowd had gathered for the centenary celebration of the "rider." Representing the German-speaking community was Harald Koch, from a German heritage organization. He spoke that the "rider" symbolized the memory of "all the soldiers and civilians of German descent who died 100 years ago." He added that this centenary commemoration was also about remembering "all the other people who lost their lives in that war. This monument should remind us of what happened and it should ensure that something like that does not happen again." Koch's words echoed universal remembrance and atonement, and he assigned meaning to the "rider" as a warning against extremism. His choice of words were still heavily criticized in the Namibian government for skirting the issue of Germans committing genocide. Minister Joël Kaapanda noted that "Koch's 'other people' were not caught in a cross-fire … they [Herero and Nama] were systematically and mercilessly exterminated."[43]

At the same time, the Namibian President Hifikepunye Pohamba proposed that the "rider" should even return to Germany, as its presence remained too divisive and disruptive in Namibia.[44] Pohamba saw that the monument symbolizes German victory over black Africans and therefore "it must be removed." Representatives of the National Heritage Council of Namibia concurred, stating that the "rider" "celebrated the victory of the Germans and it has lost its significance." It has "divided people" and that "it should no longer divide people" as an obstacle to the healing of the nation from past colonial oppression. The government also directed a message to people in the white settler community, saying that those who sympathize with what the "rider" stands for "should be happy it was not taken to the dumpsite, because it should be disposed of."[45] Asserting that time was up for the "rider," the National Heritage Council also stripped the statue of its status as a national monument, the official document giving as reason that the "rider" "does not have any significance in a liberated Namibia."[46]

Seen as a relic of the colonial past and a symbol of oppression, the "rider" was thus pushed out of sight and to the margins of the national story in 2013. Many in the white community felt outraged and upset. Some commented that the government had committed an illegal act and that the removal was simply "barbaric and short-sighted," stripping those of German descent their place in the country's heritage.[47] Yet the descendants of the settlers are still in Namibia, and their privilege at least in terms of land ownership and standard of living is still very real. In fact, the disparities of wealth in Namibia

[43] Tanja Bause, "Monument's Centenary Remembered," The Namibian, 30 January 2012; Magreth Nunuhe, "Kaapanda Lashes Out at Centenary Speech," New Era, 3 February 2012, both reprinted in The Equestrian Monument, 115–6.

[44] Ellanie Smit, "Reiterdenkmal to be Hidden Away," Namibian Sun, 22 October 2013, reprinted in The Equestrian Monument, 127.

[45] Quotes from "Reiterdenkmal Gallops Again on Christmas," The Namibian, 26 December 2013 and " … as Reiterdenkmal Disappears Overnight," Namibian Sun, 27 December 2013. See also Elvis Muraranganda, "Government Presses on with Reiterdenkmal Removal," Namibian Sun, 24 December 2013, reprinted in The Equestrian Monument, 130; Helvi Inotila Elago, "Colonial Monuments in a Post-Colonial Era: A Case Study of the Equestrian Monument," in Re-Viewing Resistance in Namibian History, ed. Jeremy Silvester (Windhoek: University of Namibia Press, 2015), 289–91.

[46] National Heritage Council of Namibia, https://www.nhc-nam.org/content/deproclamation-equestrian-statue-and-declaration-new-sites (accessed 4 January 2022). The Public Notice issued by the National Heritage Council declared that the "rider" had lost its significance already in 1915, with the end of German colonial rule, and for the second time in 1990, with Namibian independence. Republikein, 20 December 2013, reprinted in The Equestrian Monument, 129.

[47] Theresia Tjihenuna, "Anger over the Reiterdenkmal Removal," The Namibian, 7 January 2014.

are some of the steepest in the world, still echoing the racial lines set during colonial times.

Erected to push forward the German settler colonial fantasy of mastery over the land coupled with attempts to affirm German settler belonging on that land, the "rider" was meant to strengthen the sense of unity and shared destiny among the German-speaking populace. And it served that function ever since 1912. It has occupied a key place in what can be dubbed as construction of identity via nostalgic objects, physical remnants of (imagined) past glories. In this reading, it, as Joachim Zeller notes, commemorates German heroes, whose deeds "affirm 'Deutschtum' (Germanness)" in Africa, who faithfully served the German nation.[48]

What was left out of the monument also reveals the settler mentality. There were no notions of sorrow over the dead Africans or feeling of German guilt or remorse. Neither did the "rider" as such show any visible sign of German vulnerability. Even suggestions of including a fallen German soldier in the monument were refuted by the settler community. Including such a figure would have indicated a triumph for the black Africans and of German weakness. There existed a controversial precedent, the German Marine Monument raised in the coastal town of Swakopmund in 1908. It did contain both a fallen German fighter and an active combatant standing above his perished comrade, and the settlers heavily criticized it at the time for ostensibly showing the wrong message to the black population.[49]

Settlers continued to celebrate the "rider" during the apartheid era. In fact, it remained the most important memorial for the German-speaking populace. It was there and the German military cemetery at Waterberg where settlers gathered annually for commemorations and remembrance. At the 25th anniversary of the violence, all the guilt still rested on the Herero while the settlers swore to defend Germany ethnicity and futures on African soil. A settler speech given near the "rider" on the occasion declared: "This land cannot be taken from us" as the blood sacrifice of those Germans who died is a "holy seed which may not be suppressed by force and therefore German culture, the German way of life and the German language shall justly continue to flourish here for all time."[50]

Settler belonging was "for all time" and it relied on colonial violence and blood sacrifice as manifested on the "rider." During the Cold War era, the German-speakers continued to gather by the "rider" regularly to convey this message to their own community and to black Africans. As long as the "rider" stood, the German-speakers would be ok, no matter their numbers. Whites were always the minority in Southwest Africa, and the Germans were the minority among whites as more Boers moved in during the apartheid era. In 1915, the population of German Southwest Africa stood between 50,000–100,000 Africans and 14,000–20,000 Europeans.[51] So the whites formed a sizable minority. Today the demographics have shifted considerably, and among a populace of more than 2.5

---

[48] Joachim Zeller, "Symbolic Politics: Notes on the Colonial German Culture of Remembrance," in *Genocide in German South-West Africa*, 235. See also Klaus R. Rüdiger, *Die Namibia-Deutschen. Geschichte einer Nationalität im Werden* (Stuttgart: Franz Steiner Verlag, 1993).

[49] Zeller, "Symbolic Politics," 234. For more recent calls for removal and protests against the Marine Monument, see Norimitsu Onishi, "A Colonial-Era Wound Opens in Namibia," *New York Times*, 21 January 2017; "Coastal activists call for removal of Marine Denkmal," *New Era*, 17 July 2015.

[50] Excerpts from the speech by farmer Gustav Voigt from Zeller, "Symbolic Politics," 235–7, see also 243.

[51] Press, *Blood and Diamonds*, 106, 113.

million there are an estimated 100,000 whites, of whom some 30,000 claim German descent.

Besides affirming German settler belonging by repackaging the genocidal violence, the "rider" has also been a rather flexible tool of political contestation and identity politics. During the apartheid regime, the "rider" was made a national monument, but it was also used as site of protest against white minority rule. After the Old Location Uprising in 1959 – a violent clash where police shot activists protesting the apartheid regime in a racially segregated non-white district of the capitol – activists placed a sack over the "rider's" head and decorated the rest with flowers.[52] Later protests in the early 2000s saw a field of red crosses placed on the grass around the monument, and a Namibian flag pushed down the barrel of the "rider's" rifle.

Its presence increasingly questioned, the "rider" nevertheless outlasted Namibian independence in 1990, continuing to tell the story of settler presence. By then it had also became part of popular culture and tourist industry. There exists "rider" postage stamps, stickers, books, and other tourist memorabilia such as miniatures and coffee mugs. You can find the "rider" also in the logo of a local brewer, as well as in other company logos.[53]

In 2001, the Namibian Cabinet declared the intention to move the "rider" and to make room for a new museum centring on Namibia's independence struggle. This created heated opposition and growing fears over belonging, mainly from the German-speaking populace. Some, such as the Namibian German-speaking historian and activist Andreas Vogt, proclaimed that the erection of the "rider" in 1912 had been an apolitical act. He asserted that the statue formed part of a shared German and African history and heritage. He acknowledged that this included histories of violence, but that among these the German colonial war against the Herero and Nama had been just one conflict among many. Vogt argued that all Namibians ought to accept the "rider" as part of their shared heritage that included violence and they should conserve and preserve the statue. He also pointed out that the "rider" is a memorial to war heroes, thus curiously recycling the initial message of the "rider" as celebrating Germans fighting a savage threat. As such, Vogt sees the "rider" as part of a broader repertoire of similar monuments across Namibia, some of them local, others national, such as the Heroes' Acre. He argues that the heated conversation surrounding the "rider" only further attests to its importance, constantly reinterpreted over time as a living monument.[54]

Set up outside of Windhoek in 2002 as a national memorial, the Heroes' Acre forms an interesting counter-narrative to the "rider" in public space. It mythicizes the Namibian battle for freedom and independence through a teleological nation-state lens. It honours past black heroes such as Samuel Maharero and the Nama leader Hendrik Witbooi, killed by the Germans in 1905. In other words, it traces Namibian resistance and national heroism to the struggle against German colonialism. At Heroes' Acre, the Herero and Nama fighters are made part of the national story, while the Germans are

---

[52] On "Old Location" and racial divisions of Windhoek during the apartheid, see Henning Melber, "Revisiting the Wind-hoek Old Location," *Basler Afrika Bibliographien Working Paper* 3 (2016): 1–23.

[53] See *The Equestrian Monument*, 48–55.

[54] Andreas Vogt, "To Move or Not to Move," *The Namibian*, 18 July 2008. For the disputes surrounding the removal proposition, see Kuvee Kangueehi, "Reiterdenkmal Debate Divides the House," *New Era*, 23 June 2008; "Keep the Reiter-denkmal," *The Namibian*, 11 October 2013; Bob Kandetu, "Statues are Artifacts of History," *Informante*, 24 October 2013, all reprinted in *The Equestrian Statue*, 69, 142, 128–9.

Figure 4. The Heroes' Acre, a massive outdoor monument celebrating anticolonial struggles. Photo by Henrik Laaksonen. Used with permission.

aggressors, not commemorated. There is no Leutwein or von Trotha at Heroes' Acre. They – and by association all German settlers – are outsiders, not belonging to the national story. Heroes' Acre replaces settlers with black heroes (Figure 4).

A proposal in the early 2000s called for the recontextualizing of the "rider," from the one-sided commemoration of German victims to more inclusive narration that would give voice to the previously silenced Herero and Nama side of the story. This recontextualization could link the "rider" to the prisoner camp that stood nearby the *Alte Feste* during the genocide. In this way, the "rider" could be reinterpreted for the future, the proposal put.[55] There was also an earlier initiative in the 1990s for adding a complementary memorial tablet to the "rider" to acknowledge all victims of colonial violence, but neither came to no avail.[56]

Importantly, while the Namibian government removed the "rider" it also replaced it with new monuments in the key public spaces of the capitol. Where the rider used to be there now stands a gigantic statue commemorating the revolutionary and independence activist Sam Nujoma. Next to it stands the new shiny Independence Memorial Museum as well as the Genocide Memorial portraying the black victims of German aggression. These new monuments tell different stories, elaborate different heroes and narratives of belonging. They underline victory over colonization. The Genocide Memorial in particular exhibits a complete reversal of the original message of the "rider," being a monument to the victims of German colonial violence and linking the Herero and Nama sacrifice to current Namibian freedom. Thus, the "rider" is literally and symbolically substituted and because of that it is the settler and the settler colonial narratives that now face marginalization and replacement (Figure 5).

If the descendants of settlers now fear erasure, the fate of the "rider" may just mark the beginning of a new era. For example, the statue of Windhoek's German "founder" Curt von Francois is the target of an ongoing civic campaign "A Curt Farewell." Seeing the monument as a celebration of colonial rule, Namibian activists call for the removal of von Francois'

---

[55] Goodman Gwasira, Bennet Kangumu, and Gilbert Likando, "The Rider Monument: Contested Space," *The African*, October/November 2004, reprinted in *The Equestrian Monument*, 62–3.
[56] Kössler, *Namibia and Germany*, 154.

Figure 5. Substituting the "rider" and capturing its space. The Genocide Memorial, with the Independence Memorial Museum in the background, Windhoek, Namibia. Photo by Henrik Laaksonen. Used with permission.

statue from a central location on Independence Avenue.[57] Based on these recent developments it would be a logical conclusion to state that settler history and prominence perpetuates values and narratives with which Namibia no longer wishes to be associated.

Conclusion: Reinterpreting the Past in the Present

Swakomund, Namibia, 16 February 2019. "Reiterdenkmal pops at Swakomund!" Thus declares the day's issue of the newspaper *The Namibian*. A local restaurant owner in

---

[57] "Curt von Francois – Time to Go," https://ippr.org.na/blog/curt-von-francois-time-to-fall/ (accessed 28 April 2021); "A 'Curt' Farewell," https://www.change.org/p/mayor-of-the-city-of-windhoek-fransina-kahungu-a-curt-farewell?use_react=false (accessed 4 June 2021).

Swakopmund had placed a "rider" replica about the half of the original on the roof of his establishment. The move immediately drew controversy and demands for its removal. The white restaurant owner explained in the newspapers that he wanted to give a museum-type atmosphere to his place and that he erected the replica with the aim of showing visitors to his restaurant the journey that Namibia had took to attain freedom.[58] Placing a copy of a monument celebrating settler rule over black Africans and settler belonging on African soil on his roof, the restaurant owner nevertheless ended up making a provocative statement.

Looking at the experiences and narrations from the nineteenth century to the present-day, the story of the "rider" reveals the two sides of the settler identity, power and fragility: the sense of entitlement, mastery, and self-assuredness, but also continued doubt and suspicions over belonging and fears toward black Africans. For decades, the "rider" proved an adamant yet controversial survivor, occupying a key public space, editing history in ways that served the interests of the settler community that had become a small yet influential minority in the former settler colony. While substituted and out of sight today, the 2019 episode in Swakopmund shows that the "rider's" legacy remains disputed and continues to epitomize the contestations over the meanings and interpretations of the past within Namibia. While many in Namibia saw the "rider" as a festering wound at the heart of the capitol, others viewed it as a symbol of their belonging and status. For many in the black majority, the "rider" stood as a painful reminder of colonial oppression, destruction, and white supremacy. For the small white minority of German background, it was a symbol of their community and identity, indicating they had a legitimate connection to the land, that they belonged here. The "rider" has become to symbolize an ongoing battle over the country's past and identity, not only between white and black, but also involving power relations between the majority Ovambo and the minority Herero and Nama. In many ways, the "rider" signifies Namibia's failed internal reckoning with colonialism. It manifests still visible scars.

Disclosure Statement

No potential conflict of interest was reported by the author(s).

Funding

This research was supported by the funding from Academy of Finland.

ORCID

Janne Lahti ⓘ http://orcid.org/0000-0003-3475-1542

---

[58] Adam Hartman, "Reiterdenkmal Pops Up at Swakopmund," *The Namibian*, 16 February 2019; Eveline de Klerk, "Swakopmund Restaurateur Stirs Up Emotions with Reiterdenkmal Replica," *New Era*, 8 April 2019; Gina Paula Figueira, "That Horse Will Never Rise Again': An Exploration of Narratives Around the Iterations of the Reiterdenkmal Statue in Namibia," *International Journal of Heritage Studies* 27, no. 9 (2021): 10–12.

South Africa's Voortrekker Monument and 1820 Settlers National Monument: Monuments to Cultural Violence

Rebecca Weaver-Hightower and Marcus B. Weaver-Hightower

ABSTRACT

This article compares two South African monument spaces, the well-known Voortrekker Monument in Pretoria and the lesser-known 1820 Settlers National Monument in Makandha (formerly Grahamstown). While ultimately both monuments enact cultural violence through the veneration of European settler groups, they do so in contrasting ways, which may make a difference in ultimately mitigating their cultural violence. While the Voortrekker Monument presents an explicit narrative of Afrikaner supremacy literally carved in marble, the 1820 Settlers National Monument features more abstract symbolism and its leaders have long shown willingness to alter and use the monument in ways that interrupt (at least somewhat) the adulation of settler culture. Comparison of the sites, though, show that the ambivalence of the 1820 Settlers Monument may not be enough to remove the cultural violence done by such monuments.

High on Gunfire Hill above the town of Makandha (formerly Grahamstown) in South Africa's Eastern Cape, looms the 1820 Settlers National Monument. With what look to be two masts affixed to its roof, sails lowered to indicate the completion of the voyage, the monument resembles the British ships it commemorates, which in 1820 brought about 5000 settlers from Britain to – they hoped – pacify the indigenous peoples.[1] This ship-like building (see Figure 1) dominates the visual horizon for Makhandans looking toward the sea, a reminder of settlement and white settler claim on that part of Africa.[2]

---

[1] The 1820 Settlers have been widely researched. One can find an account of their arrival in South African histories Noel Mostert's *Frontiers: The Epic of South Africa's Creation and the Tragedy of the Xhosa People* (New York: Alfred A. Knopf, 1992) and in the Grahamstown Diaries series of 1820 settler autobiographies published by Rhodes University's Cory Library.

[2] Our claim of the building's resemblance to a ship is not based in any architectural intent we have found, though the flag poles that, to our eyes, resemble "masts" are "nautical flag poles" with a "yardarm," a "mast" and other elements of the pole named after similar elements on a ship's rigging. As noted by the Flag and Etiquette Committee of the US Power Squadrons boating education site, "Onshore, the 'yacht club style flagpole' with a gaff represents the mast of a ship" ("Flag FAQ," https://www.usps.org/national/fecom/faq/flag/gaffpole.html, accessed 10 May 2022). Another researcher of the Settler Monument also remarked upon the building's nautical resemblance. Thelma Neville in *More Lasting than Bronze*, her history of the Settler Monument, when once looking at the building at night, says: "the mists crept in to spread their grey curtain over the Monument so that, from below, it looked like a ship rising

Figure 1. The 1820 Settlers National Monument, exterior. Photo by Marcus Weaver-Hightower.

Inside, however, the building holds a gallery and performance spaces that host much of the annual South African National Arts Festival, an event known for its politically progressive and multicultural offerings. In its celebration of white settlement on its exterior and encouragement of multicultural gathering on its interior, the building's exterior and interior reflect an ambivalence towards a settler past that divides the region's inhabitants.

Also evidence of an ambivalence towards a settler past, the town the monument overlooks has recently been renamed. It now commemorates Makhanda ka Nxele, the warrior and prophet who in 1819 led an attack against the forces of Colonel John Graham, the brutal Scot who forcibly removed indigenous groups in the Eastern Cape and for whom the town was previously named. Though its name has now changed from reflecting the victor of the 1819 Battle of Grahamstown to the defeated but unifying Makhanda, the town remains known as "The Settler City" in tourist materials, and much of the central business district has the façade of nineteenth century European buildings.[3] Discussion has begun about also changing the name of the 1820 Settlers National Monument, though no one, to our knowledge, has suggested changing its nautical exterior, meaning that it, like the town, might have a name that would belie its historic look.[4] These internal

---

and falling with tranquil breaths" (68). In other places she refers to the Monument as a ship in describing the project, as in "keeping the Monument ship on course" (Pietermaritzburg: Natal Witness Printing and Publishing Company, 1992), 101. Similarly, Moses Lamani, tour guide at the Grahamstown camera obscura and one of the indigenous subjects of Mikhael Subotzky's 2012 film installation *Moses and Griffiths* (exhibited in among other places the Museum of Modern Art in New York), says

> The reason I dislike this building [the 1820 Settlers National Monument] is that it's just so ugly to me. And it's like a ship. Because those days actually even now – there is no sea around Grahamstown. This was supposed to be built in Port Elizabeth. Now they built it here in Grahamstown (Mikhael Subotzky, "Moses and Griffiths Composite," https://vimeo.com/406169508).

[3] Makhanda (variant spellings Makandha and Makana) was a powerful Xhosa leader in the Battle of Grahamstown, a decisive battle in the Xhosa wars, and he was incarcerated on Robben Island. He drowned on his third escape attempt but has become legendary in South Africa, with some noting parallels between Makhanda and Nelson Mandela. See Camissa People "The Other Nelson Mandela of 200 Years Ago," Camissa People Cape Slavery & Indigene Heritage, https://camissapeople.wordpress.com/2017/07/21/the-other-nelson-mandela-of-200-years-ago-makana/. See also Julie Wells, *The Return of Makhanda: Exploring the Legend* (Pietermaritzburg: University of KwaZulu-Natal Press, 2012) and Mostert, *Frontiers.*

[4] As announced on the Monument's website (https://www.foundation.org.za). Personal correspondence with a museum curator explained that the name change debate was interrupted by the Coronavirus pandemic of 2020 and a lack of funding to complete the consultation process (Nicci Spalding, email message to the author, 15 March 2021).

contradictions in these sites aimed at marking past and continued white settlement, which meant and continues to mean the displacement and oppression of indigenous peoples, capture the larger dissonance and ambivalence of the 1820 Settlers National Monument and of South African historical memory more generally.

Roughly one thousand kilometres due north, atop a hillock named "Monumentkoppie" overlooking Pretoria – one of South Africa's three capitals as the seat of executive branch – sits another monument to white settlers, the Voortrekker Monument. This complex evinces far less ambivalence about its mission than the 1820 Settlers National Monument. The Voortrekker Monument resembles a vintage "tombstone" radio of the 1930s, with its giant lunette windows and square shape. Critics have debated that the Monument represents a mélange of architectural styles, including art deco, ancient Egyptian, masonic iconography, and an homage to the Völkerschlachtdenkmal in Leipzig, Germany.[5] The monument was built in the 1940s to the Boer Voortrekkers (Afrikaans for "pioneers") from the Cape Colony in the 1830s and 1840s. Like the 1820 Setters National Monument does for British settlers, the Voortrekker Monument declares the permanence of the Afrikaner settlers it commemorates – a reminder to both Anglophone and indigenous Africans of the settlement of these Dutch-descended settlers. There has been little public discussion of changing the name or purpose of the Voortrekker monument, though there has been much analysis of the monument itself.[6]

This essay uses this much-discussed Voortrekker Monument to better understand through comparison the ambivalences of the 1820 Settlers National Monument, which has been largely overlooked by scholarship. Both the 1820 Settlers National Monument and the Voortrekker Monument continue to be in daily use; they draw tourist crowds, and their meanings are discussed regarding the "new," post-apartheid South Africa. This essay explores how both monuments, whether aligned with or despite the intentions of past builders and current managers, exist and participate in the debates and contestations of cultural violence related to colonial pasts and (post)colonial presents.

This essay builds on prior work of postcolonial and cultural studies scholars who have examined how art, artifacts, and other cultural products can be agents of cultural violence. In his foundational essay, Johan Galtung defines *cultural violence* as "those aspects of culture, the symbolic sphere of our existence – exemplified by religion and ideology, language and art, empirical science and formal science (logic, mathematics) – that can be used to justify or legitimize direct or structural violence"[7] Museum scholars recognize

---

[5] Images of the Voortrekker Monument exterior are easily found online. Cf. Elizabeth Delmont, "The Voortrekker Monument: Monolith to Myth," *South African Historical Journal* 29 (November 1993): 101. Also see Richard Evans, "Perspectives on Post-Colonialism in South Africa" (Lorna Hardwick and Carol Gillespie, *Classics in Post-Colonial Worlds* (Oxford, 2007) 141–56) and Alta Steencamp, "A Shared Spatial Symbolism: The Voortrekker Monument, the Völkerslachtdenkmal and Freemasonry," (*South African Journal of Art History* 24, no, 1 [2009]: 150–60). Both Evans and Steencamp remark on similarities between the Voortrekker Monument and the Völkerslachtdenkmal (1913) in Leipzig, Germany. Elizabeth Rankin and Rolf Michael Schneider in their two-part exhaustive treatise on the VTM, *From Memory to Marble: The Historical Frieze of the Voortrekker Monument* (Cape Town: African Minds and Berlin: Walter de Gruyter, 2019), dispute these claims (part 1, 130–5). *From Memory to Marble* is available open access from doi:10.1515/9783110668797.

[6] See Rankin and Schneider, *From Memory to Marble: The Historical Frieze of the Voortrekker Monument* for a history of public discussion of what to do with the Voortrekker monument after apartheid. The changing of place names has occurred elsewhere, however; the town formerly named "Port Elizabeth" is now Ggeberha (the Xhosa name for the river that flows through the city), while Pretoria, after great debate, decided not to change its name to Tswane. "South African city of Port Elizabeth becomes Gqeberha," *BBC News online*, 24 February 2021, https://www.bbc.com/news/world-africa-56182349 (accessed 15 March 2021).

[7] Johan Galtung, "Cultural Violence," *Journal of Peace Research* 27, no. 3 (1990): 291. See also Sarah Maddison, "Indigenous Identity, 'Authenticity' and the Structural Violence of Settler Colonialism," which examines how settler colonial

that this "symbolic sphere" can reside in museums.[8] And just as often this "symbolic sphere" can rest in monuments.[9] In our reading of these two monuments, we build on Galtung's definition to explore how agents of cultural violence, while justifying and legitimizing direct or symbolic violence. can also be complicated and contradictory sites. They can enact violence to some no matter the intentions of others. As with many elements of cultural controversy, we argue the message of monuments can be contested between the intention of the settler builders and the reception of the message by the (formerly) oppressed. The path forward for these monuments is anything but clear, but comparison of the two provides fodder for discussion about the role of settler monuments in a post-colonial world.

In South Africa, as in the US with monuments to the Civil War's Confederacy, the re-examination of monuments has its origins in continued social struggle and growing inequality. Twenty-five years after South Africa's first democratic elections, black South Africans have improved economic and political opportunities, but the continued high black unemployment rate and a geographical separation between black and white South Africans shows that massive inequalities still exist.[10] These inequalities result in anger directed against symbols of apartheid ideology that created the conditions, like statues to the imperialist Cecil Rhodes, though other symbols, like the two monuments that this essay examines, have been largely left untouched. The changing ideology in South Africa involves what Ngũgĩ w'a Thiongo calls "decolonizing the mind," a process that includes the dismantling and rebuilding of cultural systems alongside political and economic systems, as well as the use of critical lenses (like this essay) to evaluate the psychological effects of those systems and their icons.

The similarities between the monuments we examine are striking. Besides their hilltop placement, landscape dominance, and purposes as reminders for competing settlers and displaced indigenous people of white settler success, both monuments similarly contain interior visual art that addresses the journeys of both white settler groups to South Africa (though the Settler Monument art, which was not an original part of the building's design as with the Voortrekker Monument and which is mobile instead of being an intrinsic part of the building, also includes the journey of black South Africans).[11] We also recognize that, though both work within the context of cultural violence, the monuments differ

---

cultures can continue to enact structural violence through insisting on a narrow definition of authenticity of indigenous cultures (*Identities: Global Studies in Culture and Power* 20, no. 3 (2013): 288–303).

[8] Cf. Dan Hicks, *The Brutish Museums: The Benin Bronzes, Colonial Violence and Cultural Restitution* (London: Pluto Press, 2020); James M. Gore, "A Lack of Nation? The Evolution of History in South African Museum, c. 1825–1945," *South African Historical Journal* 51 no. 1 (2004): 24–46; James M. Gore "New Histories in a Post-Colonial Society – Transformation in South African Museums Since 1994," *Historia* 50, no. 1 (2005): 75–102; and Tanja Hammel, "Colonial Legacies in Post-Colonial Collections," *Shaping Natural History and Settler Society* (New York: Palgrave, 2019), 311–34.

[9] The US has provided a heated site of protest and debate on this issue, especially over monuments to the American Confederacy. Similarly, in South Africa, the "Rhodes Must Fall" movement, involving the defacement and demands for removal of monuments to colonizer and financier Cecil Rhodes, is envisioned as part of a cultural reimagination of South Africa and the structural racism of its higher education. As Giselle Ballie says in "Between Narratives of Reconciliation and Resistance," the protesters were using the statues to raise attention to problems of higher education, including access, institutional racism, white privilege, and curricula (*South African Journal of Philosophy* 37, no. 4 (2018): 423–37). See also T. M. Luescher, "Frantz Fanon and the #MustFall movements in South Africa," *International Higher Education* 85 (2016): 122–4.

[10] Drew Desilver, "Chart of the Week: How South Africa Changed, and Didn't, Over Mandela's Lifetime," Pew Research Center, https://www.pewresearch.org/fact-tank/2013/12/06/chart-of-the-week-how-south-africa-changed-and-didnt-over-mandelas-lifetime/ (accessed 10 May 2022).

[11] Rankin and Schneider call attention to two other connections between the monuments, one being in scene two of the marble frieze, which shows a Bible being presented to the departing Voortrekkers by the 1820 settlers, and the second

considerably in their relationship to settlement and contemporary social justice movements; and their differences contain important lessons for mediating cultural violence in the future. We begin by examining the motives for constructing both monuments. We then analyse how the art in both monuments works with or against the larger buildings, and we end by exploring contemporary uses of and reactions to both monuments by a multicultural South Africa and post-apartheid settler culture.

Origin Stories of Settler Violence

Both the Voortrekker and 1820s Settlers monuments were constructed to symbolize past and continued European settlement of South Africa. Both were created by settlers – the Afrikaners and British, respectively – that often competed for colonial control and indeed faced off in two wars. Because the tale of the Voortrekker Monument's design and construction has been much told, beginning with the eighty-four-page collection of history, photographs, and essays, *The Voortrekker Monument Pretoria, Official Guide* published by the Board of Control of the Voortrekker Monument in 1954 (hereafter called "Official Guide"), this essay only glosses its narrative. In brief, the Great Trek or Voortrek was in reality several journeys into the interior of the country made by groups of Dutch settlers in the early nineteenth century, seeking freedom from British colonial control and space. The *Official Guide* reports that private fundraising for the monument commemorating those journeys began in 1931 and construction in 1937, but, due to WWII, the monument did not open its doors until 1949 during the ascendancy of the conservative National Party, which constructed the nation's apartheid system.[12] An immense granite-faced concrete and steel building set upon a hilltop, the Voortrekker Monument can be seen from nearly every direction, including, as Annie Coombes remarks, from the Union Buildings in Pretoria, the 1930s-1940s seat of British colonial government.[13] A challenge to that British government, the Voortrekker Monument reminded black and white South Africans alike of Afrikaner nationalism and political and economic national control. It retains much of this symbolism today.

The Voortrekker Monument's role in literally concretizing memories of Dutch settlement and conservative Afrikaner dominance was evident from its beginning. Leading up to its groundbreaking, in 1938 civic leaders and costumed reenactors retraced "the Great Trek," culminating in a three-day celebration of the centenary of the "Battle of Blood River" (16 December 1838), in Pretoria in front of a crowd of more than 100,000.[14] A decade later, an equally impressive and well-attended festival was held for the monument's grand opening, which Robyn Autry explains was organized by United Party leaders "in an effort to deepen white unity as the basis for its official segregationist stance" and "underscore the importance of the Afrikaner settlers in laying the foundation for a united South Africa."[15] As with this celebration, every aspect of the building,

---

being the erection of a monument to that Bible in the former Grahamstown in 1962 (*From Memory to Marble*, Vol 2, 25–43).

[12] *The Voortrekker Monument Pretoria, Official Guide* (Pretoria: Board of Control of the Voortrekker Monument, 1955), 11.

[13] Annie Coombes, *History After Apartheid: Visual Culture and Public Memory in a Democratic South Africa* (Durham: Duke University Press, 2003), 28.

[14] Rankin and Schneider, *From Memory to Marble*, 75.

[15] *Official Guide*, 10. Also see *Official Guide* chapter nine, "The Centenary and Laying of the Foundation Stone" and chapter ten, "The Inauguration." Richard Evans cites the attendance at the opening as high as 400,000, with many attendees

including its architecture, art and extensive grounds, was created to stress Afrikaner ruling legitimacy, making the monument perhaps the most overt symbol of cultural violence in South Africa.

Also, early in the twentieth century but in another part of the country, another settler group was also celebrating its centenary and beginning to plan a monument. The 1820 Settlers National Monument in the Eastern Cape, was also created to legitimize white settlement, including being built upon an important defensive site during the so-called Frontier Wars. It marks the roughly 5,000 settlers brought in to pacify the indigenous population after the Battle of Grahamstown (*Egazini* or "place of bloodshed" to the Black inhabitants) the year before, in 1819, when Makana led 6000 Xhosa warriors in a daylight attack on the town, losing about 1000 warriors to the British's three soldiers. A century later, descendants of the 1820 settlers conceived, planned, and eventually built the monument overlooking Grahamstown/Makhanda, known as "the settler city" because of its many restored settler-era buildings and settler statues and monuments. The settlement in 1820 has become a touchstone identity (a brand, if you will) for the town of 67,000, which also houses Rhodes University – named for Cecil Rhodes, the mining magnate cum politician.

Though the monument was first proposed in 1920, it took half a century for it to come to fruition, opening in 1974 at the height of apartheid. Thelma Neville's *More Lasting than Bronze*, details the monument's origins: its growth from yearly Settler Day celebrations; its many planned and failed iterations, including as a tower and hall on Rhodes's campus, a hospital, and a nursing home, before the decision to build concert, theatre and conference spaces; the different controversies it weathered as a cross-cultural meeting space during apartheid; and the generations of board members, architects, and fundraisers that laboured to bring it into existence.[16] As Neville notes, from its beginning, it was proposed as a "living monument," perhaps in opposition to the already completed Voortrekker Monument. Though early proposals were for a hospital or other utilitarian space, always the name "monument" indicated that whatever its everyday use, an important part of the site's purpose was to memorialize white, English-speaking settlement. The monument's website describes its intentions as "drawing particular attention to two areas of British Settler heritage that benefit all South Africans – the English language, and the democratic tradition."[17] The website explains that its design as a cultural centre was meant to "encourage free and open debate and discussion, freedom of association, and, with state-of-the-art theatre facilities and a 940-seat theatre, to encourage freedom of expression and creativity."[18] This explicit designation as a place of free expression was likely responding to the strictures of apartheid, thus creating a narrative of an English settlement different from Dutch settlement, just as the 1820 Settlers

---

dressed as nineteenth-century settlers ("Perspectives on Post-Colonialism in South Africa" 142); Robyn Autry, "Desegregating the Past: The Transformation of Public Imagination at South African and American Museums" (PhD diss., University of Wisconsin-Madison, 2008), 122.

[16] Neville, *More Lasting Than Bronze*. Scholars can also consult original programs from Settler Day celebrations before the monument was built: Settlers Association of South Africa, "Programme, Settlers' Day, Sept. 3rd 1962," Grahamstown: 1820 Settlers' Monument Trust, 1962. A 1989 publication, *The 1820 Settlers National Monument Grahamstown* (Grahamstown, The 1820 Foundation), also contains much useful background information about the monument's grounds and artwork, though discussion of the building's nautical shape is not included.

[17] Grahamstown Foundation, https://www.foundation.org.za (accessed 27 April 2021).

[18] In 1949, the VTM also added an amphitheatre (seating 20,000) erected for the 1949 inauguration and later for Afrikaner celebrations. (Rankin and Schneider, *From Memory to Marble*, Vol 1, 444).

National Monument differed from the Voortrekker Monument, and Afrikaans from the English language. The stories of the two monuments show two white minority groups both united in a project of white supremacy but in opposition to the other in struggling over which culture and language would dominate the country and the settler narrative. Yet, the original purposes of both monuments was, and continues to be, the remembrance of the original settlers in order to mark the continuation of settlement and its attendant cultural violence.

The Buildings, Art, and Grounds: How the Monuments' Pieces Fit (or Do Not)

Both monuments were designed and constructed with great attention to detail, each structural and decorative element carrying symbolic meaning about the settlers and their descendants. The Voortrekker Monument proclaims a God-given right to exist in and even dominate South Africa, and the grounds and buildings harmonize in echoing that message.[19] Working from exterior to interior, the building is surrounded by a granite wall with sixty-four covered ox wagons in relief, symbolizing the sixty-four wagons circled into a defensive laager at the Battle of Blood River, as *Official Guide* explains, "symbolically ... protecting the tradition and sanctity of the nation against any attack."[20]

At the building's four exterior corners are statues of men, three recognizable as trek leaders and the fourth standing in for the unnamed, ordinary trekboer. At the monument's entrance, a life-sized statue of a bonneted Voortrekker mother "protects" her children.[21] As Figure 2 shows, four relief sculptures of wildebeests flank the mother and children statue, placed so that they walk away from the settlers. *Official Guide* lays bare the ideology behind the representation, explaining that the mother and children statue

> symbolizes white civilization while the black wildebeest portray the ever-threatening dangers of Africa. The determined attitude and triumphant expression on the woman's face while confidently gazing into the future, and the retreating attitude of the wildebeest, suggest that the dangers are receding and that the victory of civilization is an accomplished fact.[22]

These sculptures, along with the manicured and wagon-encircled grounds and the sentinels at each corner, assert completed white settler conquest of black indigenes.

The building itself is a massive square granite-faced structure with large lunette windows on each side and a soaring ceiling and glass-filtered light that evoke a cathedral. As Delmont notes this design "reflect[s] a desire to locate Afrikanerdom firmly within the heritage of European civilization."[23] The building features the large dome-covered Hall of

---

[19] The Voortrekker Monument website lists other elements of the grounds: a garden of remembrance, a historical garden, a remembrance wall, a niche wall, a song garden, an amphitheatre, and a picnic site among other landscape elements. Troubling this site of Afrikanerdom is a single traditional Zulu hut, which serves the purpose of reminding of the historical enemies of the Voortrekker, who are represented in the interior frieze. http://vtm.org.za/en/zulu-hut/ (accessed 10 May 2022).

[20] *Official Guide*, 57.

[21] This iconography is remarkably like that of the bonneted white "Pioneer Mother" celebrated by dozens of monuments across the US in the 1920s and 1930s. Cf. Cynthia Culver Prescott, *Pioneer Mother Monuments* (Norman: University of Oklahoma Press, 2019), chapter two.

[22] *Official Guide*, 38.

[23] Delmont, "The Voortrekker Monument: Monolith to Myth," 101.

Figure 2. The statue of the mother and child at the entrance to the VTM Pretoria. Image courtesy of Lynn Greyling (publicdomainpictures.net).

Heroes, whose marble friezes circling the interior walls tell the story of the Voortrekkers, including the Battle of Blood River, culminating in the British acceptance of Afrikaner legitimacy.

Looking down from the Hall of Heroes one sees Cenotaph Hall, featuring in its centre a large rectangular polished granite cenotaph to the Voortrekkers inscribed with "Ons vir Jou, Suid-Afrika" ("We're for you, South Africa") and on its north wall an eternal flame. *Official Guide* explains this cenotaph forms the altar ("the symbol of sacrifice") around which the rest of the building is arranged in concentric circles, waves symbolizing the sacrifice of the Voortrekkers, "extended until it eventually permeated all of South Africa."[24] Around the edges of the building's roof, a walkway offers a view of the Great Hall with its spectacular frieze and cenotaph below. The whole building is constructed so that at noon on each 16 December ("The Day of the Vow," after the oath made by the Voortrekkers to honour God if they were granted victory over the Zulu in the Battle of Blood River), the sun streams through an astronomically precise aperture to highlight the cenotaph in the monument's basement.[25] Every element of the building shows a desire to create a legacy and hints at an underlying fear of replacement in a larger nation where Afrikaners were always a numerical minority and where the Afrikaans language is now merely one of thirteen official languages instead of the official *lingua franca*. This monument was meant to make a dramatic statement about power, authority, and permanence to other white settlers and indigenous people, and in that way the Voortrekker Monument participates in cultural violence.

Likewise, the 1820 Settlers National Monument was explicitly planned and constructed to symbolize British settlement's importance, though this "statement" reveals internal conflict and ambivalence instead of a unified message of God-granted authority. The

---

[24] *Official Guide*, 34. The lower level also contains several halls dedicated to showcasing art and antiques associated with the Voortrekkers, including a large tapestry depicting scenes from the Voortrek. Cf *Official Guide* chapter seven, "The Collection of Antiques" and Chapter eight, "The Tapestry."

[25] Forecasting an intentional move away from apartheid, "the Day of the Vow" was rechristened "The Day of Reconciliation" by the post-1994 elected South African government.

1820s Settler "monument" functions as a multipurpose conference centre, meant to be a "living monument" and usable space. After extensive debate, a design was chosen that would include galleries and a large concert hall, both routinely used for South Africa's National Arts Festival; South Africa's National Science Festival, Scifest Africa; and South Africa's National Schools Festival. Despite the rhetoric Neville captured in her account of the monument's origins, where various Afrikaner and Anglophone leaders proclaimed solidarity and unity of purpose, evidence leads this essay's authors to the conclusion that this monument was designed by the descendants of the British settlers in opposition to the Afrikaners' famous Voortrekker Monument. British settler descendants, many regarding themselves as more progressive in their attitudes towards racial harmony than many Afrikaners, built a monument that would encourage gathering and art. As the website describes, it was to be "a centre of creative thought and activity, encouraging all who encounter it, to look forward with hope." In this way, the building's insides (spaces allowing multicultural gatherings, though named after famous white, English-speaking authors) are at odds with its outsides (a ship on a hill, built on a former colonial battleground).[26]

Contrasting with the explicit nineteenth-century style of the town of Makandha, the monument has a yellow-orange sand-coloured brick exterior. While in some respects it looks like any blocky mid-century government building, we argue that, when taken in as a whole – from the town below, say – the building resembles a ship the 1820s settlers would have arrived in. Its raised stern, with poop deck flared out and supported by concrete braces, overlooks the botanical gardens to the southeast, its bow to the northwest – pointed to England. Two large nautical flagpoles with crossbeams and ropes attaching them to its roof mimic the masts of the 1820 settlers' vessels (see Figure 1).[27] The exterior of the building (perhaps even more literally than the Voortrekker Monument) thus constantly reminds of invasion and continued settlement.

On the hilltop opposite the Settlers Monument is Makana's Kop, a hill behind a massive stand of trees commemorating the final battle of the Xhosa chief, Makana, in the Battle of Grahamstown. The two mirroring sites, the man-made building that looks like a ship and the tall trees marking a hill sacred to the Xhosa people, remind the community constantly of the historic struggle over the town and the Xhosa wars, a struggle still extant in the current geographical separation of the town, with the white population settled under Gunfire Hill and the township fronting Makana's Last Stand. The struggle continues, as the 2011 census shows, with seventy-nine point 2 per cent of inhabitants identifying as black, but the eight point nine per cent white minority still possessing most of the financial capital.[28]

The 1820 Settlers National Monument grounds, like the Voortrekker Monument's, tell a story of settlement. On its exterior, about 265 metres from the building, separated by a parking lot, stands a bronze statue of a settler family – a man, woman, and child –

---

[26] Neville's account interrupts its own portrayal of white unity with a few examples of conflict, reminding of the larger context of resistance within which the monument was built. One occasion where the 1820's Monument staff was at odds with the apartheid government occurred during the women's conference of 1975, for which the museum staff invited Indian and black women, a move met with criticism from the apartheid government.

[27] Cf. "Grahamstown: Architectural Wonderland" *Grocutt's Mail* (https://grocotts.ru.ac.za/2009/08/14/grahamstown-architectural-wonderland/, 14 August 2009, accessed 20 April 2021). See also note 1.

[28] Peter E Raper, Lucie A Moller, Theodorus L du Plessis, *Dictionary of South African Place Names* (Johannesburg, Jonathan Ball Publishers, 2014). Desilver, "Chart of the Week."

Figure 3. Statuary on the grounds of the Settler Monument. On the left, the Settler family and on the right, a stylized statue of a worker at the entrance (photographs by Rebecca Weaver-Hightower).

dressed to represent the 1820 settlers and placed, Neville tells, on the grounds as part of the Settler Day celebration of 1969, five years before the Settler Monument itself. Though forty-two kilometres from the sea and impeccably dressed, this family, which resembles the mother and children marking the entrance to the Voortrekker Monument, could have recently disembarked from the ship represented by the building (see Figure 3). The presumed father wears a top hat and carries two books, while the presumed bon-neted mother holds the hand of the child, a girl holding a wreath in her other hand as she gazes up at her mother. One of the father's booted feet steps forward, putting him in motion leading his family towards their new future and new home. The family, explains the publication *The 1820 Settler National Monument Grahamstown,* faces north "towards 'the unknown hinterland' which they and their descendants and other English-speaking immigrants were to help develop in many different fields."[29]

Unlike the settler family at the Voortrekker Monument, however, this statue is posi-tioned on the grounds of the monument, not at its entrance. At the 1820 Settlers National Monument's entrance looms a statue of an abstracted, oversized figure holding a pickaxe or sledgehammer above his head, his bowler hat and curled moustache signalling British-ness and that the figure is clearly from a different period than the settler family and the ship/building, another instance of the mixed messages of the Monument (see Figure 3). This abstract figure of the worker (which the *1820 Settler National Monument Grahams-town* identifies as a blacksmith) reminds visitors of what earned the 1820s British settlers

[29] *1820 Settler National Monument Grahamstown: Home of the 1820 Foundation.* Grahamstown: 1820 Foundation, 1989, 12.

the land their descendants still inhabit: hard work and stewardship of the land. Such arguments continue to be used to justify white ownership today.[30] The 1820 Settler National Monument Grahamstown quotes the piece's sculptor, Bruce Arnott, in explaining that the figure is a "'working-class hero,' symbolizing the introduction of Western artisans; as well as the powerful social and political presence that the settler groups asserted in general."[31]

Narratives of Settlement: The Interior Art

Both monuments' interior art also speaks to their overall cultural violence. Both contain interior art that, in different ways and using contrasting styles, tell a story of settlement. For the purposes of this comparison, we focus on two striking installations of art among others in both buildings: the immense marble frieze in the Voortrekker Monument's Hall of Heroes and the series of Cecil Skotnes murals in the 1820 Settlers National Monument. Again, the Voortrekker Monument pieces have been extensively studied by historians and art historians, whereas the 1820 Settlers National Monument murals have received far less scholarly attention. Yet comparing the two, we argue, illustrates how, despite many differences, the pieces of art serve comparable overall purposes.

At the Voortrekker Monument, walking past the settler mother and children statue, one enters the impressive Hall of Heroes with its vaulted ceiling and natural light, to find encircling the hall the 302 foot long, seven and one-half feet high (two point three metre high and ninety-two metre long) marble frieze ("the largest historical frieze in the world").[32] Designed by Hennie Potgieter, Peter Kirchhoff, Frikkie Kruger, and Laurika Postma, it illustrates in twenty-seven panels the events of "the Great Trek," carving an official narrative into marble. As *Official Guide* explains, the frieze "is not only a representation of historic events ... it also serves as a symbolic document showing the Afrikaner's proprietary right to South Africa."[33] Designers and sculptors planned the frieze to be realistic, with figures modelled after the actual descendants of trekkers where available and with items included that could be historically verified.

The frieze provides a linear representation of Afrikaner settlement, with a beginning, middle, and end, with the final panel showing not the victory over indigenous South Africans but over the British. Again, the idea of one "Great Trek" with a beginning, a climax, and a resolution, is also a narrative construction, because in reality four separate Treks occurred under four separate leaders.[34] As Coombes says, "The panels narrate a version of the central incidents of the Great Trek ... that became enshrined in history textbooks around the country – predominantly a tale of Boer heroism and God-fearing righteousness and of Zulu and Ndebele treachery and savagery."[35] This frieze, like the building

---

[30] The bowler hat was not invented until 1849. Laura Roberts, "The History of the Bowler Hat," *The Telegraph*, 6 October 2010, https://www.telegraph.co.uk/news/uknews/8045026/History-of-the-Bowler-Hat.html (accessed 24 April 2021). See, *Frontier Fictions: Settler Sagas and Postcolonial Guilt* (Mew York: Palgrave 2018), for more on the use of stewardship as a justification for legitimate settler land ownership.

[31] *1820 Settler National Monument Grahamstown*, 14.

[32] "The Historical Frieze" by Dr. Gerald Moerdyk, *Official Guide*, 41. This chapter gives a detailed analysis of each panel of the frieze. An even more detailed analysis can be found in Rankin and Schneider, *Monuments to Memory*. The frieze was sculpted by Italian artists in Florence who worked from the South African models created by Potgieter, Kirchhoff, Kruger, and Postma.

[33] *Official Guide*, 36.

[34] *Official Guide*, 40.

[35] Coombes, *History After Apartheid*, 28.

housing it, marks and narrates a version of events in which Afrikaner settlement is legitimate, God-given, and complete.[36]

Much has been written about the frieze, including the recent, exhaustive two volume history by Rankin and Schneider. A quick reading of one panel, however, suffices to give a sense of the deliberation and care taken in presenting this narrative that was ultimately part of the larger monument's cultural violence by, in addition to legitimizing Afrikaner rule, depicting indigenous Africans willingly ceding their right to their own space. Panel twelve, for instance, in depicting the Zulu leader Dingane signing a treaty with Trek leaders, presents the Voortrekkers gaining the space through fair negotiation rather than conquest. This is what Mary Louise Pratt, in *Imperial Eyes*, called a narrative of "anti-conquest," meaning the simultaneous disavowal and celebration of conquest. As *Official Guide* explains in its narration of another panel, Panel eight, "there were no conquerors among the Voortrekkers, no Cortez nor Napoleon, no Genghis Khan nor Tamburlaine."[37]

While central to the frieze's story, the signing event depicted and the treaty itself lack historical verification, so the panel creates a sense of verisimilitude by adding in actual items recovered from the trek. As Rankin and Schneider and others have noted, great care was taken by both to present an image that was both realistic – in historical accuracy of the items and people included in the panel, if not the actual event – and supportive of settler ideology; the Zulu, for instance, are shown kneeling so that the Voortrekkers tower above them, while Dingaan is shown holding the quill with Retief apparently showing him where to put his signature or mark, suggesting a lack of literacy (see Figure 4). Panel thirteen follows by showing Dingane betraying that treaty, implying that the indigenous people did not deserve control of their lands because, unlike the Afrikaners, they did not act in good faith. The monument thus not only asserts legitimate Afrikaner power and authority but also teaches twentieth-century Zulu to be ashamed of their duplicitous ancestor and to see the Voortrekkers as heroes. This narrative of legitimacy and superiority is one method of continued cultural violence.

The 1820 Settlers National Monument, like the Voortrekker Monument, contains art in its large interior space. The Settlers Monument includes a series of twenty-four large (two point four metres by seen point three metres),[38] painted woodcut panels grouped into four 6-panel murals, together presenting a narrative of settlement, though more thematic and abstract than chronological and realistic. The murals were commissioned in 1984, a decade after the Monument opened, to embellish what the monument website calls a "stark interior space" of unadorned brick and wood. The space had been designed, as the Monument's website explains, with an open fountain court lined by wooden statuary "designed to look like scaffolding," with "the 'scaffolding' symbolis[ing] the notion that the work of the English speaker in South Africa continues." Moreover, the wooden scaffolding resembles the crosses of the British Flag, with yellowwood chosen as the material because it was an indigenous wood used by the settlers. A decade after the monument's unveiling, this "scaffolding" was thought to need more artistic

---

[36] Cynthia Culver Prescott, Nathan Rees, Rebecca Weaver-Hightower, "This is the Place, Salt Lake City, Utah and the Voortrekker Monument Pretoria: Monuments to Settler Constructions of History, Race, and Religion," *Safundi: The Journal of South African and American Studies* 22, no. 2 (2021): 105–29. doi:10.1080/17533171.2021.1924504.

[37] *Official Guide*, 48.

[38] "Loose pages 11," *Skotnes family archive*, http://archive.cecilskotnes.com/items/show/4558.

Figure 4. Panel twelve from the Voortrekker monument frieze, showing Retief and Dingane signing the treaty which grants the Voortrekkers land to the south. Source: wikimediacommons.org.

embellishment, which led to the commissioning of the murals by the celebrated South African artist Cecil Skotnes.

As Figure 5 depicts, the interior space is now lined with four large groups of painted carvings, each two carvings wide and three carvings tall. Two groups hang on the south side of the building and two on the north side, each group stretching vertically toward the vaulted ceiling. The artist, Cecil Skotnes, a white South African, was well known for his painted wood cuts and prints, as well as his mentoring of black South African artists, his management of the influential Polly Street Art Centre, and his criticism of apartheid.[39] His selection was thus controversial, both because of the highly abstract, traditional African art-inspired style of his work and because of his political stances.

While creating a memorial of past and continued white settlement, the 1820 Settlers National Monument, through these murals, problematizes settlement, making this monument overall more dissonant and ambivalent than the Voortrekker Monument's unified story across its exterior, grounds, interior, and art. The twenty-four Skotnes woodcuts represent settlement in a complicate manner, both through their depiction of themes rather than events and through their non-representational, African-inspired visual language rather than the traditionally European Voortrekker Monument. As additions to the building after a decade, Skotnes' murals ameliorate some of the overt celebration of colonialism of the original 1820 Settlers monument, but at the same time the murals themselves present a narrative of a sort.

First, as noted above, the murals' abstract representation of settlement makes a historical reading more difficult than that encouraged by the Voortrekker Monument friezes. While little has been written about the 1820 Settlers National Monument overall or the

---

[39] The Polly Street Art Centre is credited for influencing numerous important black South African artists. CF E. J. DeJager "Contemporary African Art in South Africa," *Africa Insight* 17, no. 3 (1987): 209–13. See Freida Harmsen, "Cecil Skotnes," *Our Art* 3 (1977): 152–60, for a biography of Skotnes and further analysis of his neo-primitive style. Harmsen's essay was published before the 1820 Settlers National Monument panels were created.

Figure 5. The panels on the South and North sides of the atrium, left to right. For scale, one can see the chairs in the background on the right. Photographs by Rebecca Weaver-Hightower. Readers can view the panels – though not in the same order in which they were hung – on the Cecil Skotnes website at http://cecilskotnes.com/panels-for-the-1820-settlers-monument-grahamstown (accessed 10 May 2022).

panels in particular, the Skotnes family website explains that, when the panels were commissioned:

> Detailed historical realism, which some Council members favoured, was rejected. Instead the complex work ... would "present, in bold symbolic manner, the dynamic nature of the British-speaking experience in Africa, from the settlement to their current involvement in the creation of a common society in which African and European elements will blend – as in Skotnes's [sic] distinctive work."[40]

That is, the Council members resisted a realistic visual narrative, along the lines of the Voortrekker Monument, which had been opened to the public thirty-five years earlier. The Council members, as art critic Freida Harmsen explains, wanted a narrative of "the Settlers' arrival, living conditions and their contribution to the development of South Africa," but their rejection of literal historic representations suggests an unease with overt celebration of settlement, even inside a larger building resembling a settler ship.[41] The panels' depictions are not literal, but they do contain figures, animals, architecture, and boats that create the sense of a story, even if one not easily discerned. The figures are faceless and often androgynous, with the white figures appearing mummified or flayed (though other figures' race is ambiguous), some with what seem to be African-styled

---

[40] The Skotnes family website contains a comprehensive discussion of the panels as part of Skotnes' other work (http://cecilskotnes.com/panels-for-the-1820-settlers-monument-grahamstown/). The website here is quoting from Frieda Harmsen's "Artist Resolute," in *Cecil Skotnes*, ed. Frieda Harmsen (Cape Town: South African Breweries). 11–63.

[41] Harmsen, "Artist Resolute."

masks over their white faces. Again, we see more ambivalence about the settlement project here than in the Voortrekker Monument frieze, as these panels show a version of settlement that doesn't totally valorize the white settler nor demonize the indigenous person, even while marking the presence of the 1820 settlers and the pacification they sought to achieve, a "blend" of African and European in both style and presence not found in the Voortrekker monument.

Second, the abstract murals don't present a narrative as linear as that of the Voortrekker Monument friezes, though, as a description of the panels reprinted on the Skotnes family website describes, the "allegorical" panels were intended to portray "the Settlers' arrival, living conditions and their contribution to the development of South Africa" – a timeline of a sort.[42] The murals' groupings, though not captioned on or by the murals themselves, are identified on the Skotnes family website as corresponding to the seasons and a general narrative of settlement. The first section, autumn and winter, "deals with wars prior to 1820, both in Europe and South Africa." The second six panels, "The Frontier," show "new beginnings for all, both black and white–an allusion to spring." The third six panels, "Towards a New Society" and summer, show "harmony and equal rights"; and the final section, not identified with any season, but rather depicting arts and creativity, show "the means through which people can attain the ideals of unity and freedom."[43] The narrative about the settlement of South Africa is not as direct as that of the Voortrekker friezes; and it was added later, making it not a part of the original concept. One gets the sense that the builders of the 1820 Settlers National Monument attempted to create a monument in opposition to the Voortrekker Monument, but they could not help creating similarities because of the colonialist nature of white settlement in South Africa.

A reading of two specific panels gives a further sense of dissonance with the site overall. For instance, the most clearly representational of the panels comes in the first grouping, "New Beginnings," associated with Autumn and winter, and is entitled "Departure" (see Figure 6). This panel shows two high masted sailing ships, echoing the masts of the building and the 1820 settlers it memorializes, with eight white figures in the foreground, one a smaller figure. The white figures, presumably the 1820 settlers, have either just disembarked from the ships and are now on the shore of their new home, in the colonial space later known as South Africa, as the ships depart behind them, or it could be that the figures are about to embark from England and head to their new home (the panel's title is "Departure" as identified on the mural poster). In either case, the shore behind/in front of them is red, perhaps suggesting the bloodshed inherent

---

[42] http://cecilskotnes.com/panels-for-the-1820-settlers-monument-grahamstown/. This reading of the panels as presenting a narrative was disputed at the time by South African author Guy Butler, who was instrumental in the development of the Monument and who recorded in his journals his thoughts and reactions to the monument and its building. Guy Butler, "Notes on the Skotnes Murals," June 1986.

[43] A poster of the mural (http://www.artnet.com/artists/cecil-skotnes/murals-1820-settlers-national-monument-3r9nJgfJZrKdplBt0o-hmw2) identifies the groupings and panel titles more specifically (see fig # and fig 3, from left to right): Group A: "Beginnings" (with panels entitled "Bondage," "Cruelty," "Starvation," "Exile," "Departure," and "Arrival"); Group B: "The Frontier" (with panels entitled "The New Land: Its Spirits," "The New Land: Its Ancient Forms," "Cattle," "The Horse," "Confrontation I," and "Confrontation II"), Group C: "Towards a New Society" (with panels "Mother Africa," "Fruits of the Earth," "Right of Assembly," "Hope for Justice," "Industrial Labour," and "The Architect"); and Group D: "The Arts" (with panels "Poetry," "Theatre," "Song," "Music," "Language Man's Greatest Gift," and "The Creative Spirit"). Rosalie Breitenbach and Guy Butler, in *The 1820 Settlers National Monument, Grahamstown,* provide further explanation of several panels.

Figure 6. "Departure" on the left and "Arrival" on the right, from the panels by Cecil Skotnes in the interior of the 1820 Settlers National Monument. Image reproduced from cecilskotnes.com with permission of the Skotnes family.

in settlement, and the figures' faces resemble African masks, making them appear more ghostly and ethereal than real, with looks of sadness and anxiety, not joy at their departure. One might read the art as problematizing the monument's overall project of celebration as described on the monument's website, forecasting the debates occurring post-apartheid about the role of white settlers/settlement in the new South Africa.

The panel's companion, hung just beside it to the right, is entitled "Arrival" (see Figure 6 above). The figures in "Arrival" are less ghostly in appearance, with darker skin and clothing tones, in a smaller boat, and the colours are warmer, suggesting the African sun. This could be the smaller craft meant to ferry sunburnt settlers from the masted ship to the African shore, or this image could show the arrival of black South Africans to the to-be-settled-space, because one of the primary arguments of settler legitimacy is that *all* South Africans, black and white, were settlers from elsewhere – either Europe or elsewhere in Africa. Again, the figures' masks make it difficult to ascertain their emotions about arrival. The panel's interpretation is open, again creating a lack of a clear settlement narrative even within the larger narrative of British cultural importance.

Contemporary Uses and Reactions

Sabine Marschall notes in "Setting up a Dialogue: Monuments as a Means of 'Writing Back'" that monuments will always be reinterpreted by constantly changing cultures, sometimes forming spaces of resistance as well as predictable interpretation divergences stemming from differences in culture and positionality.[44] Though the Voortrekker Monument is now open to other uses (its website, for instance, mentions weddings, concerts,

---

[44] Marschall "Setting up a Dialogue: Monuments as a Means of 'Writing Back'," *Historia* 48, no. 1 (2003): 309–25.

antiques fairs and church services, as well as burial sites), the building still primarily serves as a space of memorializing conquest.[45] The building's unapologetic purpose could be explained by the very real fears of Afrikaners concerned with losing their culture and language. Afrikaners are isolated as contemporary settlers, largely existing only in South Africa (though many emigrated post-apartheid to other Anglophone nations).

In contrast, the 1820 Settlers National Monument commemorates British settlers, who are connected to a global diaspora, with little fear of their language and culture "dying out" in the near future. The 1820 Settlers National Monument was created to be a multi-use building, one that encouraged gathering and education for large festivals and public events, instead of existence as a singular object. In 1994 the 1820 Settlers National Monument suffered a fire that led to serious damage, causing two years of construction costing millions of rand, and led to a re-opening and rebranding, most famously with a speech given by then-president Nelson Mandela who included the 1820 Settlers National Monument among "monuments which open the past to scrutiny; recalling it in order to illuminate it and transform it into part of our living and changing society; and merging the tradition from which they emerged with the rich diversity of South Africa's cultures."[46] Mandela's statement captures the result of the tangled aesthetics and messaging of the 1820 Monument, which is allowing a rupture in history instead of pasting over the cracks with a unified fiction.

In other ways one might contrast the two monuments. The Voortrekker Monument seems largely concerned with representation and education about the history of the Voortrekkers and the maintenance of the Afrikaner culture and language. The 1820 Settlers National Monument seems more ambivalent about its overall relationship to settlers, even to the extent of potentially changing its name. In January 2019, *Grocott's Mail*, the local newspaper (and the oldest surviving independent newspaper in SA), announced a contest being held to rename the monument.[47] The Monument, as the Grahamstown Foundation website explains, needs a new name and conceptual ethos because its present name is, "for many South Africans, alienating and seen by many as monument to conquest and colonisation." The invitation for public participation goes on to say that the "ethos and operations" of the Monument should be based on "the collective values of post-1994 South Africa" as enshrined in South Africa's Constitution, "rather than solely the values and ideals of the British Settlers who arrived in this area in the 1820s."[48]

Comparison of the two monuments provides a snapshot of South Africa in the twenty-first century, the push/pull of responses to monuments and cultural violence that we are seeing elsewhere in the world, as well. When put side by side, one notices between the Voortrekker Monument and the 1820 Settlers National Monument

---

[45] Rankin and Schneider, *From Memory to Marble*, Vol 1, 409–21.

[46] See M. Goldswain, "1820 Settlers National Monument Reinstatement," *Architect and Builder* 2, no. 2 (1997): 10–13. Mandela's brief speech can be found at http://www.mandela.gov.za/mandela_speeches/1996/960516_settlers.htm. Rankin and Schneider note that this speech bears similarity to one Mandela gave in Afrikaans on a visit to the VTM site in 2002 (Vol. 1, 424).

[47] See Grocutt's Mail Contributors, "Concern About Living Monument Name Change," *Grocutt's Mail*, 10 January 2019, https://grocotts.ru.ac.za/2019/01/22/concern-about-living-monument-name-change/.

[48] Grahamstown Foundation, "Change of Name 1820 Settlers Monument Invitation for Public Participation," https://uploads.strikinglycdn.com/files/d7ebd792-7c79-4fe2-9a56-560cc29909cb/name%20change%20call.pdf (accessed 10 May 2022).

similarities that one might otherwise see only in terms of distinctions. Both monuments were constructed by white settler groups to memorialize their origin story
and continued heritage. Both are imposing hilltop buildings placed on sites of historic
violence, and both include impressive artistic installations placed around a large
interior hall presenting a narrative of settlement, even if one narrative is more easily
discerned. Both sites were intended for gathering, the Voortrekker Monument for
the Afrikaner-focused Day of the Vow and the 1820 Settlers National Monument for
an annual Settlers Day and now a range of artistic events, many now involving
black artists. Despite their differences and the 1820 Settlers National Monument's
clear ambivalence about its founding purpose, it, like the Voortrekker Monument, is
also inevitably a site of cultural violence, both in tribute to the white minorities who
historically won the wars for control of South Africa and who for generations generally
participated or were complicit in the oppression of black South Africans and others.
Through this comparison, we discover that cultural violence is insidiously built into
existing structures that seem benign, or are even beneficial to the community, like
the 1820 Settlers National Monument, a community building that hosts community
events. The site and its art may make nods to multiculturalism, but it is still promoting
similar messages of settler dominance as the Voortrekker monument.

Still, from a perspective of justice and strategy, sparks of nuance exist between the two
sites – perhaps contrasting cultural positions on the challenges that South Africa faced
and still faces – that hold hope that the cultural violence of settlement might slowly,
perhaps glacially, be wiped away. While we regard it largely as a site of cultural violence
in its current form, the 1820 Settlers National Monument has shown a structural ability
and, more importantly, willingness to morph into a site of inclusion and reconciliation.
Just as it invited an anti-apartheid artist during the height of apartheid to introduce
African visual languages into its central space, and just as it has offered to change its
name, the Monument to the 1820s settlers might one day pull down the masts from its
roof. It might one day erect a statue to Makhanda and the warriors and families lost to
invasion.[49] Because it can alter names and spaces more easily than other monuments
might alter marble and granite, we see in the 1820 Settlers National Monument and in
the people who have led it the anti-racist work towards healing the wounds wrought
by cultural violence.

Acknowledgements

The authors thank the staff of the Amazwi South African Museum of Literature (formerly the
National English Literary Museum, Grahamstown), Makana Tourism, The National Arts Festival
and the Grahamstown Foundation, and Pippa Skotnes for their assistance. We also wish to thank
the anonymous peer reviewers for their excellent and thorough recommendations.

Disclosure Statement

No potential conflict of interest was reported by the author(s).

---

[49] A memorial to the Xhosa warriors who died in the Battle of Grahamstown, the Egazini Memorial, unveiled in 2001 and
significantly updated in 2015, lies near Fort England Hospital in Makhanda. This and other Black memorials can be seen
at http://sawarmemorials.ed.ac.uk.

The Ajnala Massacre of 1857 and the Politics of Colonial Violence and Commemoration in Contemporary India

Mark Condos ⓘ

ABSTRACT

In February 2014, an amateur archaeological team unearthed thousands of bones and other remains from an old well in the town of Ajnala, located in the Indian state of Punjab. These remains are believed to belong to 282 Indian sepoys who were summarily executed en masse on 1 August 1857 under the orders of Deputy Commissioner Frederic Cooper, during the height of the Indian Uprising of 1857. The discovery of the bodies has not only reignited fierce debates about the violent history of the British Empire in India, but also offers an interesting glimpse into some of the ways that Indian history and national identity are currently being remade and negotiated in relation to the colonial past. This article is about the contested historical narrations, memories, and ongoing efforts to commemorate the Ajnala Massacre. It reveals how the history and public memory of colonial violence remain poorly understood, and the ways that calls for the recognition of previously forgotten, absent, or erased memories can prompt difficult and highly politicized discussions about the meaning of history, identity, and politics.

Introduction

On 28 February 2014, an amateur archaeological team led by Surinder Kochhar unearthed the remains of 22 bodies from an old well in the town of Ajnala, located in the Indian state of Punjab.[1] After the first remains were uncovered and pulled out of the well, the traditional Sikh *jaikara* ("shout of victory") of *"Bole so nihal, Sat Sri Akal!"* ("Shout aloud in ecstasy, true is the Great Timeless One!") resounded through a large crowd that had gathered for the event.[2] Over the next two days, Kochhar and his team excavated thousands of bones, including 90 skulls, 170 jaw bones, and more than 5,000 teeth, as well as bits of jewellery and old coins.[3] According to the residents of Ajnala, these are the remains of 282 Indian soldiers, known as sepoys, who mutinied against their British superiors

---

[1] "After 1857, 22 Bodies Extricated from Shadeedan da Khu," *The Times of India*, 28 February 2014, https://timesofindia. indiatimes.com/city/chandigarh/After-157-years-22-bodies-extricated-from-Shaheedan-da-Khu/articleshow/ 31183298.cms (accessed 20 September 2020).

[2] Asit Jolly, "The Remains of 1857: Remnants of 282 Indian Soldiers Executed in 1857 Reveal the Brutality of the British Raj," *India Today*, 7 April 2014, https://www.indiatoday.in/magazine/controversy/story/20140407-remains-of-indian-soldiers-of-1857-war-british-raj-801784-1999-11-30 (accessed 20 September 2020).

[3] "The Black Hole," *The Indian Express*, 16 March 2014, https://indianexpress.com/article/india/india-others/the-black-hole/ (accessed 21 September 2020).

during the Indian Uprising of 1857. On 1 August 1857, British Deputy Commissioner Frederic Cooper summarily executed these sepoys, and had their bodies dumped into the well. Although the residents of Ajnala have demonstrated a renewed interest in uncovering and memorializing this history, the fate of the sepoys was and continues to be generally forgotten by both British and Indian audiences when it comes to commemorating and memorializing the momentous events of the Indian Uprising.

The Indian Uprising of 1857 was one of the most significant anti-colonial revolts of the nineteenth century.[4] Both sides committed atrocities during this conflict, but the British resorted to particularly brutal tactics and exemplary forms of punishment in a desperate attempt to suppress the rebellion and reassert control. They tied rebels and mutineers to mouths of artillery, and literally blew them to pieces. The British also destroyed entire villages, slaughtering civilian populations indiscriminately.[5] Within this catalogue of horrors, the massacre at Ajnala has been brushed aside as yet another example of the violent excesses of British colonial rule.[6] It has also been overshadowed by more well-known and highly politicized colonial atrocities, particularly the infamous Jallianwala Bagh Massacre of 1919, whose recent centenary celebrations highlighted how the legacies of British rule are still hotly contested in postcolonial India today.[7] Unlike Ajnala, Amritsar boasts a prominent "Martyrs' Memorial" monument, surrounded by gardens, as well as a "Martyrs' Gallery" and museum, all located on the site of the massacre.[8] In August 2021, Indian Prime Minister Narendra Modi unveiled a highly controversial set of expensive renovations to the Jallianwala Bagh memorial site, including a new sound and light show and embellished murals covering the previously austere and sombre entrance into the site. Although these cosmetic changes drew widespread criticism from historians and others as a form of "Disneyfication," they reveal how certain aspects of history are given privileged national attention and resources, while others like Ajnala are forgotten (Image 1).[9]

---

[4] There is a voluminous literature on this subject, but some key studies include: Rudrangshu Mukherjee, *Awadh in Revolt, 1857–1858: A Study in Popular Resistance* (Delhi: Oxford University Press, 1984); William Dalrymple, *The Last Mughal: The Fall of a Dynasty, Delhi 1857* (London: Bloomsbury, 2006); Mahmood Farooqui, *Besieged: Voices from Delhi 1857* (Delhi: Penguin, 2010); Crispin Bates and Marina Carter et al., eds., *Mutiny at the Margins: New Perspectives on the Indian Uprising of 1857*, 6 vols. (New Delhi: Sage, 2013–14); and Kim A. Wagner, *The Skull of Alum Bheg: The Life and Death of a Rebel of 1857* (London: Hurst, 2017). While many British people today still refer to it as the "Mutiny," suggesting this was little more than a treacherous, dishonourable, criminal outbreak, Indian nationalists refer to it as the "Indian War of Independence," and often deploy deeply emotive, hagiographic language when referring to the *shaheeds* ("martyrs") and "heroes" who fought in it. For a summary of some of the salient shifts in these various representations, as well as divergent Indian and British interpretations and mythmaking surrounding these events, see Pramod Kumar Srivastava, "Nationalism Imagined? Hidden Impacts of the Uprising of 1857," *South Asia Research* 38, no. 3 (2018): 229–46; Kim A. Wagner, "The Marginal Mutiny: The New Historiography of the Indian Uprising of 1857," *History Compass* 9, no. 10 (October 2011): 760–6; and Astrid Erll, "The 'Indian Mutiny' as a Shared Site of Memory: A Media Culture Perspective on Britain and India," in *Memory, History, and Colonialism: Engaging with Pierre Nora in Colonial and Postcolonial Contexts*, ed. Indra Sengupta (London: German Historical Institute, 2009), 17–48.
[5] See, generally, Wagner, *The Skull of Alum Bheg*.
[6] One exception to this lacuna is Wagner: ibid., 157–8, 159, 180, 223.
[7] See Kim A. Wagner, *Amritsar 1919: An Empire of Fear and the Making of a Massacre* (New Haven, CT: Yale University Press, 2019); Vidya Ram, "Jallianwala Bagh Massacre: The Unending Wait for an Apology from Britain," *The Hindu*, 6 April 2019, https://www.thehindu.com/news/international/jallianwala-bagh-massacre-the-unending-wait-for-an-apology-from-britain/article26756834.ece (accessed 1 October 2020); "Jallianwala Bagh Centenary: UK MPs Discuss Issuing Apology but Government Refuses to do so," *Scroll.in*, 10 April 2019, https://scroll.in/latest/919561/jallianwala-bagh-centenary-uk-mps-discuss-issuing-apology-but-government-refuses-to-do-so (accessed 13 April 2019).
[8] Wagner, *Amritsar 1919*, 263–4.
[9] "Jallianwala Bagh: Indian Outrage over Revamp of Memorial," *BBC News*, 31 August 2021, https://www.bbc.co.uk/news/world-asia-india-58382434 (accessed 31 August 2021); Kim A. Wagner, "Jallianwala Bagh Victims' Memory

Image 1. The Well at Ajnala. Inside of the well following the excavation. Photo by Harvinder Chandi-garh.

Source: Wikimedia Commons.

Some of the residents of Ajnala, however, are determined to rectify this commemora-tive lacuna. Speaking a few days after the discovery of the bodies in 2014, Amarjit Singh Sarkaria, the head of the Gurdwara Shaheed Ganj Managing Committee, which assisted with the excavation, put it this way: "The whole of Ajnala was crying today. Nobody thought about these martyrs for 157 years. They deserve all prayers and will be laid to rest as per faith."[10] Since unearthing the bodies, Kochhar, the Gurdwara Committee, and other residents of Ajnala have petitioned both the state and central authorities in India to honour these "martyrs" through various commemorative activities, including the construction of a memorial monument and museum.[11] In January of 2015, the Com-mittee laid the foundation stone for a memorial monument situated atop the well in an attempt to reclaim these sepoys from this commemorative neglect and integrate them into India's national public memory. Yet, their efforts were beset by a number of difficul-ties. These included a lack of interest from government authorities who are reluctant to fund this endeavour, as well as disputes between Kochhar and the Gurdwara Committee. The commemorative project also involved difficult questions raised by professional

---

Deserves Better. Disneyfication isn't Preservation," *The Print*, 31 August 2021, https://theprint.in/opinion/jallianwala-bagh-victims-memory-deserves-better-disneyfication-isnt-preservation/725084/ (accessed 3 November 2021).

[10] Manjeet Sehgal, "Remains of 100 Indian Soldiers Excavated from Well in Punjab," *India Today*, 2 March 2014, https://www.indiatoday.in/india/story/punjab-well-ajnala-amritsar-remains-martyrs-revolt-of-1857-183315-2014-03-02 (accessed 20 September 2020).

[11] "The Black Hole."

archaeologists and scientists about whether the remains can be scientifically verified due to the improper methods used to unearth and preserve the remains.[12]

This article is about the contested historical narrations, memories, and ongoing efforts to commemorate the Ajnala Massacre. It reveals how the history and public memory of colonial violence remain poorly understood, and the ways that calls for the recognition of previously forgotten, absent, or erased memories can prompt difficult and highly politicized discussions about the meaning of history, identity, and politics. Taking inspiration from Shahid Amin's pioneering study on the Chauri Chaura "riot" of 1922, this article seeks to unpack the Ajnala Massacre as an historical event; a metaphor for colonial and anti-colonial narratives of empire; and as a site of contested memory.[13] In so doing, it argues that histories and memories of colonial violence are shaped as much by the politics of the present as they are by the scale and nature of the events themselves. The article begins by contextualizing these contestations within the wider "culture wars" currently being fought over the legacies of empire in both Britain and India. From there, the article explores both the facts of the massacre as well as the symbolic meanings attached to it within colonial narratives, particularly those produced by Cooper himself, who was responsible for the first efforts to "memorialize" this event. Next, the article considers how the ongoing efforts by the Sikh inhabitants of Ajnala to obtain wider recognition for the massacre and the sacrifice of these "martyrs" sits uncomfortably at the crossroads of highly contentious debates in India about history, national identity, and commemoration. Indeed, the divergent traditions of remembering and commemorating this massacre reveal not only radical differences between British and Indian commemorative traditions, but they also raise important questions about the ability of memory and history to overcome internal regional and religious differences across postcolonial India today.

Imperial Memory Wars

The last several decades have seen a resurgence of interest in the history of European imperialism, and have been characterized by increasingly fierce debates about the violent legacies of empire, decolonization, and the ways both former imperial powers and colonized nations have reoriented and reinvented themselves within the postcolonial present.[14] Today, these "imperial history wars," as described by Dane Kennedy, have also become an integral component of the wider culture wars raging across society.[15] Perhaps unsurprisingly, one of the key battlefields of these culture wars are the physical vestiges of empire: its cities and buildings, street names, and, of course, its monuments. As Dominik Geppert and Frank Lorenz Müller have pointed out, imperial "sites of memory" retain

---

[12] "No British was thrown into Kalianwala Khuh," 9 May 2014, *Hindustan Times*, https://www.hindustantimes.com/punjab/no-british-was-thrown-into-kalianwala-khuh/story-ao32bLd54vUFuMuvpQJDgN.html (accessed 8 May 2021).

[13] See Shahid Amin, *Event, Metaphor, Memory: Chauri Chaura 1922–1992* (Berkeley: University of California Press, 1995).

[14] Robert Gildea, *Empires of the Mind: The Colonial Past and Politics of the Present* (Cambridge: CUP, 2019); Dane Kennedy, *The Imperial History Wars: Debating the British Empire* (London: Bloomsbury, 2018).

[15] The ongoing controversy surrounding Nigel Biggar's "Ethics and Empire" project at Oxford, and the furious response to Bruce Gilley's article, "The Case for Colonialism," are two high-profile examples of this: James McDougall and others, "Ethics and Empire: an Open Letter from Oxford Scholars," *The Conversation*, 19 December 2017: https://theconversation.com/ethics-and-empire-an-open-letter-from-oxford-scholars-89333 (accessed 19 December 2017). There has also been a proliferation of various anti- and pro-colonial polemics, including Shashi Tharoor, *Inglorious Empire: What the British Did to India* (London: Hurst, 2017); and Jeremy Black, *Imperial Legacies: the British Empire around the* World (New York: Encounter Books, 2019).

continued relevance and a lasting capacity to elicit strong emotional responses from those who experience them.[16] We can see this quite vividly in the ways that once-dominant Eurocentric historical narratives and commemorative practices are currently being challenged by those seeking to incorporate more diverse perspectives and experiences from groups who have been hitherto marginalized or forgotten. In many cases, these movements directly challenge enduring narratives about the "positive" aspects of imperialism by highlighting instead the violent, brutal, and oppressive practices that sustained empire. In the UK, for example, the removal and replacement of the statue of slave trader Edward Colston in Bristol in 2020 provoked a furious right-wing backlash, prompting Robert Jenrick, the Secretary of State for Housing, Communities and Local Government, to vow to "save Britain's statues from woke militants" and "baying mobs."[17]

Since independence in 1947, Indians have removed, relocated, or re-appropriated colonial commemorative monuments and public spaces, while also erecting new memorials to their own national heroes.[18] In so doing, Indian nationalists have sought to deliberately repudiate what they see as the humiliating colonial narratives of the past, and to replace them with patriotic assertions of postcolonial nationhood. In the case of 1857, individuals who were once vilified by the British as "mutineers," or "traitors" have been transformed by nationalists into noble "freedom fighters" who fought in the "First War of Independence." One of the most poignant examples of this process began on 15 August 1947, the day India gained its independence, when a large crowd stormed the Memorial Gardens in the city of Kanpur (Cawnpore) and defaced the iconic angel statue that lay at the heart of the site's Memorial Well. Completed in 1865 to commemorate the massacre of over a hundred British women and children in July 1857, the Kanpur memorial was widely considered the most sacred and important site of colonial memory in all of India.[19] For many Indians, however, the memorial and its strict prohibition barring entry to non-Europeans served as a stinging reminder of colonial racial hierarchies and humiliation. In 1948, the memorial was relocated to the grounds of the Memorial Church in the Kanpur Cantonment. The following year, the gardens that surrounded the memorial were also renamed Nana Rao Park, in honour of Nana Sahib, a key rebel leader during 1857 and the alleged mastermind behind the massacre.[20] For the centenary celebrations of the Uprising in 1957, the city erected a new monument on the exact site

---

[16] Dominik Geppert and Frank Lorenz Müller, "Beyond National Memory. Nora's *Lieux de Mémoire* across an Imperial World," in ibid. (eds.), *Sites of Memory: Commemorating Colonial Rule in Nineteenth and Twentieth Centuries* (Manchester: Manchester University Press, 2015), 4–6.

[17] "Edward Colston Statue Replaced by Sculpture of Black Lives Matter Protester Jen Reid," *The Guardian*, 15 July 2020, https://www.theguardian.com/world/2020/jul/15/edward-colston-statue-replaced-by-black-lives-matter-protester (accessed 16 July 2020); Robert Jenrick, "We Will Save Britain's Statues from the Woke Militants Who Want to Censor Our Past" *The Telegraph*, 16 January 2021, https://www.telegraph.co.uk/news/2021/01/16/will-save-britains-statues-woke-militants-want-censor-past/ (accessed 17 January 2021); "Statues to Get Protection from 'Baying Mobs,'" *BBC News*, 17 January 2021: https://www.bbc.co.uk/news/uk-55693020 (accessed 17 January 2021).

[18] See, generally, Deborah Cherry, "The Afterlives of Monuments," *South Asian Studies* 29, no. 1 (2013): 1–14; and Stephen Heathorn, "The Absent Site of Memory: The Kanpur Memorial Well and the 1957 Centenary Commemoration of the Indian 'Mutiny,'" in *Memory, History, and Colonialism*, 73–116.

[19] On the significance of the Cawnpore Massacre and Memorial see: Patrick Brantlinger, *Rule of Darkness: British Literature and Imperialism, 1830–1914* (1988; Ithaca, NY: Cornell University Press, 1990), chap. 7; Andrew Ward, *Our Bones are Scattered: The Cawnpore Massacres and the Indian Mutiny of 1857* (London: John Murray, 1996); Lydia Murdoch, "'Supressed Grief': Mourning the Death of British Children and the Memory of the 1857 Indian Rebellion," *Journal of British Studies* 51, no. 2 (April 2012): 364–92; and Sebastian Pender, *The Commemoration and Memorialisation of the "Indian Mutiny," 1857–2007* (Unpublished PhD Diss., University of Cambridge, 2014).

[20] Heathorn, "The Absent Site of Memory," 73–116.

previously occupied by the Memorial Well. It was dedicated to Tatya Tope, one of the great heroes of the "First War of Independence."[21] In that same year the city of Meerut, where the Indian Uprising began, also marked the centenary celebrations by erecting a 100-ft white, marble tower, known as the Shaheed Smarak ("Martyrs Memorial"), in honour of the sepoys who began the "First War of Independence."

Yet, despite these iconoclastic repudiations of colonial commemorative narratives and their attendant sites of memory, the overall reaction of Indians towards their colonial past has been much more ambivalent. As Maria Misra has pointed out, vestiges of the Raj continue to shape the physical and cultural landscape of India today, and ordinary Indians treat many prominent colonial symbols and monuments with a combination of indifference or even sympathetic nostalgia[22] It is also difficult to disentangle attempts to refashion India's postcolonial national heritage from the complex, intense, and sometimes violent contests that are currently being fought over its political, cultural, social, linguistic, and religious character. As Romila Thapar has demonstrated, communal identities and ideologies have had a profound impact on the writing and interpretation of Indian history, which has often been mobilized in order to advance contemporary political goals.[23] Thus, even attempts to reclaim and refashion colonial monuments and narratives often take on a majoritarian character in the ways these are communicated to India audiences.[24]

To take one obvious example of this at work in the context of Ajnala, the "First War of Independence" was a term popularized in 1909 by Vinayak Damodar Savarkar, a right-wing Hindu nationalist, who later insisted that India belonged to Hindus.[25] The veneration by the Hindu right of "freedom fighters" and "martyrs" who fought against the British in 1857 and in the subsequent freedom struggle of the twentieth century, has been intimately tied up with their wider efforts to exclude other religious and social minorities in India, most notably Muslims.[26] History, heritage, and commemoration are being weaponized in order to propagate an exclusively Hindu vision of Indian culture and nationhood. The ongoing efforts by the Sikh inhabitants of Ajnala to construct a memorial to the massacred sepoys must thus be understood in this broader context of building locally-specific nationalist narratives that seek to reshape conventional understandings of Indian national identity and patriotism, both internally and in the face of India's former colonizers.

Mutiny and Massacre: Ajnala as Event and Colonial Metaphor

The discovery of the bodies at Ajnala helped fuel fierce debates about the violent history of the British Empire in India. Ajnala has been readily compared to the more well-known Jallianwala Bagh Massacre at Amritsar.[27] There, Indian soldiers under the command of

---

[21] Maria Misra, *Vishnu's Crowded Temple: India since the Great Rebellion* (New Haven, CT: Yale University Press, 2007), 6; Heathorn, "The Absent Site of Memory," 73–4.

[22] Maria Misra, "From Nehruvian Neglect to Bollywood Heroes: The Memory of the Raj in Post-war India," in Geppert and Müller, *Sites of Memory*, 187–206.

[23] Romila Thapar, "Communalism and the Historical Legacy: Some Facts," *Social Scientist* 18, no. 6-7 (1990): 4–20; ibid., *The Past as Present: Forging Contemporary Identities Through History* (New Delhi: Aleph, 2014).

[24] Amin, *Event, Metaphor, Memory*, 200.

[25] V.D. Savarkar, *The Indian War of Independence* (London: s.n., 1909). On the phenomenon of Hindutva, see Christophe Jaffrelot, *The Hindu Nationalist Movement and Indian Politics, 1925 to the 1990s* (1993; London: Hurst & Co., 1996).

[26] Misra, "From Nehruvian Neglect to Bollywood Heroes."

[27] "The Black Hole."

Brigadier-General Reginald E. Dyer opened fire on an unarmed crowd, killing an estimated 379 people and wounding at least 1,200 others. In this reading, it is easy to see Cooper's actions at Ajnala as part of a much longer tradition of brutal, racialized colonial violence systemic to British rule.[28] An alternative perspective, however, insists that these kind of incidents were "exceptional" moments, resulting from erratic actions of individual officers.[29] As the culture wars over the legacies of Britain's imperial past continue to rage across India and the UK, it seems important to reflect on how the undeniable violence of empire was justified by those who committed and supported these kinds of actions, and how this history has been interpreted and commemorated since. Whereas the inhabitants of Ajnala today are working to have the sepoys recognized as Indian heroes and victims of British cruelty, nineteenth century British audiences saw this event in a much different light. Britons in both India and the metropole widely praised Cooper's actions as a legitimate and necessary response to the atrocities attributed to Indian rebels. Indeed, Cooper himself attempted to fashion this massacre as a deliberate response to the massacre of British women and children at the hands of Indian rebels in Kanpur in July 1857.

The Indian Uprising began on 10 May 1857, when Indian sepoys stationed in the cantonment town of Meerut in northern India mutinied against their British officers after rumours circulated that the cartridges used for their new Enfield rifles were greased with cow and pig fat. Both Hindus and Muslims saw this as a deliberate attack against their religious customs and cultural traditions, prompting them to rise up and murder their British officers, along with any other European or Christian civilians they encountered, including women and children. The mutineers proceeded to Delhi, and a general uprising erupted as aggrieved peasants and elites alike rose up in a bid to oust their British masters. The sepoys who were killed at Ajnala belonged to the 26th Native Infantry (N.I.) regiment, which was stationed at the Mian Mir (Meean Meer) cantonment, just outside the city of Lahore. On 13 May 1857, fearing spreading disaffection throughout the army, British officers disarmed the 26th, along with several other regiments stationed at Mian Mir.[30] On 30 July, the nearly 635-man strong 26th N.I. rose up and killed their commanding officer, along with the regiment's sergeant-major, and two Indian officers.[31] The sepoys, along with a band of camp followers, then proceeded north, taking advantage of a large dust storm to conceal their movements.[32]

Immediately following this outbreak, the British despatched soldiers from both Lahore and Amritsar to pursue the mutineers, and enlisted the help of Sikh villagers in hunting down the sepoys.[33] The following day, villagers from the settlement of Dadian (Doodean) spotted the sepoys near the Ravi River and quickly sent word to the tehsildar (revenue collector) of one of the neighbouring districts, a man named Pram Nath.[34] After

---

[28] Wagner, *Amritsar 1919*; Kim A. Wagner, "'Calculated to Strike Terror': The Amritsar Massacre and the Spectacle of Colonial Violence," *Past & Present* 233, no. 1 (November 2016): 185–225.

[29] Ferdinand Mount, "They Would Have Laughed," *London Review of Books* 41, no. 7 (April 2019): 9–12.

[30] Ibid., 265.

[31] For the complex reasons sepoys mutinied, see: Wagner, *The Skull of Alum Bheg.*

[32] Roberts to Montgomery, 17 August 1857, *Government Records, vol. 7:1-2 – Punjab: Mutiny Records Correspondence* (Lahore: Punjab Government Press, 1911), pt. 1, para. 2, 387 [hereafter *Punjab: Mutiny Records vol. 7*].

[33] Introduction by Mr. Montgomery, Parliamentary Papers (PP), 1859 (238) XVIII.307, *Papers Relating to Mutiny in Punjab, 1857*, para. 64, 39 [hereafter *Papers Relating to Mutiny in Punjab*].

[34] Cooper to Roberts, 5 August 1857, *Punjab: Mutiny Records vol. 7*, para. 2, 390.

assembling local policemen and volunteers, Nath's force attacked the sepoys, around 150 of whom died in the bloody skirmish or drowned trying to escape. The remaining sepoys fled, and about 200 managed to swim across part of the river to a small island. Bloodied, exhausted, and demoralized from their ordeal, most of the sepoys surrendered willingly to Cooper and his men after they arrived on the scene. The sepoys thought they would be tried by court-martial.[35] With the aid of the villagers, Cooper and his men marched the sepoys nearly 10 kilometres to Ajnala, where they were then locked up in the *thana* (police station) and several other old buildings for the night (Image 2).

Early the next morning, 1 August 1857, Cooper sent his Muslim horsemen back to Amritsar, under the generous pretence of allowing them to celebrate Eid al-Adha.[36] In all likelihood, Cooper's real motivation for sending away these more experienced Muslim soldiers was that he doubted their loyalty, and feared they might rise up against him when they saw what he had in store for the captured sepoys. Once the Muslim soldiers were gone, Cooper ordered his remaining Sikh troopers to bring the prisoners out in groups of ten. The prisoners were bound together, marched before a firing squad, and summarily executed without a trial or hearing of any kind. By 10 am, 237 sepoys had been killed, and their bodies dumped into a large well by the village sweepers.[37] This left 45 still to be executed, but when Cooper and his men opened up their prison cell, they discovered that almost every-one inside had already died, mostly likely from a combination of heat stroke and suffocation after being locked inside the crowded cell with the only window provid-ing any sort of fresh air tightly closed and barricaded.[38] Cooper later mused how he had inadvertently re-enacted and inverted one of the most infamous massacres in the history of British India: the Black Hole of Calcutta.[39]

Cooper's actions met with strong approval from both John Lawrence, the Chief Com-missioner of Punjab, and even Governor-General Charles Canning.[40] Robert Montgomery, the Judicial Commissioner of Punjab, personally wrote to Cooper to convey his hearty congratulations for this "success."[41] When describing the slaughter of the 26th N.I. at Ajnala, Cooper adopted a gloating, self-satisfied tone:

> The execution at Ujnalla commenced at daybreak, and the stern spectacle was over in a few hours. Thus, within forty-eight hours from the date of the crime, there fell by the law nearly 500 men. All the crowds of assembled natives, to whom the crime was fully explained, con-sidered the act "righteous," but incomplete; because the magistrate did not hurl headlong

---

[35] Some sepoys tried to escape from the island, and Cooper estimates that at least 35 drowned in the river: ibid., paras. 14, 16, 391–2.

[36] Frederic Cooper, *The Crisis in the Punjab, from the 10th of May until the Fall of Delhi* (London: Smith, Elder and Co., 1858), 161.

[37] Cooper to Roberts, 5 August 1857, *Punjab: Mutiny Records vol. 7*, paras. 27–30, 393–4.

[38] Memorandum by Frederic Cooper, enclosed in Cooper to Roberts, 19 February 1858, *Government Records, vol. 8:1-2 – Punjab: Mutiny Records Correspondence* (Lahore: Punjab Government Press, 1911), pt. 1, para. 15, 274–5 [hereafter *Punjab: Mutiny Records vol. 8*]. There is some discrepancy in the numbers of sepoys who died at Ajnala here. In many cases, the total is given as 282, but in this report, Cooper states the number was 285.

[39] Cooper, *The Crisis in the Punjab*, 163. For the mythology surrounding this event see: Partha Chatterjee, *The Black Hole of Empire: History of a Global Practice of Power* (Princeton, NJ: Princeton University Press, 2012).

[40] John Lawrence instructed Robert Montgomery, the Judicial Commissioner, to personally write to Cooper and convey his "especial thanks" for "the very satisfactory manner in which he managed to capture and execute so large a body of mutineers": Brandreth to Montgomery, 21 August 1857, *Punjab: Mutiny Records vol. 7*, para. 1, 405; Temple to Edmon-stone, 25 May 1858, *Papers Relating to Mutiny in Punjab*, para 57, 20.

[41] Qtd. in Cooper, *The Crisis in the Punjab*, 168.

Image 2. Frederic Cooper.

Source: *Government Records, vol. 7:1-2 – Punjab: Mutiny Records Correspondence* (Lahore: Punjab Government Press, 1911), 389.

into the chasm, the rabble of men, women and children, who had fled miserably with the mutineers: they marvelled at the clemency and the justice of the British.[42]

We can see here in this passage how Cooper's destruction of the 26th was conceived of first, and foremost, as a spectacular form of communicative violence designed to instil terror and fear into Indian audiences. Yet rather than being an expression of colonial strength and invincibility, Cooper's actions – like those of many colonial officials who enacted other kinds of similarly brutal, exemplary violence – can be more convincingly explained as products of weakness, fear, and panic.[43] As Robert Montgomery later put it, this was a moment when British power in Punjab was "literally in extremity," and only the harshest and most severe measures could save it.[44] Even so, Cooper was

---

[42] Cooper, *The Crisis in the Punjab*, 163.

[43] Wagner, *Amritsar 1919*; Mark Condos, *The Insecurity State: Punjab and the Making of Colonial Power in British India* (Cambridge: CUP, 2017); and Thomas R. Metcalf, *Ideologies of the Raj*. The *New Cambridge History of India*, III.4 (Cambridge: Cambridge University Press, 1998), 44.

[44] Statement of Facts Connected with the Execution of the 26th Native Infantry, PP, 1859 (125) XXIII.499, *Letter from Sir. R. Montgomery to Lord Stanley, April 1859*, and *Statement of Facts Connect with Execution of 26th Native Infantry*, para. 6, 3 [hereafter *Letter from Montgomery*].

careful to justify this violence by emphasizing its legal and "righteous" character. "The punishment for mutiny is death" was a common refrain uttered by British officers during the Uprising, and was thus deemed the only justification required.[45] As Montgomery pointed out in a letter to Lord Stanley, the newly-minted Secretary of State for India: "they were murderers, mutineers and rebels, in the broadest sense. As such they were taken in *flagrante delicto*, and for such an offence the punishment of death is adjudged both in law and morals."[46]

The "righteousness" of Cooper's actions was further established by his decision to spare the women and children camp followers who had fled with the sepoys. Here, Cooper was alluding to one of the most infamous events of the Indian Uprising: the Kanpur (Cawnpore) Massacre, which had taken place just over two weeks earlier on 15 July. The slaughter of European women and children at Kanpur became the supreme signifier of Indian savagery and barbarism, and provided the most potent emotional rallying cry for the brutal, and often indiscriminate, retributive violence unleashed by the British during the suppression of the Uprising.[47] By emphasizing his decision not to emulate the "fiends" at Kanpur, Cooper sought to establish the moral legitimacy of his own massacre as a legitimate form of justice. At the same time, he also portrayed the executions at Ajnala as a deliberate and carefully choreographed re-enactment and inversion of the Kanpur Massacre. "There is a well at Cawnpore," he proudly declared, "but there is also one at Ajnala!"[48]

Cooper's efforts to style the Ajnala Massacre as a response to Kanpur can be seen as part of the first effort to commemorate or memorialize this massacre. By constructing this narrative, Cooper imbued the massacre with a potent symbolic significance. This was not just the just and deserved punishment of mutineers, but was a righteous form of retribution for the crimes and indignities suffered by the British race. Following the executions, Cooper ordered the village sweepers to erect what might be considered the first "monument" to the massacre. After filling in the well with charcoal, lime, and dirt, the sweepers created a large burial mound, in front of which Cooper intended to erect a commemorative stone tablet engraved with the words *the grave of the mutineers* written in Gurumukhi, Persian, and English in order to "long preserve in the pergunnah [district] the record of their just fate."[49] Although it is not clear whether Cooper ever got around to installing this macabre marquee, he noted with satisfaction how the burial mound could be seen from a great distance away due to its high position along the nearby road.[50] He obviously delighted in the symbolic power of the site, believing it would serve as an enduring monument to British "justice" that would strike terror into the hearts of all who would oppose them. Ultimately, neither Cooper nor his compatriots ever got around to erecting a more polished "monument" to the massacre, but this

---

[45] Introduction by Mr. Montgomery, *Papers Relating to Mutiny in Punjab*, para. 65, 39.

[46] Statement of Facts Connected with the Execution of the 26th Native Infantry, *Letter from Montgomery*, para. 5, 3.

[47] Jenny Sharpe, *Allegories of Empire: The Figure of Women in the Colonial Text* (Minneapolis: University of Minnesota Press, 1993); Ward, *Our Bones are Scattered*; Gautam Chakravarty, *The Indian Mutiny and the British Imagination* (Cambridge: Cambridge University Press, 2004). For an analysis of the way Indian rebels understood this violence, see Rudrangshu Mukherjee, "'Satan Let Loose Upon Earth': The Kanpur Massacres in India in the Revolt of 1857," *Past & Present*, 128 (Aug. 1990): 92–116.

[48] Cooper, *The Crisis in the Punjab*, 167.

[49] Ibid., paras. 31–2, 394.

[50] Ibid.

is hardly surprising. Although Cooper's actions were widely applauded both in India and the metropole, a minor public scandal erupted in March of 1859 when the Liberal MP, Charles Gilpin, denounced him in Parliament and claimed the massacre represented "almost the very blackest page in the emphatically black book of the Indian rebellion."[51] Britons at the time were also more concerned with commemorating their own trauma and martyrdom by highlighting the atrocities committed by Indian rebels at places like Kanpur, rather than the brutal violence they had enacted in revenge.[52] If they had done so, large swathes of northern India would have been dotted with such memorials.

It is important to emphasize that Cooper's decision to massacre the sepoys of the 26th N.I. at Ajnala was not an isolated incident, but was part of a much wider culture of imperial violence that emphasized the need for strong executive authority and swift, exemplary spectacles of punishment during times of crisis. Writing some years after the incident at Ajnala, Thomas Rice Holmes hit back against those who criticized Cooper's actions. "For this splendid assumption of responsibility," Holmes wrote, "Cooper was assailed, as other men of his mettle, both in the East and the West Indies, have been, by the vulgar cries of ignorant humanitarians."[53] Holmes' reference to "other men of his mettle" was a nod to Governor Edward Eyre, who had been at the centre of a prolonged, high-profile controversy after his brutal handling of the 1865 Morant Bay Uprising in Jamaica.[54] Although Eyre was ultimately acquitted from any wrongdoing his trial represented something of a turning point when it came to the British public's acceptance of large-scale, indiscriminate violence being used to suppress colonial revolts and uprisings. Fifteen years after Cooper's executions at Ajnala, another Punjab officer named John Lambert Cowan offered a similar defence of his decision to summarily execute 49 Namdhari Sikhs (known pejoratively as "Kookas") by cannonading, following a failed attack by them against the Muslim princely state of Malerkotla. However, whereas Cooper's actions had been widely supported and ultimately upheld by his superiors in both India and Britain, Cowan found himself severely reprimanded and removed from his position.[55] Following the infamous Jallianwala Bagh Massacre of 1919, General Dyer offered the same defence as Cooper and Cowan, arguing that his actions had been necessary to prevent the horrors of a second "Mutiny" from unfolding. Thus, as Kim Wagner has demonstrated, rather than being exceptional, Jallianwala Bagh was the culmination of this wider logic of colonial violence.[56]

Remembering the Sepoys: Ajnala as Postcolonial Metaphor and Memory

Sites of memory are also sites of forgetting, and those moments where they are neglected, lost, or "lain fallow" are instructive of the need for concealment, or attempts to overcome deep-seated trauma.[57] In the years following the events of 1857, the Ajnala

---

[51] *Hansard*, HC Deb. 14 March 1859, vol. 153, col. 146.

[52] On British colonial trauma, see: Christopher Herbert, *War of No Pity: The Indian Mutiny and Victorian Trauma* (Princeton, NJ: Princeton University Press, 2008); and Chakravarty, *The Indian Mutiny and the British Imagination*.

[53] T.R.E. Holmes, *A History of the Indian Mutiny, and of the Disturbances which Accompanied it among the Civil Population* (London: H. Allen & Co., 1883), 373.

[54] R.W. Kostal, *A Jurisprudence of Power: Victorian Empire and the Rule of Law* (Oxford: OUP, 2008).

[55] Condos, *The Insecurity State*, chap. 3; and Wagner, "'Calculated to Strike Terror.'"

[56] Wagner, *Amritsar 1919*; ibid., "'Calculated to Strike Terror.'"

[57] Dominik Geppert and Frank Lorenz Müller, "Beyond National Memory. Nora's *Lieux de Mémoire* across an Imperial World," in ibid. (eds.), *Sites of Memory: Commemorating Colonial Rule in Nineteenth and Twentieth Centuries*

Massacre gradually faded from collective memory in both Britain and India, but was kept alive, to some extent, at the local level. Following the massacre, the well became known as *Kalianwala Khuh* ("The Well of the Blacks"). The burial mound erected atop the well was still visible in the early twentieth century, but it had eroded and resembled an elevated sand hill. In 1957, the centenary celebrations for 1857 were even held on this site in the presence of the Chief Minister, Pratab Singh Kairon. In 1972, the residents of Ajnala built a gurdwara (a Sikh place of worship) over the well, and in 2007 the 150th anniversary commemorations of the Uprising were observed at the gurdwara.[58] In 2012, the towns-people of Ajnala formed a committee "to honour the martyrs by disinterring their remains from the well."[59] The committee built a new gurdwara nearby, and petitioned the Government of Punjab, the Archaeological Survey of India, and the central Government of India for assistance with the excavation. Their requests were ignored.

In the absence of any official support, the townspeople began excavation work on 28 February 2014. Following the discovery of the bodies, the committee renamed the well as the *Shaheedan da Khu* ("The Well of Martyrs") and again petitioned government authorities for support in constructing a memorial and museum in honour of the soldiers.[60] Although the excavation attracted widespread media attention in India, prompting several government authorities to visit the site, more substantial support never really materialized. The Punjab state government pledged to help construct a memorial and museum, but reportedly invested just Rs. 3 lakhs (roughly £3,150) in the project, meaning the Gurdwara Shaheed Ganj Committee had to assume the responsibility for constructing both the memorial and museum.[61] They have also repeatedly and unsuc-cessfully petitioned the Punjab state government to grant the sepoys official status as martyrs, and to be accorded full military honours.[62] In a 2017 interview with *The Times of India*, the Committee's President, Amarjit Singh Sarkaria, expressed disappointment with the lack of interest from successive state governments to grant them martyr status. "It was due to their sacrifice that we are enjoying the freedom," Sarkaria stated.[63] As of writing this article, the well in Ajnala is still not specifically listed as a pro-tected site, according to the Archaeological Survey of India, but the historic buildings of the Old Tehsil at Ajnala are.[64]

The apparent lack of interest from both the Punjab state government and the Govern-ment of India raises a number of questions about why there has been so little support for this commemorative project. From a historical point of view, any attempt by Punjab to celebrate its role in the "First War of Independence" or the Indian freedom struggle more generally is problematic. Unlike the North-Western Provinces and Awadh (what is

---

(Manchester: Manchester University Press, 2015), 9. See also Paul Ricoeur, *Memory, History, Forgetting,* trans. Kathleen Blamey and David Pellauer (Chicago: University of Chicago Press, 2004).

[58] Chaman Lal, "A Matter of Martyrs," *The Hindu,* 2 August 2014, https://www.thehindu.com/features/magazine/a-matter-of-martyrs/article6274960.ece (accessed 20 September 2020).

[59] Ibid.

[60] Ibid.

[61] G.S. Paul, "Govt Forgets, Residents Step in," *The Tribune,* 29 October 2017, https://www.tribuneindia.com/news/archive/features/govt-forgets-residents-step-in-488838, (accessed 28 September 2020).

[62] Yudhvir Rana, "Grant Martyr Status to Soldiers who died at Ajnala in 1857," *The Times of India,* 1 August 2017, https://timesofindia.indiatimes.com/city/chandigarh/grant-martyr-status-to-soldiers-who-died-at-ajnala-in-1857/articleshow/59853471.cms (accessed 20 September 2020).

[63] Ibid.

[64] Protected Monuments in Punjab, *Archaeological Survey of India,* https://asi.nic.in/protected-monuments-in-punjab/, (accessed 12 November 2021).

modern-day Uttar Pradesh), which saw widespread and sustained revolts against British authority by aggrieved peasants, dispossessed elites, and rebellious sepoys, there was nothing close to any kind of mass uprising or popular movement in Punjab in 1857–58.[65] The Punjabi peasantry, especially the Sikhs from the central Majha region, where Ajnala is situated, shared little sympathy with the Hindustani sepoys who had helped defeat them less than ten years prior in the Second Anglo-Sikh War (1848–49). On the contrary, Punjabis actively supported the British cause by helping to track down and eliminate mutinous regiments, as in the case of the 26th N.I., or by taking up service with the British forces to retake territories lost to the rebels in the North-Western Provinces and Awadh. The soldiers Cooper used to execute the sepoys of the 26th were recently-recruited Sikhs from the same region, which presents a particularly delicate issue for the Sikhs of Ajnala seeking to commemorate these martyrs.[66] Following the Uprising, Punjab was rewarded for its loyalty, becoming the main recruiting ground for the new Indian Army and the recipient of an array of preferential economic and political policies designed to ensure the province remained the loyal bulwark to British rule that it did until very late in the freedom struggle.[67] In modern-day Pakistan, which inherited the lion's share of Punjab during Partition in 1947, celebrations of 1857 as the "First War of Independence" are extremely muted, and some Pakistanis actually continue to commemorate certain British figures as "heroes."[68]

For the reigning right-wing Hindu Bharatiya Janata Party (BJP) Government of India, the Ajnala Massacre holds little political or ideological interest because the commemoration or mythologization of this history can do little to advance their goal of transforming India into a Hindu Rashtra (nation). Traditionally, the Hindu right has tended to focus on celebrating iconic, Hindu "martyrs" who fought in the cause of freedom – figures like Nana Sahib or the Rani of Jhansi[69] – but the mixed religious backgrounds of the sepoys of the 26th N.I. makes this more complicated.[70] BJP government officials have also shown more interest recently in re-writing India's ancient history in order to emphasize the cultural and scientific achievements of the ancient Vedic period – sometimes making rather outlandish claims that their Hindu ancestors invented aircraft or cosmetic surgery.[71] Alongside this, the Hindu right has also shown itself to be much more concerned with emphasizing the historical oppression and crimes committed by India's Muslim Mughal rulers, rather than its British colonial overlords.[72] The fact that the most vocal calls for a commemorative

---

[65] Wagner, *The Skull of Alum Bheg*.

[66] Cooper, *The Crisis in the Punjab*, 161.

[67] Tan Tai Yong, *The Garrison State: Military, Government and Society in Colonial Punjab, 1849–1947* (New Delhi and London: Sage, 2005); Ian Talbot, *The Punjab and the Raj 1849–1947* (New Delhi: Manohar, 1988).

[68] Haroon Khalid, "1857 Revolt: Why Pakistan Ignores the Rebels and Honours Three British Officials Instead," *Scroll.in*, 20 May 2016, https://scroll.in/article/808375/1857-revolt-why-pakistan-ignores-the-rebels-and-honours-three-british-officials-instead (accessed 23 September 2020).

[69] Savarkar, *The Indian War of Independence*, 22–34, 307–16. The recently-released historical epic, *Manikarnika: The Queen of Jhansi* (2019) offers a more contemporary example of this phenomenon.

[70] Most of the sepoys appear to have been Hindus, but there were some Muslims as well: Cooper to Roberts, 5 August 1857, *Punjab: Mutiny Records vol. 7*, para, 28, 394.

[71] Rupam Jain and Tom Lasseter, "By Rewriting History, Hindu Nationalists Aim to Assert their Dominance over India," *Reuters*, 6 March 2018, https://www.reuters.com/investigates/special-report/india-modi-culture/ (accessed 4 October 2020); Vinaya Deshpande, "'Rishi has Given Guidelines to Make Planes,'" *The Hindu*, 4 January 2015, https://www.thehindu.com/news/cities/mumbai/first-man-to-build-and-fly-an-aircraft-was-indian/article6753840.ece (accessed 4 October 2020).

[72] The rancorous controversy over the destruction of the Babri Masjid Mosque, or the vile attacks launched against American scholar Audrey Truschke's work on the Mughal Emperor Akbar are all examples of this: Vidya Subrahmanian,

monument and museum at Ajnala come from the region's local Sikh organizations are also unlikely to increase the chances that this project becomes any kind of priority for the current BJP regime. The decision by the Martyrs Memorial Committee to cremate the remains of the sepoys at Ajnala, according to Hindu and Sikh burial customs, is also a somewhat sensitive issue. Some of the sepoys massacred at Ajnala were Muslims, who bury their dead, but it is impossible to differentiate Hindu, Sikh, and Muslim remains.[73] In this sense, the commemorative efforts of the residents of Ajnala seem to have fallen prey, at least in part, to the communal fault lines which have plagued India during both the colonial and postcolonial periods.[74] Finally, India has not always shown the greatest concern with preserving its cultural heritage. For years now, the Ministry of Culture and its attendant organizations in charge of preserving and maintaining historic monuments and other cultural artefacts have remained underfunded. Historic sites are threatened by rising levels of pollution and India's challenging climate, while priceless archival documents have in turn been lost or destroyed due to neglect and lack of training.[75] The appalling human tragedy currently unfolding in India as a result of the global pandemic makes it unlikely that this situation will change any time soon.

Archaeological and forensic analyses of the remains have also cast some doubt on whether these remains belong to the 26th N.I. In 2016, the Punjab Government's Department of Archaeology and Museums commissioned a team of researchers led by J.S. Sehrawat from Panjab University to conduct a forensic analysis of the human remains and material objects found in the well. The initial report produced by Sehrawat and his team concluded that the material objects found alongside the remains – bracelets, necklaces, arm bands, and coins and medals bearing the likeness of Queen Victoria – strongly suggested that these belonged to the sepoys of the 26th who were executed by Cooper in 1857.[76] However, Sehrawat's report also noted that "some amateur local historians" believe the remains were victims of Partition violence in 1947, while others believe they belong to victims of other violent episodes separate from either 1857 or 1947.[77] In October of 2017, Sehrawat's preliminary analysis of the DNA tests on the remains indicated that they belonged to individuals hailing from Bihar, Uttar Pradesh, and West Bengal.[78] This would tend to confirm the historical narrative, since the sepoys from the 26th N.I. were most likely Purbiyas, who were recruited from these regions.

"Babri Masjid's Destruction Laid the Foundation of Modi's New India of Today," *The Wire*, 6 December 2018, https://thewire.in/politics/babri-masjid-narendra-modi-bjp (accessed 4 October 2020); Audrey Truschke, "'Some of the Hate Mail is Chilling': Historian Audrey Truschke on the Backlash to her Aurangzeb Book," *Scroll.in*, 25 May 2017, https://scroll.in/article/838539/aurangzeb-is-controversial-because-of-indias-present-not-past-says-audrey-truschke (accessed 27 May 2017).

[73] According to Chaman Lal, the Martyrs Memorial Committee was aware of these difficulties, and included rituals from Hindu, Sikh, and Muslim traditions during the cremation ceremony in recognition of this: Chaman Lal, "Honouring the Martyrs 157 Years Later – Cremation of 282 Martyrs on 1st August 2014" (unpublished research paper), https://www.researchgate.net/publication/280405241_Ajnala-The_Blackwell_story (accessed 9 May 2021).

[74] On the history and legacies of communalism, see: Gyanendra Pandey, *The Construction of Communalism in Colonial North India* (Delhi: OUP, 1990; David Ludden, ed., *Contesting the Nation: Religion, Community, and the Politics of Democracy in India* (Philadelphia: University of Pennsylvania Press, 1996).

[75] Maria Thomas, "The Good, the Bad, and the Ugly of Heritage Conservation in India," *Quartz India*, 18 April 2018, https://qz.com/india/1254201/world-heritage-day-the-good-the-bad-and-the-ugly-of-conserving-history-in-india/ (accessed 4 October 2020); Dinyar Patel, "In India, History Literally Rots Away," *The New York Times*, 20 March 2012, https://india.blogs.nytimes.com/2012/03/20/in-india-history-literally-rots-away/ (accessed 23 March 2012).

[76] Jagmahendar Singh Sehrawat, Raj Kamal Pathak, and Jaspreet Kaur, "Human Remains from Ajnala, India, 2014," *Bioarchaelogy of the Near East* 10 (2016), 86.

[77] Ibid., 83.

[78] "The Well of 1857 Truth," *The Tribune*, 29 October 2017, https://www.tribuneindia.com/news/archive/features/the-well-of-1857-truth-488818 (accessed 28 September 2020).

In 2019, a peer-reviewed study published by Sehrawat and Monika Singh analyzing the dental remains again suggested that these remains came from the sepoys of the 26th N.I.[79] However, a more comprehensive forensic analysis subsequently performed by Sehrawat and his colleagues has cast some doubt on their earlier findings, suggesting the remains may belong to ethnic groups hailing from modern-day Pakistan and Iran, including Pashtuns.[80] If the remains do, indeed, belong to groups from these regions, this would undermine both the historical record, as well as the claims by the residents of Ajnala that they should be commemorated as "Indian" heroes. The results of an even more extensive DNA analysis are still forthcoming, but, as Sehrawat and his colleagues have acknowledged, the "non-scientific" methods of excavation used by the amateur team that uncovered the remains has made it quite challenging to analyze them accurately.[81] As a result, it may not even be possible for existing scientific methods to provide a definitive answer to this question.

In a sense, the remains at Ajnala have become floating signifiers, open to different meanings and significance, depending on who is staking claim to them. For many of the residents of Ajnala, the historical record and archaeological evidence "prove" they are heroes and martyrs from 1857. For scientists, like Sehrawat, the remains only become "legible" and imbued with significance through verifiable, scientific quantification. For government authorities, whether at the state or federal level, these remains only become significant insofar as they can be weaved into the wider historical narratives and identities. At the state level, Punjab's complicated history with colonialism, particularly the vital role it played in suppressing the Uprising of 1857, makes it somewhat awkward for the government to highlight the province's role in the "First War of Independence." As for the lack of resonance with the Central Government, there is little here for the BJP to exploit in order to advance their Hindutva agenda, since the sepoys were from mixed religious backgrounds and were not massacred at the hands of Muslim tyrants. Ultimately, Ajnala demonstrates the difficulties of crafting and imposing coherent, unified narratives of the past in a pluralistic country like India, which has so many complex, sometimes competing, traditions, identities, and histories.

Conclusion

A circular memorial now stands atop the well at Ajnala. An inscription written in Gurumukhi reads: "The memorial of 282 martyred soldiers of 1857 when they were killed and dumped here." A nearby stone marker, adorned in the colours of the Indian national flagreads in English: "Salute to Martyrs of 1857 26 Bengal Inf." An arched gateway above one of the roads to Ajnala reads *Kaalianwala Shaheedi Khu, Yaadgari Gate* (the "Remembrance Gate of the Martyred"), and a new gurdwara, The Gurdwara of the Martyred and of the Martyred Well, has also been built near the site. Inside the gurdwara, a large collection box decorated in blue rests before the Guru Granth Sahib (the central

---

[79] J.S. Sehrawat and Monika Singh, "Forensic Odontological Sex Determination of Ajnala Skeletal Remains Based on the Statistical Equations Generated from the Odontometrics of Known Teeth," *Forensic Science International: Reports* 1 (November 2019).

[80] J.S. Sehrawat, Niraj Rai, Wolfram Meier-Augenstein, "Identification of Ajnala Skeletal Remains using Multiple Forensic Anthropological Methods and Techniques: A Bioarchaeological Report," *Journal of Archaeological Science: Reports* 32 (August 2020), 102434.

[81] Ibid.

Image 3. Kalianwala Khu. The Ajnala Memorial under Construction. Photo by Harvinder Chandigarh. Source: Wikimedia Commons.

Sikh holy text used for prayers) so that people can donate money for the maintenance of the *Shaheedi Khu* (the "Martyrs' Well"). Yet, despite these efforts, the Ajnala Massacre remains largely absent from national memory (Image 3).

How are we to make sense of the Ajnala Massacre, its contested meanings, and as a site of memory? As an event, the massacre was yet another example of the brutal violence that was central to colonial rule. As a metaphor, the shifting meanings and significance attached to the massacre by British and, subsequently, by Indian audiences demonstrate the malleability of historical narratives, and the ways that history is mediated by the politics of the present. the marginalized position of this event within the history of British India reminds us that the systemic violence of empire still remains poorly understood and is often brushed aside as the "exceptional" excesses of a few "bad apples." Contemporary British audiences are still struggling to come to terms with much more well-known colonial atrocities or instances of brutal callousness, such as the Jallianwala Bagh Massacre or the 1943 Bengal famine. So, it remains to be seen whether Ajnala will begin to figure more prominently in these discussions.[82] And, even if it does, the increasingly polarized debates surrounding the legacies of empire do not augur particularly well for the possibility of a more nuanced and critical reckoning with this history. For Indian audiences,

---

[82] See, for example, the backlash that has accompanied the publication of Sathnam Sanghera, *Empireland: How Imperialism has Shaped Modern Britain* (London: Viking, 2021).

Image 4. "The Remembrance Gate of the Martyred." Photo by Professor Chaman Lal.

Ajnala cannot be easily weaponized by either the Hindu Right against its internal enemies, or the Congress and its supporters who have equally nothing to gain from excoriating British rule. Ajnala is also difficult to insert into the already considerably rich historiographical and commemorative traditions of 1857. There are no great heroes, like Mangal Pandey, Nana Sahib, Tatya Tope, or the Rani of Jhansi, to equal the villainy of Cooper and rally the nation. As Shahid Amin reminds us, it is impossible to ever fully escape the hegemonic power of both colonial and nationalist narratives when writing the history of highly politicized events such as this (Image 4).[83]

As a site of memory, the well at Ajnala has also thus far resisted any fixed, singular meaning. The lack of consensus among locals about who the bodies belong to, coupled with the absence of any kind of authoritative, verifiable scientific analysis to support one particular historical narrative has meant that the bodies have become floating signifiers, empty vessels upon which individuals and groups can ascribe their own meanings and significance. For many of the inhabitants of Ajnala, these are the bodies of heroic martyrs, who died in the cause of Indian freedom, but it is unclear if this particular narrative will gain greater traction or resonance beyond the locality. Recently, Chris Moffat has suggested that history is an inheritance and the figures of the past continue to "haunt" the present, demanding our engagement with it.[84] It remains to be seen whether and how the ghosts of the sepoys at Ajnala will be heard.

Acknowledgement

I would first like to thank the editors of this special edition, Cynthia Prescott and Janne Lahti, for inviting me to contribute to this volume, and for their incisive editorial commentary. Reeju Ray, Derek Elliott, and Kim Wagner, also all provided helpful and constructive feedback on earlier

---

[83] Amin, *Event, Metaphor, Memory*, 118.
[84] Chris Moffat, *India's Revolutionary Inheritance: Politics and the Promise of Bhagat Singh* (Cambridge: CUP, 2019).

drafts of this piece, while the anonymous reviewers helped me sharpen and clarify aspects of its analysis. Finally, I am grateful for the assistance of Chaman Lal, who shared photographs and reflections from his visit to Ajnala, and also to Satvinder Juss.

Disclosure Statement

No potential conflict of interest was reported by the author(s).

ORCID

Mark Condos ⓘ http://orcid.org/0000-0001-7211-4224

Belgian Monuments of Colonial Violence: the Commemoration of Martyred Missionaries

Idesbald Goddeeris

ABSTRACT
Present-day scholarship on Black Lives Matter and the decolonization of public space has largely focused on the monuments that have raised societal criticism. Commemorative markers for missionaries have so far largely fallen beyond these debates. This article asks why this has been the case, how missionaries are remembered and in which ways they connect to the present-day criticism of problematic memorials. More particularly, it analyzes the memorialization of martyrs, i.e. missionaries who were killed during their mission, and works with the case of Belgium, a country that has witnessed campaigns against statues of Leopold II and his collaborators in the Congo Free State.

The article reveals that the only direct references to colonial violence in Belgian public space are tributes to martyred missionaries. Although explicit reference to martyrdom has gradually faded (but not completely disappeared), colonial language and frames have not, white individuals' commitment and victimhood being emphasized and contrasted with collective and anonymous indigenous savagery. At the same time, the article demonstrates the complexity of dealing with these monuments. They also serve as sites of mourning and family reunion and honor individuals that are not associated with colonialism but, on the contrary, are being venerated beyond Europe.

Missionary history has for a long time been written by clergy, who mostly elaborated on the cases of "their" congregations and often presented achievements in an almost hagiographical way. However, present-day researchers increasingly emphasize the inextricable links between mission and empire. Colonialism went far beyond political, economic or military dominance and included cultural, social and psychological hegemony. Missionaries were crucial actors in achieving the latter. They spread a discourse of European and Christian superiority that portrayed local populations as childish, primitive and backward. They reinforced racial classifications and created rifts between pagans and believers. They transformed social structures by introducing new concepts (from agricultural cooperatives to the nuclear family) and moral standards (such as chastity; in spite of the fact that missionaries are now increasingly being associated with sexual abuse).

They separated children from their environment and turned them into controllable subjects. And in the metropole, they were key actors in the mobilization for and legitimation of the colonial project.[1]

Little wonder that missionary statues have recently been under attack in several countries. Already before the Black Lives Matter summer of 2020, some monuments depicting white priests towering over adoring indigenous worshippers were criticized for their racist setting. A statue in the Dutch city of Tilburg has regularly been the subject of societal debate; one in a district of the Belgian city of Antwerp has received a contextualizing plaque in 2015; and a monument in St. Louis, Missouri, for a Belgian Jesuit who in the mid-nineteenth century worked among Native Americans was removed in the same year.[2] During Black Lives Matter, the iconoclasm in California especially targeted the Spanish Franciscan Junípero Serra, who had spread Catholicism throughout the region in the eighteenth century (and had been canonized in 2015) and was accused of having destroyed local cultures. His statues in Los Angeles, San Francisco and Sacramento were torn down by protesters. One in Ventura was removed as a precaution by the city council, and the Serra statue in Palma, Spain, on his native island of Mallorca, was defaced with red paint and the word "racista".[3]

However, not all missionaries have fallen into disgrace. The residents of the Greenlandic capital Nuuk in July 2020 voted to preserve the statue of the Danish missionary Hans Egede, which had been vandalized with red paint and the inscription "decolonize".[4] Moreover, many more statues for missionaries have not been questioned at all. On the contrary, some of them remain widely celebrated in their former mission areas. Their parishes, congregations or educational institutions even erect new monuments.[5] Secularized and non-Christian authorities also honor missionaries, for instance for their linguistic research and their nation-building, as happens with Johann Ernst Hanxleden, Benjamin Bailey, Hermann Gundert and Ferdinand Kittel in the South Indian states of Kerala and Karnataka.

Present-day scholarship on Black Lives Matter and the decolonization of the public space has largely neglected these aspects. Much of the literature focuses on monuments

---

[1] Karen Vallgårda, "Were Christian missionaries colonizers? Reorienting the debate and exploring new research trajectories," *Interventions* 18, no. 6 (2016): 865–886; Mak Geertje, Monteiro Marit & Wesseling Elisabeth, "Child Separation. (Post)Colonial Policies and Practices in the Netherlands and Belgium," *BMGN - Low Countries Historical Review* 135, no. 3–4 (2020): 4–28.

[2] Namely the statue of Peter "Peerke" Donders in Tilburg (Waldy, "Ophef over het standbeeld van missionaris Peerke Donders in Tilburg," NPO Radio1, https://www.nporadio1.nl/nieuws-en-co/onderwerpen/77084-2021-05-20-ophef-over-het-standbeeld-van-missionaris-peerke-donders-in-tilburg (accessed 15 March 2022), of Constant De Deken in Wilrijk (Idesbald Goddeeris, "Colonial Streets and Statues: Postcolonial Belgium in the Public Space," *Postcolonial Studies* 18, no. 4 (2015): 397–409; and of Pieter Jan De Smet in Saint Louis (Nathan Rubbelke, "Complaints prompt Catholic university to remove statue of priest praying over Indians," The College Fix, https://www.thecollegefix.com/complaints-prompt-catholic-university-to-remove-statue-of-priest-praying-over-indians/ (accessed 15 March).

[3] Abel R. Gomez, "Statues topple and a Catholic church burns as California reckons with its Spanish colonial past," The Conversation, https://theconversation.com/statues-topple-and-a-catholic-church-burns-as-california-reckons-with-its-spanish-colonial-past-142809 (accessed 15 March).

[4] Mikkel Schøler, "Greenland Decides to Keep Egede Statue in Place," Over the Circle, https://overthecircle.com/2020/07/22/greenland-decides-to-keep-egede-statue-in-place/ (accessed 15 March).

[5] Some examples: KN Redactie, "Keniaanse parochie eert Nederlandse priester met beeld," Katholiek Nieuwsblad, https://www.kn.nl/nieuws/lokaal/keniaanse-parochie-eert-nederlandse-priester-hij-gaf-zichzelf-voor-anderen/ (accessed 15 March); Jayzl Nebre-Villafania, "Relief of Fr. Jules Sepulchre," Wikipedia, https://en.wikipedia.org/wiki/File:Relief_of_Fr._Jules_Sepulchre_in_the_Philippines.jpg (accessed 15 March); Tim Moore, "Statue of Gustavo Le Paige," Alamy, https://www.alamy.com/stock-photo-statue-of-gustavo-le-paige-outside-the-archaeological-museum-in-san-35918282.html (accessed 15 March); Idesbald Goddeeris, *Missionarissen: geschiedenis, herinnering, dekolonisering* (Leuven: LannooCampus, 2021): 138–141 (with examples of statues for Belgian missionaries in Congo and India).

that have received the most criticism. Communication scientist Christiana Abraham explains that monuments are not neutral, but "can be viewed as forceful forms of selected memory framing socially constructed public consciousness".[6] Philosopher Caesar Alimsinya Atuire refutes common presumptions, for instance that few people notice statues, that they are an important part of our collective history, that it is unfair to judge persons from the past with today's criteria, and that the fact all humans have flaws, or that many statues have aesthetic and historical value can excuse problematic monuments.[7] Landscape architect Kamni Gill and others discuss how contested monuments should be dealt with.[8]

In this article, I will highlight commemorative markers for missionaries who have so far largely fallen beyond the debate and explore why this has been the case, how they are remembered and in which ways they connect to the present-day criticism of problematic memorials. I will do so by focusing on the commemoration of a particular group: martyrs, i.e. missionaries who were killed during their mission (see below for a more elaborated definition). This choice immediately suggests the complexity of memorialization. On the one hand, most of the martyred missionaries came to an end in periods of violent resistance against colonial rule or foreign interference: circumstances that were long condemned but are now gaining more and more sympathy, or at least understanding, in spite of the use of violence. On the other hand, the martyrs themselves compel admiration for their perseverance in faith. The adoration for martyrs stretches back to antiquity and was revived by Pope John Paul II who in an apostolic letter from 1994 called to keep the memory alive of Christian martyrs in the twentieth century and established the New Martyrs Commission.[9] Martyrdom is also cherished in other religions (e.g. Judaism and Islam) and secular groups (e.g. revolutionary movements and independence fighters), but this falls beyond the scope of this study.[10]

By examining both the markers themselves – including the iconography and the texts on pedestals – and the coverage of their establishment and celebration in newspapers, I will analyze the commemoration of martyred missionaries in the public space and find out why they have been ignored. Is this because they are less overtly disturbing, for instance less connected with colonial discourse and racist representation? Or because they were erected in other, for instance more recent eras? Or because they are located in less populated villages or less public spaces (e.g. churches), far from the cities where much of the protest so far had been concentrated?

The article examines the case of Belgium. As I explain in the first section following this introduction, Belgium has already since the beginning of the century been the scene of campaigns against statues of Leopold II and his collaborators in the Congo Free State, but a larger number of monuments for missionaries have almost entirely been kept out

---

[6] Christiana Abraham, "Toppled Monuments and Black Lives Matter: Race, Gender, and Decolonization in the Public Space. An Interview with Charmaine A. Nelson," *Atlantis* 42, no. 1 (2021): 3.

[7] Caesar Alimsinya Atuire, "Black Lives Matter and the Removal of Racist Statues. Perspectives of an African," *Inquiries into Art, History, and the Visual* 21, no. 2 (2020): 449–467.

[8] Kamni Gill, Imke van Hellemondt, Janike Kampevold Larsen, Sonia Keravel, Bruno Notteboom and Bianca Maria Rinaldi, "Towards a Culture of Care," *Journal of Landscape Architecture* 15, no. 2 (2020): 4–5.

[9] See the introduction in Andrea Riccardi, *Il secolo del martirio. I cristiani nel Novecento* (Milan: Mondadori, 2000 and 2009); Jan Willem van Henten and Ihab Saloul, "Introduction," in *Martyrdom: Canonisation, Contestation and Afterlives*, ed. Ihab Saloul and Jan Willem van Henten (Amsterdam: Amsterdam University Press, 2020): 16.

[10] Jay Winter, *War beyond Words. Languages of Remembrance from the Great War to the Present* (Cambridge University Press, 2017), 122, 125 and 137; van Henten and Saloul, "Introduction", 11–32.

of the debate. The same applies to martyrs, which will be the focus of the second section. I will give an overview of missionaries who died a violent death and are commemorated in the public space and discuss the criteria for martyrdom and how this evolved over time. The third and the fourth section will focus on martyrs in two particular mission destinations: China and Congo. These two cases facilitate a comparison between a Belgian colony (Congo) and a region that was not formally colonized (China). In the conclusion, I will demonstrate that martyrs – and especially those in China and Congo – constitute the largest group of honored missionaries. Even more, their commemorative markers are the only references to colonial violence in the Belgian public space.

Belgium's Colonial Past and Heritage

The Black Lives Matter protests of the summer of 2020 have resonated across the globe. English-language media and scholarly literature have especially focused on the US and the UK, but also regularly refer to Belgium.[11] This should come as no surprise. The Congo Free State – the Belgian king Leopold II's private property established at the Conference of Berlin (1885) – is reputed to have been one of the most violent colonial regimes. In the early twentieth century, fierce international criticism led to the take-over by the Belgian state and the transformation into the Belgian Congo. One hundred years later, Adam Hochschild's bestseller *King Leopold's Ghosts* and Peter Bate's documentary *Congo: White King, Red Rubber, Black Death* renewed public attention. As a result, monuments to Leopold II and his so-called Congo pioneers, i.e. Belgians who died in the Congo Free State, have since 2004 regularly been vandalized with red paint or graffiti. Authorities have always fixed the damage, although at least nine cities and municipalities have contextualized "their" monuments with information plaques.[12] The criticism even crossed borders and a #LeopoldMustFall movement at Queen Mary, University of London, in 2016 successfully campaigned for the removal of two plaques commemorating Leopold II's visit in 1887.[13] In Belgium itself, it was only in the summer of 2020 that local authorities for the first time removed some monuments, inter alia in Mons, Ekeren (Antwerp), Leuven, and Ghent.[14]

The great attention to the public space in Belgian postcolonial debates is also caused by the sheer number of colonial statues in Belgium, which results from a deliberate propaganda campaign in the interwar period and the 1950s in order to rehabilitate Leopold II and to find support for the colonial project. Matthew G. Stanard has studied this extensively in two monographs, the first on Belgian colonial propaganda and the second on the country's memory of its colonial past. This second book highlights monuments and street names and includes a link to an online spreadsheet of all markers.[15] Stanard counts 442 markers that celebrate colonizers and/or the colony in general. He could

---

[11] Abraham, "Toppled Monuments," 2; Gill and others, "Towards a Culture of Care," 4.

[12] Ostend (September 2016), Geraardsbergen (December 2016), Ghent (March 2017), Hasselt (May 2018), Ekeren (August 2018), and Mechelen (May 2019). See Goddeeris, *Missionarissen*, 156–157.

[13] CIGH Exeter, "Leopold Must Fall," Imperial & Global Forum, https://imperialglobalexeter.com/2016/06/28/leopold-must-fall/ (accessed 15 March); Belga, "A London university removes plaques in honour of Leopold II," The Brussels Times, https://www.brusselstimes.com/news/belgium-all-news/40517/a-london-university-removes-plaques-in-honour-of-leopold-ii/ (accessed 15 March).

[14] Idesbald Goddeeris, "Black Lives Matter in Belgium (June-July 2020). A catalyst in postcolonial memory?", *Rosa Luxemburg Stiftung. Dossiers*, https://www.rosalux.eu/en/article/1796.black-lives-matter-in-belgium-june-july-2020.html.

[15] Matthew G. Stanard, *Selling the Congo: A History of European Pro-Empire Propaganda and the Making of Belgian Imperialism* (Lincoln NE: University of Nebraska Press, 2011) and Matthew G. Stanard, *The Leopard, the Lion, and the Cock.*

confirm that 309 of them are still standing: at least 145 monuments and 164 streets in Belgium refer to Congo (and Ruanda-Urundi). Of these, 129 are located in Flanders (the northern and Dutch-speaking half of Belgium), 112 in Wallonia (the southern and largely French-speaking part) and 68 in Brussels (the bilingual capital in the center).[16]

Among them, he found 20 markers for missionaries, namely 9 street names, 3 collective monuments, 3 statues, 4 other memorials, and 1 plaque. This, however, is a huge underestimation. In Flanders alone, I located public remembrances for 91 missionaries who worked in the Congo: 22 monuments, 27 plaques, 48 street names and 3 other markers.[17] This is almost as many as the 118 markers for secular colonials that Stanard counted in Flanders.[18]

There are even many more monuments for missionaries who worked in regions other than Congo, such as China, India, the United States, and Latin America. In all, the Flemish public space has 157 markers for 102 missionaries beyond Congo. This number is amplified by the huge attention to Father Damien, a missionary who in the 1860s went to Hawaii, in 1873 settled in the leprosy colony of Molokai, and in 1889 died from the disease.[19] Damien, who was an international celebrity already during his lifetime and was canonized in 2009, has at least 54 monuments and streets in Flanders. But even if we exclude him, there are more than twice as many commemorative markers for missionaries (in Congo and beyond) than for secular colonials.

Regarding the commemoration of missionaries, Flanders seems to take a unique position. The other regions in Belgium – Brussels and Wallonia – pay far less tribute to missionaries: whereas Flanders has 257 markers for missionaries, Brussels has only 5 monuments and statues for Father Damien and 1 street for another missionary, and Wallonia just a few markers for Father Damien and 6 for other missionaries.[20] Of the latter, two died a martyr death; in addition, there is also a memorial for the Congo martyrs in Gentinnes, Walloon Brabant (see below).

The vast amount of commemorative markers for missionaries in Flanders is explained by the fact that the greatest portion of Belgian missionaries came from that region. In 1948, for instance, Wallonia provided just 16.4% of the missionaries in Belgian Congo.[21] The two regions indeed differ: whereas Wallonia industrialized earlier and had a more socialist and less religious past, Flanders had a more rural and Catholic character until post-industrial transformations from the 1960s onwards. Also from an international perspective, Flanders stands out. Its number of missionary vocations was extremely high: in 1940, Flemings accounted for less than 1% of global Catholics, but provided almost 10% of the Catholic missionaries.[22] The huge presence of missionaries in the public space also seems unmatched in other countries.

Colonial Memories and Monuments in Belgium (Leuven: Leuven University Press, 2019). The link on https://lup.be/collections/contact-91252/products/108258.

[16] Stanard 2019 and https://lup.be/pages/digital-appendix-the-leopard-the-lion-and-the-cock.

[17] On top of that, 5 more worked in Congo, but also in other colonies. See Goddeeris, *Missionarissen*.

[18] The total of 129 minus the three streets, two collective monuments, three statues and three memorials for missionaries in Flanders. See Goddeeris, *Missionarissen*, 30 for the details.

[19] A discussion of Father Damien from a postcolonial angle: Pennie Moblo, "Blessed Damien of Moloka'i: The Critical Analysis of Contemporary Myth," *Ethnohistory* 44, no. 4 (1997): 691–726.

[20] Goddeeris, *Missionarissen*, 30 and 183 (footnote 12).

[21] Jean-Luc Vellut, "Les Belges au Congo (1885–1960)," in *La Belgique: sociétés et cultures depuis 150 ans (1830–1880)*, ed. Albert d'Haenens (Bruxelles: Creadif, 1980), 263.

[22] Dries Vanysacker, "Historisch overzicht van de katholieke Belgische en Nederlandse missies (negentiende-twintigste eeuw)," *Trajecta. Tijdschrift voor de geschiedenis van het katholieke leven in de Nederlanden* 5, no.4 (1996): 322–323.

Martyred Missionaries

Martyrdom has no clear definition.[23] Within Christianity, the concept mostly refers to people who were killed because of their faith, but this is often broadly interpreted. The numerous books on twentieth-century martyrdom following John Paul II's revived interest include icons such as Charles de Foucauld (who was assassinated by kidnappers in Algeria in 1916) and Óscar Romero (the archbishop of San Salvador who was assassinated in 1980 for defending the poor against an unjust economic system, rather than because he was Christian).[24] Importantly, martyrdom evolved over time. This section will give historical background to Belgian missionaries who died a violent death and examine who were labeled as martyrs, when this happened and how this label evolved over time.

Already in the early modern period, some missionaries from what is now Belgium died violent deaths. Louis Fraryn (Ludovicus Flores), a Dominican who in 1602 went to the Philippines and later moved to Japan, in spite of the fact that the Tokugawa shogunate had issued a ban on missionaries in 1614, was burned at the stake in 1622 in Nagasaki. Adriaan Willems (Joris Van Geel), a Capuchin who in 1651 joined a Portuguese mission near the Congo estuary, died of his wounds after he had been attacked by locals. Both these missionaries were venerated as martyrs, and attempts were made to beatify them (which happened with Fraryn in 1867 but failed with Willems in the 1930s and 1940s).[25] Both are now remembered in the public space, but the reference to their martyrdom has disappeared. The plaques of the Louis Fraryn Avenue in Antwerp only label him as a "missionary in Asia"; the plaques of the Joris Van Geelstraat in Oevel, Westerlo, do not identify him; and the statue for the latter that was erected in 1994 calls him a "missionary in Central Africa" and has a quote from the Bantu dictionary Van Geel authored.

The same applies to the above-mentioned Father Damien. Whereas he was sometimes considered a martyr in the past because he gave his life for the lepers,[26] he is now being remembered as a saint, an apostle, the Greatest Belgian, or, most commonly, a missionary. Charles John Seghers, in contrast, is called "the first martyr of Alaska" on a plaque at his birth house in Ghent that, given its outdated spelling, was created before the mid-twentieth century. This bishop of Vancouver Island was shot in Alaska in 1886, but "the murder was no more than the act of a paranoid schizophrenic."[27]

None of these four missionaries – Fraryn, Van Geel, Damien and Seghers – are connected to colonialism. The Louis Fraryn Avenue received its name in order to memorialize

---

[23] A discussion of different definitions in Van Henten and Saloul, "Introduction", 15 and 27.

[24] Susan Bergman, *Martyrs. Contemporary Writers on Modern Lives of Faith* (San Francisco: HarperCollins, 1996); Robert Royal, *The Catholic Martyrs of the Twentieth Century. A Comprehensive World History* (New York: The Crossroad Publishing Company, 2000); Riccardi, *Il secolo del martirio*. Bergman has separate chapters on Jesuits in El Salvador in 1989 and on the Boxer Rebellion; Riccardi one on martyrdom and mission (covering Asia, Oceania, Africa and Latin America). About Romero, see also Todd M. Johnson and Gina A. Zurlo, "Christian Martyrdom as a Pervasive Phenomenon," *Society* 51, no. 6 (2014): 679–685.

[25] Zana Aziza Etambala, "Poging tot beatificatie van martelaar Joris van Geel en de Belgische koloniale geschiedschrijving (1930-1948)," *Koninklijke Zuidnederlandse maatschappij voor taal- en letterkunde en geschiedenis* 55 (2002): 287–305; Pio Tommaso Masetti, *Leven en marteldood van den gelukzaligen Ludovicus Flores van Antwerpen* (Mechelen: Van Velsen, 1867); Guilielmus Rommens, *Geschiedenis der apostolische zending en marteling van den zaligen Ludovicus Flores, predikheer, geboortig van Antwerpen, en van zijne gezellen, martelaren van Japan* (Leuven: Peeters, 1868).

[26] Constant Eeckels, *De martelaar van Molokaï: Vier episodes uit het leven van pater Damiaan, met voorspel en verheerlijking* (Roeselare: Deraedt-Verhoye, 1938); Steven Debroey, *Wij, melaatsen: leven en martelaarschap van Pater Damiaan* (Leuven: Davidsfonds, 1958).

[27] Charles G. Steckler, "Seghers Charles John," Dictionary of Canadian Biography, http://www.biographi.ca/en/bio.php?id_nbr=5825 (accessed 15 March).

a former Dominican monastery on that spot and because Fraryn was one of the most famous Dominicans born in Antwerp. Van Geel's statue had been conceived on the occasion of the 1000th anniversary of his birthplace Westerlo, which aimed to honor one of its most famous inhabitants.[28] The missionaries in North America are seen as allies of the Native Americans and opponents of the US and Canadian authorities rather than as agents of expansionism.[29] And the work of Fr. Damien has been completely decontextualized from Western interventionism in Hawaii, the history of leprosy, and the strategy of segregating diseased and other people in the colonies.[30]

Similarly, missionaries in China are rarely bracketed together with imperial history, in spite of the fact that there were clear connections. It was immediately after the end of the Second Opium War in 1860 that the first Belgian missionary institution – the Congregation of the Immaculate Heart of Mary, commonly named Scheut after the Brussels suburb where its origins lie – was founded and sent its first priests to China, more particularly to Inner Mongolia. In 1872, the Belgian province of the Franciscans did the same in southwest Hubei, Central China. They were followed by Franciscan sisters and, in the early twentieth century, some other congregations.[31]

These China missionaries met with a lot of resistance, which often turned violent. Five Belgian missionaries were assassinated during the Boxer Rebellion of 1900.[32] Another one was murdered in December 1901 when he tried to liberate Christian women that the Boxers had captured and sold.[33] In 1904, three others were the victim of a conspiracy against the missions (according to their superiors) or of a conflict between Catholic and Protestant Chinese (according to the local authorities and the French consul).[34] At least six missionaries died a violent death in the warlord era following the collapse of the Chinese empire.[35] Three were killed during the Japanese occupation, the Second World War and the civil war.[36] All in all, at least eighteen Belgian China missionaries died a martyr death.

In Congo – along with Rwanda-Urundi the only Belgian colony – there were many more martyrs. Especially in the early years and decades, many missionaries died at a young age of disease or violence. However, they are honored as "Congo pioneers", along with secular colonialists who died in the Congo Free State, rather than as martyrs. The concept of "Congo martyr" is reserved for the missionaries who were killed in the years immediately

---

[28] Julie Nijs, *De ware helden van ons Rooms katholieke landeke. Monumenten van missionarissen in België* (Leuven: unpublished MA Thesis KU Leuven, 2016): 40.

[29] Catherine O'Donnell, *Jesuits in the North American Colonies and the United States. Faith, Conflict, Adaptation* (Leiden: Brill, 2020).

[30] Moblo, "Blessed Damien of Moloka'i"; John Tayman, *The Colony. The harrowing true story of the exiles of Molokai* (New York: Scribner, 2006); Edmond Rod, *Leprosy and Empire: a Medical and Cultural History* (Cambridge University Press, 2006); James L. Haley, *Captive Paradise. A History of Hawaii* (New York: St. Martin's Press, 2014); Goddeeris, *Missionarissen*, 130–135.

[31] Thomas Coomans, "Unexpected Connections: The Benedictine Abbey of Maredsous and Christian Architecture in China, 1900–1930s," *Revue Bénédictine* 131, no. 1 (2021): 270; Pipeleers Ludo & Snoeks Leon (2000), *Limburgse martelaren. Geloofsgenoten ook voor deze tijd* (Hasselt: Wereld-Missiehulp, Stelimo & Missio-Limburg): 18.

[32] Désiré Abbeloos, Amand Heirman, Jan Mallet, Jozef Segers, and Amandina of Schakkebroek.

[33] Staf Beelen, *Remi Van Merhaeghe C.I.C.M., Waregem 1869 - Xiayingzi 1901: zendeling in de Ordos en martelaar van de Boksersopstand* (Leuven: Ferdinand Verbiest Stichting, 2001).

[34] Carine Dujardin, *Missionering en moderniteit: de Belgische minderbroeders in China 1872–1940* (Leuven: Universitaire Pers Leuven, 1996), 224.

[35] Julianus Adons in 1922; Kamiel Ruyffelaert in 1926; Trudo Jans, Rupertus Feynaerts and Bruno Van Weert in 1928; and Marinus Adons in 1931.

[36] Jozef Dangreau in 1939, Aloïs Abeloos in 1944, and Constant Dom in captivity in 1947.

following Congo's independence in 1960. Whereas many Belgians left the former colony during the crisis,[37] missionaries tended to stay and became primary targets for anti-imperial resistance. Renaat De Vos, a White Father (i.e. belonging to the Congregation of the Missionaries of Africa) was killed in February 1961 as retribution for the assassination of Lumumba. Twenty members of the Congregation of the Holy Spirit were executed on New Year's Day 1962 in Kongolo, in the north of the present-day Tanganyika province, during the war with the secessionist province Katanga. However, most victims fell in 1964 and 1965 during the Simba rebellion. This was a communist uprising assisted by Che Guevara and other advisors from Cuba and the Soviet Union. The resistance spread across different regions, but was especially concentrated in the northeast. In early August 1964, rebels seized the city of Stanleyville (present-day Kisangani) and proclaimed the People's Republic of Congo. The more than 1,300 foreigners they held hostage were liberated in November by Belgian paratroopers and American aircraft. A year later, the Congolese army defeated the Simbas. A total of 392 foreign civilians died in the insurrection, of whom 268 were Belgian nationals. Clergymen constituted almost half of them: 156 Catholic missionaries (of whom 81 were Belgian, 36 Dutch and 10 Italian) and 30 Protestants had been killed.[38]

In the following years and decades, there are more examples of Belgian missionaries dying violent deaths. Brother Arnold Knevels, who was stabbed in Burundi in 1980, is called a martyr on a commemorative plaque in his native village of Bocholt.[39] Others, however, are not explicitly related to martyrdom in the public space. The Jesuit Herman Rasschaert, who was stoned in India in 1964 when he protected Muslims in a Hindu pogrom, is only labeled as a missionary on the plaques of a street named after him in his birth place Aalst.[40] The same applies to two fathers who were killed by robbers in South Africa in 1975 and 1999,[41] and to four fathers who were assassinated in Latin America, one murdered by the army in Colombia in 1985, three others in the Guatemalan Civil War in 1980, 1982 and 1994.[42]

The fact that many recent markers – not only for recent missionaries, but also for Father Damien and early modern missionaries – no longer refer to martyrdom, is in line with Jay Winter's finding that "in Western Europe, the term martyr (with some exceptions) has faded rapidly and irreversibly from use in the twentieth century". However, Winter dates the start of the long-term decline of the concept in English books in the 1870s, and sees similar evolutions in France and Germany, with prominent reappearance in those two countries during the two world wars.[43] This section has revealed later examples of the language of martyrdom in Belgium, lying exactly between England, France and

---

[37] Emmanuel Gerard and Bruce Kuklick, *Death in the Congo. Murdering Patrice Lumumba* (Cambridge MA: Harvard University Press, 2015).

[38] Dries Vanysacker, *Vergeten martelaars. Missionarissen in het oog van de Simba-opstand in Congo, 1964–1966* (Leuven-Den Haag: Acco, 2015), 26–27.

[39] "Moord op missionarissen," *Reformatorisch Dagblad*, 22 February 1980; "Liste Chronologique des Pères et Frères morts de mort violente," Missionnaires d'Afrique, http://www.peresblancs.org/assassines.htm (accessed 15 March).

[40] The title of a biography, in contrast, calls him a "Missionary-Martyr": Robert Houthaeve, *Recht, al barste de wereld! Herman Rasschaert Missionaris-Martelaar 1922–1964* (Moorslede: 1995).

[41] Omer Devos (street name in Kortrijk) and Albert Peleman (a commemorative stone in the church of Berlare).

[42] Hubert Gillard (street in Gingelom), Walter Voordeckers (plaque and street in Grobbendonk, street in Turnhout), Serge Berten (monument, park and walking trail in Menen) and Alfons Stessel (street and monument in Leuven).

[43] Winter, *War beyond Words*, 124–125. Winter especially writes on the world wars and includes an analysis of the memory of the Armenian genocide and the Shoah, but he has searched the use of the word "martyr" in general and does not exclude missionaries.

Germany. Some missionaries – e.g. Seghers after 1887 and Knevels after 1980 – are called martyrs in the public space; others – e.g. Willems and Father Damien – in biographies from the 1930s to the 1950s. In the next two sections, the analysis of the commemoration of missionaries who died a violent death in China and Congo will make clear whether these examples are an exception or whether the memory of martyred missionaries indeed faded much later in Belgium.

Commemorative Markers for China Martyrs

The first commemorative markers for missionaries who fell in China were constructed before 1960, when Belgium was still a colonial power. Mechelen, an historic city between Antwerp and Brussels, in 1933 hung a memorial plaque at the birth house of the Verhaeghen brothers and five years later established a life-size statue on the adjacent square.[44] The inscription on the latter is brief but telling: "Verhaeghen Brothers. Friars. Martyrs. China. 19 July 1904". The text at the birth house is less legible, but also says that they "died as martyrs". Hasselt, the capital city of the province of Limburg, in 1953 erected a monument to another family of China missionaries: four Adons brothers and their mother. It honors them as "heroes of the China mission" and "paragons of the purest sacrifice spirit", but also mentions that two of them were martyred in 1921 and 1931 and that a third one was sentenced to death in 1951 (Illustration 1).

Other markers from that era are more closely linked to colonial propaganda. The Pater Segersstraat in Sint-Niklaas is near streets referring to Congo: the Kongostraat and the Baron Dhanisstraat (dedicated to Francis Dhanis, one of Leopold II's main collaborators in Congo). Segers, a local missionary who was assassinated during the Boxer Rebellion, in 1950 also received a memorial plaque in the Minor Seminary, his former high school.[45] Other schools, too, hung such panels to recognize alumni who died as martyrs in China: for instance in Tielt (also in 1950) and Eeklo.[46] This was not only to honor them, but also to mobilize youth for the missions: schools were primary sites for colonial propaganda.[47] Such campaigns had their effect: the mysticism of martyrs contributed to new vocations.[48]

The iconography and language of these early markers for martyrs in China are quite explicit. The Adons monument has scenes in which an armed Chinese man is ready to slaughter a missionary defending himself with a cross, and another missionary blesses a Chinese man with a spear, apparently accepting the violent fate that awaits him. The Segers plaque mentions that he was tortured and buried alive. The representation of

---

[44] "Monseigneur Theotimus en zijn Broeder Eerwaarde Pater Fredericus Verhaeghen," *Gazet van Antwerpen*, 13 October 1933, 3 and "Monument van de Gebroeders Verhaegen wordt in ere hersteld," *Het Nieuwsblad*, 12 March 2010; "Gebroeders Verhaeghen," Mechelen Mapt, http://mechelen.mapt.be/wiki/Gebroeders_Verhaeghen (accessed 15 March).

[45] "Gedenkplaat-onthulling," *Het Nieuws van den Dag*, 15 December 1950, 4.

[46] Both buildings were recently demolished. See: "Bisschoppelijk college Heilige Vincentius," Onroerend Erfgoed, https://inventaris.onroerenderfgoed.be/erfgoedobjecten/51867 (accessed 15 March) and Eddie Verbeke, *Cha-Tse-Ti 1904* (Tielt: Heemkundige kring De Roede, 2020), 117 and 125.

[47] Stanard, *Selling the Congo*, 135ff.; Bram Cleys, Jan De Maeyer, Carine Dujardin & Luc Vints, "België in Congo, Congo in België: weerslag van de missionering op de religieuze instituten," in *Congo in België: koloniale cultuur in de metropool*, ed. Vincent Viaene, David Van Reybrouck & Bambi Ceuppens (Leuven: Universitaire Pers Leuven, 2009), 155–156.

[48] Carine Dujardin, "Van pionier tot dienaar. Profiel van de Belgische missionaris in historisch perspectief (1800–1989)," in *Rond Damiaan. Handelingen van het colloquium n.a.v. de honderdste verjaardag van het overlijden van pater Damiaan, 9–10 maart 1989*, ed. Robrecht Boudens (Leuven: Universitaire Pers Leuven, 1989), 141.

Illustration 1. A part of the Adons brothers monument in Hasselt (1953)

the Chinese as martyrs' brutal murderers, without any reflection on their motives, is typical of the late nineteenth and early twentieth century. East Asians were often depicted as cruel villains, connecting to old stereotypes such as Fu Manchu and the Yellow Peril.[49]

Interestingly, the celebration of martyrs in China did not fade over time. In the 1960s, when several streets were named after China martyrs, this may relate to the killing of missionaries in Congo.[50] Later, new markers emerged on the occasion of anniversaries. In the late 1970s, two missionaries killed in China fifty years earlier were honored with a plaque at the entrance of their parish churches.[51] In 2000, three others who fell victim to the Boxer Rebellion were immortalized on the occasion of their death centenary.[52]

Unlike the pre-1960 monuments, these recent markers for martyrs in China are no longer located in central cities. The streets named in the 1960s are in two Western Flemish towns and a municipality of the nearby city of Oudenaarde and, apart from Désiré Abbeloos, all the other markers are in the eastern province of Limburg. Moreover,

---

[49] Colin Mackerras, *Western images of China* (Oxford University Press, 1999).

[50] Remi Vanmeerhaeghestraat (Waregem) in 1960; Robberechtstraat (Tielt) in 1964; Pater Ruyffelaertstraat (Oudenaarde) in 1965.

[51] Trudo Jans in Zussen in 1977, on the occasion of the centenary of his birth; Bruno Van Weert in Vlijtingen undoubtedly in 1979, fifty years after his death. Records of the latter inauguration, clearly dating from that time, are on "Herdenking Pater Bruno Vanweert," YouTube, https://www.youtube.com/watch?v=mQi5AzNALk0 (accessed 15 March).

[52] Désiré Abbeloos received a memorial plaque at his birth house in Opwijk, Jan Mallet a bust in Hechtel (his second monument; see "Parochiekerk Sint-Lambertus," Onroerend Erfgoed, https://inventaris.onroerenderfgoed.be/erfgoedobjecten/80466 (accessed 15 March)), and Sister Amandina saw a revival of her cult in her native Schakkebroek (Herk-de-Stad) after her canonization in 2000, along with 119 other (non-Belgian) martyrs of the Boxer rebellion.

most of these places are villages. They even seem to have inspired each other, some of them being located close to each other.

An important difference is, of course, that these markers were erected long after the martyr's death: sometimes fifty, but most often one hundred years later. Apparently, the memory of China martyrs has remained vivid for a long time. The major initiators are local history associations, parishes and municipality councils. All of these actors use missionaries as figures to ascribe their villages with a more global past. In some places, attention has continued to date. The church of Zussen has a permanent exhibition of some of Trudo Jans's paraphernalia; the annual Saint-Paul's Horse Parade in Opwijk in 2000 for the first time honored Désiré Abbeloos and has since made it a tradition.[53]

The language on the commemorative markers has softened down during the past decades. The present-day plaques of the street names created in the 1960s do not provide further explanation. The plates from the 1970s call the honored missionaries "martyrs", but do not refer to the circumstances of their death or their Chinese murderers. The ones from 2000 are even more neutral. In Opwijk, it reads that "he was Scheut missionary in Inner Mongolia and died for the Christian faith on 22 August 1900, during the Boxer Rebellion". In Hechtel, it clarifies "that he was killed", has the quote "Having to die, fair enough, may God's will be done", and also adds that "This world needs noble and brave people. One of them is Father Jan Mallet, Scheut missionary. August 2000".

However, newspapers articles on the inauguration of the monuments or the commemoration of the missionaries keep emphasizing the cruel circumstances of their martyr's death. Jan Mallet "was murdered in a gruesome and cowardly manner by a secret grouping". Julianus Adons was "killed by 73 spear stabs". His brother Marinus "was arrested, tortured and released again, but shot dead barely three days later. His body was retrieved after as many as two weeks." Trudo Jans was "assassinated by bandits, armed with knives and lances". And Désiré Abbeloos was, along with three hundred soulmates, "persecuted by a clandestine sect. They took refuge in a church, which was set on fire". "He was buried alive".[54]

In other words, even at the turn of the century, the old representation of China missionaries as victims of brutal savages had not completely faded. Nobody asks what missionaries were doing in China in the first place, nor do they link this to expansionism and colonialism. Still in 2017, a tourist guide from the city of Mechelen wrote an article on the Verhaeghen brothers statue in which he compared old hagiographies with more recent literature and elaborated on the different versions about the circumstances of their death, but did not highlight the Chinese perspective. On the contrary, he concluded that the two brothers rightly received a statue and a street name.[55] It was only in 2020 that a local historian from Tielt who wrote a new biography on the China martyr of his

---

[53] E.g. "Paardenprocessie wordt op nieuwe leest geschoeid," *Het Nieuwsblad*, 24 June 2016 and "Paardenprocessie over andere boeg," *Het Nieuwsblad*, 8 June 2017. See a picture on Paul Onselaere, "Opwijk de 112e Sint-Paulusprocessie," Editiepajot, https://editiepajot.com/regios/17/articles/38021 (accessed 15 March).

[54] "Van missionaris tot 'westerse duivel'", *Het Nieuwsblad*, 24 August 2000, 14; "33 Limburgers gemarteld en gestorven voor geloof", *Het Belang van Limburg*, 11 July 2000, 1; "Missiebisschop Trudo Jans stierf marteldood in China", *Het Belang van Limburg*, 11 September 1993, 19; "Pater Abbeloos gaf zijn leven voor zijn geloof, net als Damiaan", *Het Nieuwsblad*, 4 November 2009, 24; "Paardenprocessie trekt door straten", *Het Laatste Nieuws*, 21 June 2014, 22.

[55] Rik Belmans, "De gebroeders Verhaeghen, martelaren-missionarissen uit Mechelen," *Klapgat-Echo* 321 (2017), 3–14.

town showed some empathy with the Chinese anti-western rebellions: "just as we have movements resisting foreign intervention, the same also happened there."[56]

Commemorative Markers for Congo Martyrs

Almost immediately after missionaries were murdered in the violence following the Congolese independence, some of their native villages erected commemorative markers.[57] Two congregations set up collective memorials: the Spiritans in Gentinnes in 1967 and the Crosiers in Hasselt in 1970.[58] The former was conceived after twenty confrères had been murdered in Kongolo on 1 January 1962, but by the time of its inauguration it included the names of all other missionaries who were assassinated in Congo in the first years after independence.[59]

In the following decades, new markers continued to pop up. At least six other monuments were established in the 1970s.[60] Commemoration plaques were hung up in 1989, 1990, 1994 and 2000; and roadside chapels were built or reorganized in 2002 and 2010.[61] In some places the same missionary was honored several times. Karel Bellinckx received a street in 1965 and a monument in 1974, Godfried Kraewinkels and Rik Snijkers a street no later than 1968 and a commemoration plaque in 1990. Jozef Beckers was not only remembered with a monument and a Pater Beckersstraat, but also with a Butastraat (after the place where he was killed) and a Kruisherenstraat ("Crosiers Street", after his congregation).

These markers were not evenly spread over the country. Wallonia has only four: the Kongolo memorial in Gentinnes (in the province of Walloon Brabant), a Nicolas Hardy street in Herve and a plaque for the same in neighbouring Elsaute, Thimister-Clermont (both in the province of Liège) and a plaque for Clément Burnotte in Vielsalm (province of Luxemburg). In Flanders, two provinces celebrate only one Congo martyr each,[62] another one five,[63] and the two most peripheral ones many more. Western Flanders in the west has 15 markers for missionaries who were assassinated in Congo in the early 1960s; Limburg in the east even 23. This ties in with the findings regarding the China martyrs from the second half of the twentieth century onwards. It is partly related to the fact that many missionaries came from these regions, which were more rural, traditional, and religious. Another explanation is the lack of other heroes that these places

---

[56] "Eddie Verbeke uit Tielt schrijft boek over pater Georges Robberecht," *Krant van West-Vlaanderen*, 27 March 2020.

[57] A street for Karel Bellinkx in Koersel (Beringen) in 1965, a plaque for Jozef Wouters in Stevoort (Hasselt) in 1966 and a monument for Jozef Beckers in Eversel (Heusden) in 1966.

[58] The monument honors 23 Crosiers. Most of them were Dutch nationals; only the seven Flemish are included in our count. Apart from Leo Ignoul, they are also celebrated in their native municipalities.

[59] Its memorial wall lists 216 names, including the 186 who died in the Simba rebellion. Vanysacker, *Vergeten martelaars*, 201–202.

[60] For Jozef Van den broucke and Julia Vandendriessche in 1973, for Karel Bellinckx in 1974, for Marie-Thérèse Vandorpe in 1974, for Roger t'Jaekens in 1976, for Theo Schildermans and Michel Vanduffel in 1978, and for Chris Van Dael in 1980.

[61] For Eugeen Pauwelijn in 1989, Godfried Kraewinkels and Rik Snijkers in 1990, Constant Lenaers in 1994, Theresa Simons in 2000, Désiré Pellens in 2002, and for Robert Carremans in 2010.

[62] Broeder de Zwaeflaan in Erembodegem (Aalst, Eastern Flanders) and the monument for Jean Lenselaer in Nossegem (Zaventem, Flemish Brabant).

[63] Pater A. Verlindenstraat in Gierle (Lille), Gebroeders Doxplein in Lier, Pater Renaat de Vosstraat in Mortsel, and Pater Hensstraat and a commemoration plaque in Oostmalle (Malle).

can celebrate: most markers are located in small boroughs or municipalities, which do not have many other people to give their place an historical importance. Last but not least, there also seems to have been a cascade effect. Many markers are located in neighboring municipalities, which may have inspired each other.[64]

Also, regarding the style, the most recent generation of monuments – for instance to China martyr Jan Mallet in Hechtel (2000) and Congo martyr Désiré Pellens in Pelt (2002) – are strikingly similar (see illustration 2). The ones to Congo martyrs from the 1960s and 1970s, however, are different (see illustration 3). They are cast in concrete or metal rather than stone or bronze and have a figurative character instead of depicting the lamented missionary. In Pittem, a phoenix in stainless steel symbolizes resurrection; in Pelt, a large and tapered stone represents Jesus pointing at eternal life while two adjacent smaller stones stand for the two commemorated martyrs. At some places, the missionary's portrait is carved in a bas-relief; but most of the monuments only depict their images in small pictures, just like on a tomb. This does not seem accidental: these monuments function as empty graves in the public space.

Plaques serve a similar function. Many of them hang within or outside church buildings.[65] Installed by the parish, they are testament to the importance that worshippers attach to the martyr and function as a mobilization factor for mission work. Monuments and street names were erected by local associations and the concerned missionaries' friends and relatives, and approved of by the municipality council. In several places, dozens of people convene every year to mark the day of the killing (or of the missionary's birth). The monuments, in other words, also keep serving as sites of commemoration, family reunion, and mourning.

At first sight, this seems innocuous. However, the language on the pedestals or the plaques is not always neutral. The information mostly concerns the missionary's biography. It sometimes (but not always) adds that he/she was assassinated and, quite often, that he/she was a martyr. The latter word is used on plates dating from the 1960s to the twenty-first century.[66] If there is more text, it univocally highlights virtues, such as innocence and commitment. Jeroom Vandemoere in De Haan "died as martyr of the rebellion in the 33rd year of his life", which not only emphasizes his young age, but also implicitly makes a connection with Jesus Christ, who also died at that age. Sister Maria Simons and other missionaries from the parish of Hamont "placed their life in the service of the world church". Also, bravery is often suggested. Désiré Pellens from Pelt "still returned [to Congo] in 1961, although 'it was safer that he would not go back'". Brother Kuypers in Bree "remained at his post in peril of death out of love for his seminarians and Christians."

---

[64] There are indeed clear clusters of neighboring municipalities honoring Congo martyrs: 1) in northern Limburg Pelt, Hamont-Achel, Bocholt, Bree and Maaseik; 2) in central Limburg Heusden-Zolder, Beringen and Hasselt; 3) at the seacoast Bredene and De Haan; 4) in central Western Flanders Ardooie, Pittem and Tielt; and 5) in southeast Western Flanders Ingelmunster, Oostrozebeke, Wielsbeke and Harelbeke.

[65] Only the ones for André Verschaeve (Moorslede) and Jozef Wouters (Stevoort, Hasselt) are located at their birth house.

[66] The plates in Elsaute, Ingelmunster, Oostmalle and Stevoort seem old and supposedly date from the 1960s. The ones in Runkst and Ooigem were erected in 1970 and 1974; the one in Maaseik in 1990; and the street name plaques of the Pater Pellensstraat, the Pater Schildermansstraat, the Pater Vandaelstraat and the Pater Vanduffelstraat all date from after 2019, when the municipalities of Neerpelt and Overpelt were merged into Pelt. All these markers explicitly use the word martyr.

Illustration 2. The monuments for Jan Mallet in Hechtel (2000; left) and Désiré Pellens in Pelt (2002; right)

This white innocence is contrasted with black savagery. Apart from references to Congo or the Simba rebellion, the context of the assassination is rarely elaborated upon, but sometimes the barbaric character of the killings is emphasized. The nameplate of the Father Beckers Street in Heusden, for instance, clarifies that he was "horribly killed in Buta and thrown into the Buta river". The same discourse is used in newspaper articles on the commemoration of the martyrs. In Bondo, "the fathers were to proceed in a row to the Rubi river, where they were slaughtered in a bestial manner". In Kongolo, the missionaries' dead bodies "were mutilated with choppers and poison arrows". In Wamba, Karel Bellinckx was "heavily tortured" and then "finished off by gun shots".[67]

Notably, Congolese perspectives, and more specifically the causes of the violence and the reasons for the murders, are not mentioned even once. Whereas dozens of markers honor the eighty Belgian missionaries who were killed, the hundreds of thousands Congolese victims to the Simba rebellion are completely ignored. The Kongolo Memorial mentions four Congolese clergymen, but their names are eclipsed by their Western colleagues. Even Belgian scholarly literature on the violence in Congo in the early 1960s only works with Belgian clerical sources and adopts their explanation of the events without questioning its bias.[68]

---

[67] "Pater Robert Carremans in Belgisch-Congo omgebracht", *Het Belang van Limburg*, 21 August 1993; "33 Limburgers gemarteld en gestorven voor geloof", *Het Belang van Limburg*, 11 July 2000; "Eerbetoon in boekvorm aan pater Karel Bellinckx", *Het Nieuwsblad*, 25 February 2014; "Boek over Pater Karel Bellinckx", *De Streekkrant*, 26 February 2014.
[68] Dries Vanysacker, *Vergeten martelaars*, 26 and 202; Zana Etambala, "Les missions catholiques et les émeutes de Léopoldville, 4 janvier 1959," in *Religion, colonization and decolonization in Congo, 1885–1960. Religion, colonisation et décolonisation au Congo, 1885–1960*, ed. Vincent Viaene, Bram Cleys and Jan De Maeyer (Leuven: Leuven University Press, 2020), 285–311.

Illustration 3. The monuments for Jozef Van den Broucke and Marie-Juliana Vandendriessche in Pittem (1973; left) and for Theo Schildermans and Michel Vanduffel in Pelt (1978; right)

Conclusion

Belgium has dozens of monuments for martyred missionaries, mostly for those who were killed in China in the first half of the twentieth century and in Congo during the first five years after the former Belgian colony became independent in 1960. The 18 China martyrs that are honored with 27 different markers (4 monuments, 3 statues in churches, 8 memorial plaques and 12 street names)[69] are especially remarkable. On the one hand, fewer than 800 Belgian missionaries went to China, which is less than a tenth of the approximately 10,000 Belgian missionaries who settled in Congo.[70] On the other hand, there were not only far fewer missionaries, but also fewer martyrs in China than in Congo. About 20 Belgian missionaries were killed in China, whereas more than 80 of them met the same fate in Congo. Almost all of the China martyrs are commemorated in the public space, whereas only half of the Congo martyrs – 40 individuals – are recognized with 13 monuments, 22 street names and 15 other markers.

Both regarding China and Congo, martyrs constitute the largest group of missionaries honored in the public space. Other important, but smaller categories – regarding both China and Congo – are pioneers, bishops, key figures and returnees who earned credits in Belgium. Women are tremendously underrepresented: whereas there were almost as many missionary sisters as fathers and brothers, they make only 12% of the total number of markers in the public space. Again, martyrs are the largest group. Of the 16 honored female missionaries, 5 died a martyr death and 4 perished in the Congo Free State.[71]

These commemorative markers for martyred missionaries are the only sites in Belgium remembering colonial violence. In this way, they illustrate Belgium's one-sided public space regarding the colonial past. Even a year after the Black Lives Matter protest, the country has not a single monument for Congolese victims or independence fighters, apart from two minor street names for Patrice Lumumba, which were erected just before municipality elections in 2018.[72]

Of course, the commemorative markers for martyred missionaries cannot be put in the same league as the monuments for Leopold II and his Congo pioneers. Most of the latter were the result of deliberate propaganda by authorities and colonial veterans. A few markers for China martyrs were part of this campaign, but most of the monuments and street names for martyred missionaries were erected by congregations, parishes, local history clubs and, last but not least, family members. They did not explicitly seek to glorify the colonial project, but honored priests who had given their life in the missions. The commemorative markers were not only sites of pride of a local hero, but also places of mourning for a belated friend or relative. Moreover, many plaques are hung at the wall of churches and a couple of monuments are on territory of monasteries or religious institutions, which are open to the public, but cannot be considered space as public as, for instance, a market square or a city hall.[73] For all these reasons, the markers for martyred missionaries also show the complexity of postcolonial memory.

---

[69] Goddeeris, *Missionarissen*, 43–44. The commemorative markers for Aloïs Abeloos (street and plaque in Zaventem), Jozef Dangreau (plaque in Ostend), Constant Dom (street in Broechem), Amand Heirman (plaque and street in Berlare), Kamiel Vandekerckhove (plaque in Ingelmunster) are not included in this article's analysis because the dates of their creation is unknown. However, their language and iconography do not refute the conclusions.

[70] Luc Vints, "Congo en de katholieke kerk (1885–1960)," in *100x Congo. Een eeuw Congolese kunst in Antwerpen*, ed. Els De Palmenaer (Kontich: BAI, voor het MAS Antwerpen, 2020), 115.

[71] Goddeeris, *Missionarissen*, 45 and 56–57.

[72] Idesbald Goddeeris, "Mapping the Colonial Past in the Public Space. A Comparison between Belgium and the Netherlands," *BMGN - The Low Countries Historical Review* 135, no. 1 (2020): 83.

[73] Some monasteries also honor their members who were assassinated in Congo, for instance with a wall of honor (in Gits) or a chapel (in Ingelmunster), but since this is not publicly accessible, these are not included in this article's analysis. See Omer Tanghe, *Hun stem in steen. Westvlaamse missionarisroute. Monumenten, gedenkstenen, begraafplaatsen, straatnamen en biografische gegevens van Westvlaamse missionarissen* (Tielt: Lannoo, 1984), 52–53 and 56–57.

The commemoration of missionaries who died a violent death is still framed in the language of martyrdom, in contrast to Jay Winter's conclusion about the vanishing of this narrative in Western Europe. It is true that the explicit use of the word martyr has gradually decreased from the mid-twentieth century onwards. Even more, the honored missionaries are increasingly secularized: they are no longer perceived in religious terms, for instance as agents of proselytization, but rather as architects of development and as messengers of charity. Formerly emphasized characteristics such as piety and devotedness have been replaced by less religious ones, such as bravery and innocence. Yet, reference to martyrdom did not completely disappear and even persists in the twenty-first century.

Equally paradoxical is the fact that the commemoration of missionaries is still very much alive. Still in the twenty-first century, people erect new monuments for missionaries and have annual celebrations to commemorate individual martyrs. Of course, one should not overestimate the turnout: pictures of such events reveal that, at a maximum, dozens of people attended them.[74] On the contrary, it is important to emphasize the local character of the markers and the celebrations. Many of them are located in rural areas, often even in the peripheral parts of Belgium. It seems that those villages have few other heroes to place in the limelight and that they even may have inspired each other. At the same time, this local character also accounts for the fact that the markers remain under the radar. Fewer people visit the places and the local population is still much whiter than in urban or semi-urban areas, where people with a migrant past ignited protests against colonial monuments.

However, these monuments' iconography and language, just as the narratives with which they are described in media, are still clearly affected by colonial framings, emphasizing white individuals' commitment and, in the case of martyrs, victimhood, and contrasting these virtues to collective and anonymous indigenous savagery. This so far has remained unnoticed.

The question remains how to deal with these monuments, or with the remembrance of martyred missionaries in general. Jay Winter suggests "that the language of human rights and not that of martyrdom is the appropriate register", but talks specifically about the Armenian genocide.[75] Church historians, in contrast, keep using the concept of martyr. The renewed attention following John Paul II's call has created a fascination for numbers of martyrs, which in turn leads to far-reaching conclusions. A retired American psychiatrist who has done research on Catholic martyrdom concludes that "the Church lost more people and property to the Nazis than Jews ever did", and "the Roman Catholic Church indeed is the most persecuted organization in history".[76]

Not everybody is that extreme, though. Jan Willem van Henten and Ihab Saloul emphasize the constructivist character of martyrdom. Every period has its own canon of martyrs, who may be appropriated by some groups, but contested by others. The volume they edited has many examples from Christian, Jewish, Muslim and secular spheres, but

[74] For instance KVH, "Familie herdenkt moord op paters," Het Nieuwsblad, https://www.nieuwsblad.be/cnt/3o3mca1e (accessed 15 March) (Overpelt 2012); Rita Vanhove, "Vermoorde pater Beckers herdacht," Het Belang van Limburg, https://www.hbvl.be/cnt/dmf20150601_01708400 (accessed 15 March) (Heusden 2015); and "Vermoorde missionarissen herdacht," Internetgazet, https://www.internetgazet.be/pelt/herdenking-vermoorde-missionarissen.aspx (accessed 15 March) (Pelt 2020).
[75] Winter, War beyond Words, 138.
[76] Samuel A. Nigro, "The Catholic Martyrs of The Twentieth Century: A Comprehensive World History - A Review Article," Journal of Psychology and Clinical Psychiatry 5, no. 2 (2016): 3.

does not pay attention to martyred missionaries.[77] The latter's memory seem to be even more complex. Whereas many martyrs opposed powerful institutions or dominant discourses,[78] missionaries were somehow part of these. In addition, some of them garnered admiration that stretches beyond Europe. In 2019, the bishop of Kongolo initiated the process of beatification of the missionaries that were assassinated in his city on New Year's Day 1962.[79]

Still, these views are not in direct opposition to the findings of Black Lives Matter scholars. Atuire, for instance, explains that "when public space is adorned with figures with which black people cannot identify, even if they are not aware of the full story of these persons, a feeling of alienation is created." He does not call to remove, and certainly not to destroy them, but argues that "the public sphere should be a place in which all the members of the community can feel at home or at least represented."[80] Abraham is on the same page: "Decolonising public spaces have to be part of a larger process demanding that these public sites of knowledge become more democratic."[81] In other words, they advocate more diversity in the public space. They acknowledge the problematic nature of certain, especially racist monuments, but also offer solutions, such as artistic redesigning or non-white reinterpretation.[82]

Interestingly, this is currently happening with the statue of Father De Deken, the single monument of a missionary in Belgium that had been criticized so far (and, as mentioned in the introduction, received a contextualizing plate in 2015). In January 2018, the Ghanaian artist Ibrahim Mahama organized a discussion evening in an Antwerp art gallery and created a new statue in the symbolic material of black rubber, which has since been exhibited in several Belgian museums. In June 2020, activists projected pictures of chained Congolese and the message "white silence = violence" on the wall behind the original statue.[83] The statue still stands, but the memory has been enriched with different narratives. One may assume that commemorative markers for martyrs will undergo a similar fate in the future. This has actually already happened spontaneously. The language on martyrdom has softened down over the last decades and some commemorative plaques have been removed from the public space following unrelated construction projects.[84]

Disclosure statement

No potential conflict of interest was reported by the author(s).

---

[77] van Henten and Saloul, "Introduction", 19–21.

[78] Ibid., 22.

[79] "RD.Congo. Beatification of twenty martyr missionaries on track," SouthWorld, https://www.southworld.net/rd-congo-beatification-of-twenty-martyr-missionaries-on-track/ (accessed 15 March).

[80] Atuire, "Black Lives Matter," 459 and 466.

[81] Abraham, "Toppled Monuments," 30.

[82] Gill and others, "Towards a Culture of Care," 5.

[83] HW, "On Monumental Silences," M HKA, https://www.muhka.be/collections/artworks/o/item/20804-on-monumental-silences (accessed 15 March); "Beeldenstorm zónder vandalisme, maar met sterke visuele boodschap: "Geef meer aandacht aan koloniale periode"," Het Laatste Nieuws, https://www.hln.be/antwerpen/beeldenstorm-zonder-vandalisme-maar-met-sterke-visuele-boodschap-geef-meer-aandacht-aan-koloniale-periode~a10b82f6/ (accessed 15 March).

[84] More precisely in Tielt and Eeklo; see footnote 50.

Index

Note: Figures are indicated by *italics*.